Managing Today's University

Frederick E. Balderston

Managing Today's University

Strategies for Viability, Change, and Excellence

SECOND EDITION

Jossey-Bass Publishers • San Francisco

Substantial discounts on bulk quantities of Jossey-Bass books are available to corporations, professional associations, and other organizations. For details and discount information, contact the special sales department at Jossey-Bass Inc., Publishers. (415) 433-1740; Fax (800) 605-2665.

For sales outside the United States, please contact your local Paramount Publishing International Office.

TCF Manufactured in the United States of America on Lyons Falls Pathfinder Tradebook. This paper is acid-free and 100 percent totally chlorine-free.

Library of Congress Cataloging-in-Publication Data

Balderston, Frederick E.
    Managing today's university : strategies for viability, change, and excellence / Frederick E. Balderston—2nd ed.
       p.   cm. (The Jossey-Bass higher and adult education series).
    Includes bibliographical references (p.) and index.
    ISBN 0-7879-0072-9
    1. Universities and colleges—Administration.   I. Title.
LB2341.B26   1995
378.1—dc20   94-25143
                                                   CIP

SECOND EDITION
HB Printing   10 9 8 7 6 5 4 3 2 1

The Jossey-Bass

Higher and Adult Education Series

Contents

Preface

Universities are remarkably flexible and resilient organizations. But financial stringency and conflicting demands on their resources have produced serious new stresses within them. In the past, these institutions were capable of growing in many directions without having to assess mission or scope and without being specifically accountable, financially or otherwise, to funding agencies, the tax-paying public, faculty, or students. That period has ended, and universities are now asked to justify themselves. Accountability is difficult to achieve. The problems of identifying and measuring the components of such complex organizations or of analyzing and evaluating performance are enormous. These problems are further complicated by uncertainties about how to identify and demonstrate the quality and quantity of education, research, and public service. Each year, large numbers of graduates receive degrees, research is conducted in many fields and through many organizational arrangements, and public service programs are offered to numerous clients. But the task of justifying the continued investment in higher education is formidable.

This book is a successor to the first edition of *Managing Today's University*, published in 1974. The above paragraph, repeated verbatim from that edition, still holds true. Many topics treated earlier remain relevant and worthwhile, but the universities face a significant new agenda for the next twenty years or so. The present volume addresses the new array of problems that have arisen, as well as the classic task of managing the university in ways that will help its members achieve their academic and institutional goals.

The 1974 edition depended on the work of the Ford Foundation Program for Research in University Administration, which from 1968 through 1973 supported analytical research and policy analysis on major questions of university resources and management. There remains here a significant intellectual debt to those who worked in that program. The Carnegie Commission on Higher Education and its successor, the Carnegie Council on Policy Studies in Higher Education, were located in Berkeley under the leadership of Clark Kerr. As a member of the technical advisory committees of both, I gained insights that promoted clearer thinking about universities and their missions, opportunities, and problems.

This revised edition benefits from the extensive literature that has appeared over the past twenty years concerning university management and planning. It draws also on what I have learned from continued research and teaching in strategic management and from my institutional duties in administration and advisory work.

Audience

Managing Today's University is intended for those who share a special concern for the role of the university and its enduring contributions to society—citizens and trustees, students and faculty members, legislators and commission members, devoted alumni and energetic critics—as well as for administrators, budget analysts, economists, and planners who have specific professional and technical involvements with the subject.

University decision makers and policy makers, in common with executives and politicians everywhere, focus on what they must respond to in the immediate context. This is the *symptomatic agenda*. University presidents, provosts, and deans, originally recruited from their professorial duties, operate in the commonsense realm of institutional administration. They often draw on the technical expertise of planners, economists, and budget analysts; when they have time, they may dip into contemporary management writings of the accessible kind. Decision makers coping with the symptomatic agenda often rely on the shrewd guess or the fragment of available data, allied with the advice that is given. Deeper analysis would often not be cost-effective in time or money, and it might well miss the all-important nuances of timing, consensus-building, and credible communication that are essential to the president's survival.

The *substantive agenda*, on the other hand, draws concepts, analytical frameworks, and methods from the relevant systematic literatures. Managerial economics and finance provide ways to optimize resource usage and to deal with time paths and uncertainty. Theories of organizational behavior offer analysis of organizational structure and function and of human motivation and incentives. The guidance of legal experts is indispensable for issues as far apart as the environmental impact statement for a new building or the determination of a policy to prevent sexual harassment. To the analytically sophisticated, the marshaling of empirical evidence must meet positive professional standards if the evidence is to be used to support a policy position, prove an analytical relationship, or predict the consequences of an action.

Both the symptomatic and the substantive viewpoints have their value, and both have their drawbacks. The symptomatic approach may satisfy the decision maker temporarily but fail to provide hope of a durable solution to the problem, as that approach is often based on inadequate evidence and may misstate the real problem that a deeper analysis would uncover. It is also biased toward the preoccupations of the particular decision maker, whereas the problem facing the university *as a permanent organization* will likely outlast that decision maker.

The substantive approach, as we have said, is often not cost-effective in time or money. An analytical method may miss the central problem if the problem does not fit the available analytical paradigm. All too often, the analysis and the proposed solution, even if on the mark, are expressed in jargon impossible for decision makers to understand.

There is a conscious juxtaposition of the substantive and the symptomatic in the treatment of each topic in this book. Where necessary, technical vocabulary is used, but it is translated and interpreted for the different audiences of those interested in universities. Most chapters contain examples of reported decisions or expressions of a policy perspective. Their purpose is to keep the discussion grounded in the realities of university management and policy making. The book will succeed if it is helpful and persuasive to a variety of audiences, and if the topics and their treatment convey something more than transient insight.

Overview of the Contents

Part One, in six chapters, covers the basics of university organization. Chapter One introduces ways to organize for management. Chapter Two discusses the values of the university (including that contemporary challenge, "diversity"). Chapter Three, on governance, and Chapter Four, on leadership and the presidency, offer a framework for directing the institution. Chapter Five, on academic organization, and Chapter Six, an analysis of the array of administrative functions and representational entities, lay out complexities of university operation that place a premium on patience and skill. Of these chapters, Chapters Three and Four are entirely new. I deleted the 1974 chapter on policy analysis as not urgently needed when compared with new topics.

The four chapters of Part Two deal with various aspects of the acquisition and management of university resources. Chapter Seven, on budgets and budgeting, introduces the main issues of allocating and managing resources. Chapter Eight ties together the issues of revenues and enrollment, which are intertwined because enrollment levels and their changes both generate revenue and, in operating activities, absorb it. Tuition and financial aid, topics perennially important to private universities and now urgent for public ones as well, are discussed in Chapter Nine. Key resources, discussed in Chapter Ten, include the faculty, building space and equipment, and library and other academic support resources.

The 1974 edition of the book contained two chapters—"Cost Analysis" and "Varieties of Financial Stress"—whose analysis is now absorbed in the above set of substantive chapters. Chapter Nine, on tuition, is entirely new. Chapters Eight and Ten resulted from a reorganization as well as an updating of resource-related material.

Part Three brings together in three chapters issues of university academic focus and quality. Graduate education, discussed in Chapter Eleven, is a distinctive part of the research university's mission, and its effectiveness is crucial to the institution. Chapter Twelve, on university research and creative activity, discusses the other distinctive aspect of the university as an institution. Chapter Thirteen is devoted to issues of quality and quality assessment, an important and contentious challenge to universities.

The 1974 edition contained a separate chapter, "Institutional Data Systems," that I did not include here. Some earlier materials on market indicators are now subsumed in the new Chapter Thirteen. New also are Chapters Eleven and Twelve, which embody the policy perspective that I seek to maintain in the present book.

The three chapters of Part Four focus on strategic issues and coordination. Growing concern with efficiency and productivity in the university is the subject of Chapter Fourteen, where the question is posed: what measures can the university adopt to prevent its unit costs (in constant dollars) from rising over time? Chapter Fifteen deals with retrenchment and management of cutbacks, offering a focus for this difficult topic in the agenda of the 1990s.

Finally, in Chapter Sixteen, I consider the capstone question of defining and achieving strategic direction for the university as a whole. Coordination among the elements of a university's strategy, and trade-offs between competing uses of resources, are of the essence. The task is urgent for every institution, as it is impossible to do everything academic and at the same time do it well. The chapter then looks forward to the effective university of the future. That emerging institution will accord due weight to the university's values and tradition but will adopt new elements of organization and technology in the conduct of academic programs and in administrative services, in order to come as close as possible to meeting goals of resource efficiency.

Chapters Fourteen and Fifteen are entirely new. Chapter Sixteen is a substantially redesigned version of the 1974 edition's concluding chapter.

With this assemblage of topics on university policy making and management, I seek to bring forward the most critically important questions (and guidance toward answers) for the executive decision maker, the trustee, the influential faculty leader and adviser, and those who provide analytical support. Concept and technique alone will not provide the answers, which in the nature of the case must depend on the particular circumstances of the institution, its tradition and priorities, and its robustness (and that of its leadership) under stress.

The University as an Information and Learning Organization

The university is the "information and learning organization" par excellence, society's main repository of systematic knowledge and its main contributor to tomorrow's scientific and humanistic understanding. The university is designed precisely for that mission. I venture the guess that the few years remaining of this century, and all of the next, will see information and learning organizations dominate in the advanced countries and be important in transitional societies as well. Other types of enterprises and institutions may therefore need to pay special attention to the university as the archetype of the organization where discovery and transmission of knowledge are both the reasons for existence and the occasion for enduring satisfaction.

Acknowledgments

Many friends and colleagues provided helpful critiques and suggestions. Intensive discussions with Alceste Pappas and Barbara Horst helped to set the initial agenda of new topics, which determined that this book had to be more than an update of the 1974 book. Particular chapters benefited from critical reading by Nelson Polsby and Bruce Cain, Joseph Cerny and Marisa Nerad, Janet Ruyle, Marian Gade, Neil Smelser, Gary Matkin, Cheryl Haigh, Richard West, and Richard Katz. Joyce Wan did fine work in bibliographical search during a part of a summer.

Janet Ruyle, formerly assistant director of the Center for Studies in Higher Education at Berkeley, put her wide professional experience to the task of verifying data, editing text, and completing large numbers of bibliographical references. Gale Erlandson, senior editor of the Higher and Adult Education Series at Jossey-Bass, exerted a rare blend of patience and persistence in guiding the book through many vicissitudes. Ann Richardson made crucial suggestions regarding both style and substance.

I want to acknowledge with deep gratitude the high professional competence and thoroughness of two external reviewers, President Kenneth Mortimer of the University of Hawaii System, and Professor Joseph Kauffman. They pointed out weaknesses in the earlier manuscript version, and I sought to respond to their many suggestions.

Conversations and debates too numerous to mention helped to deepen my appreciation of the challenges that universities face and the necessity of more powerful and far-reaching solutions to problems. Clark Kerr continues to be a formidable mentor concerning frameworks and trends in all of higher education, and it has been a privilege to work with him on current California Master Plan issues.

Involvement in university affairs has been a family matter. Canby Balderston, my father, was a professor and dean at the University of Pennsylvania for many years. He allowed me as a child to listen and observe on many occasions, and so my education began early in the matters discussed here. My son Daniel, a professor at Tulane University and chair of the Department of Spanish and Portuguese, has provided many insights. John Brooke, my son-in-law, is a history professor at Tufts University. He too offered a useful and needed corrective against the economist's temptation to believe that most serious problems are solved by rational deployment of scarce resources.

All this said, any errors of fact or interpretation are mine, with the recognition that one comes to a point of view with enormous debts to the literature of the field, to the varied insights of scholars and practitioners, and to the lessons flowing from participation in numerous institutional actions and events.

Judith Balderston and I assisted the higher education authorities of Indonesia over a period of half a dozen years. At the end of this interval, we edited and published the proceedings of a 1991 working conference on Indonesia's university reforms (Balderston and Balderston, 1993). This was our last opportunity to share ideas about universities, for the present book came to fruition too late to benefit from her acute intelligence as a reader, critic, and partner.

Berkeley, California   Frederick E. Balderston
February 1995

The Author

Frederick E. Balderston served on the regular faculty in the Haas School of Business, University of California, Berkeley, from 1953 to 1991. As professor emeritus, he continues to teach a graduate course in strategic planning. From 1966 to 1970, he served as vice president, business and finance, and then as vice president, planning and analysis, in the central administration of the university's nine-campus system, and he continued part-time as special assistant to the president until 1975. From 1968 to 1973, he and then-president Charles Hitch were coprincipal investigators of the Ford Foundation Program for Research in University Administration, headquartered at Berkeley. He also served as a member of the technical advisory committees of the Carnegie Commission on Higher Education and the Carnegie Council on Policy Studies in Higher Education.

Balderston has held other academic posts: as research associate in economics at the Massachusetts Institute of Technology; as visiting professor at Carnegie-Mellon University; as visiting scholar at Handelshögskolan in Stockholm (the Stockholm School of Economics) and at the University of Amsterdam. In fall 1985, he was a fellow at the Netherlands Institute for Advanced Study.

In 1963, Governor Edmund G. ("Pat") Brown appointed Balderston to be California savings and loan commissioner, and he served in that capacity until 1965, on leave from his faculty post. He subsequently continued his interest in financial research and wrote *Thrifts in Crisis* (1985). In 1991, he testified on the savings and loan industry to the House Banking Committee's Subcommittee on Financial Institutions. From 1986 through 1991, he was an adviser to Indonesia's Ministry of Finance on problems of financial regulation.

On his return to faculty duties in 1970, Balderston resumed the chairmanship of Berkeley's Center for Research in Management Science. He served as associate dean of the Business School for a total of three and a half years, and he was active on numerous committees of the business school, the Berkeley Academic Senate, and the Universitywide Academic Senate.

Balderston was coauthor (with A. C. Hoggatt) of *Simulation of Market Processes* (1961) and numerous articles in the field of marketing. He wrote the first edition of *Managing Today's University* (1974) after returning to the faculty from his administrative duties.

Balderston and his wife, Judith Balderston, also advised Indonesia's director general of higher education on Indonesia's higher education reforms. They organized a conference on the subject and then edited a monograph, *Higher Education in Indonesia: Evolution and Reform* (1993).

Balderston has consulted for various public and private organizations and has served on numerous boards. He was a board member of the National Center for Higher Education Management Systems for six years and of Deep Springs College for five years. A member of the Nature Conservancy's national board of governors for six years, he continues on the board of the California Nature Conservancy. He was a member of the board of directors of Golden West Financial Corporation from 1974 to 1988. Having served during World War II as an ambulance driver in the American Field Service (AFS), he became a life trustee of AFS Intercultural Programs, Inc. Balderston has served on the board of directors of the Bernard Osher Foundation since 1979. He was appointed executive vice president and executive director of the foundation in June 1994 and is actively involved in its management.

Balderston received a B.A. degree (1948) in economics from Cornell University and a Ph.D. degree (1953) in economics from Princeton University.

Managing Today's University

Chapter One

Organizing for Management

Universities are our greatest and most enduring social institutions. This book is devoted to their more effective management. The book draws much of its factual and analytical material from the major research universities in the United States, identified as Research Universities I in the latest revision of the Carnegie classification of institutions of higher education (Carnegie Foundation for the Advancement of Teaching, 1994). These 88 institutions (just 2.4 percent of the total) have the widest span of academic programs and the largest array of degrees granted, from B.A. and B.S. degrees through M.A. and professional school master's programs to the Ph.D. and other doctoral degrees (Evangelauf, 1994, pp. A17, A21). Thus, they are the most complex among the U.S. population of over thirty-six hundred higher education institutions. In many ways, they are also the most visible nationally and pose the most far-reaching issues of funding and policy.

Research Universities II (37 in number) and Doctoral Universities I and II (52 and 59, respectively) face most of the same problems of management as those encountered by the "top" institutions. In all cases, there is intense pressure to maintain or improve current quality and reputation. Research Universities I already have arrived at the apex of an undeniable "pecking order" of academia, and they struggle to remain in that select group, whereas most of the other doctorate-granting institutions are driving toward more intensive research, larger graduate programs, and broader recognition of their academic qualities.

In the next tier of the Carnegie classification are the Master's

(Comprehensive) Universities and Colleges I (439) and II (93). Many of these are highly ramified institutions with large enrollment; they share many management issues with the doctorate-granting institutions, and our discussion of academic organization, leadership, budgeting, and other problem areas will apply to them as surely as it does to the research universities. Thus, it is hoped that this book will be useful to all those who have official responsibilities in higher education, and to those who seek to be influential in its institutions. Where there is a need to adjust our analysis to deal with important differences of institutional mission, we will make note of it.

The significant universities vary greatly in age, size, legal form of organization, institutional style, and mode of financing. Yet they have in common the coupling of teaching and research, the offering of a diversity of programs up to the most advanced stages of systematic learning, and the implicit commitments to humane ideals and scholarly interests that cross the boundaries of governments. They are (mostly, but not entirely) focused on the young and paid for by the old, through government and private sponsors. They are supposed to endure forever, and they make their budgets one uncertain year at a time.

Today, universities in all parts of the United States and in much of the rest of the world have other features in common. Their sponsors consider them too important to leave alone in a world where knowledge counts, too costly to forget about, and yet dangerous to tinker with. Universities must thus make new accommodations to coordination and control; they face new requirements for planning, and demands for explicit, rational management.

Need for Management

Historically, the university grew as an institution, not as an enterprise or service agency. It is an institution in the sense that it makes strong claims of loyalty and effort on those involved with it, while it defends its distinctive, autonomous place in society and the right to choose its members, settle its aims, and operate in its own way. But now the university has become a mixture of institution, enterprise, and agency. This is partly because it has assembled a broad and confusing range of activities and operations, but a further reason is that the major parties at interest view it in different ways: the faculty and students, as an institution; the trustees and some administrators, as an enterprise; and the governmental sponsors, as an agency. Conflicts of purpose, law, motivation, and style flow from these differing views.

University budgets have risen in the past five decades at a much faster rate than the GNP. This growth is the result of enrollment expansion, program elaboration, productivity problems, new responsibilities, and inflation. Universities have put mounting pressure on their sponsors, and now they face counterpressures—both for planning and control and for severe budgetary constraint. Many universities are having to stabilize or even retrench in their activities and budgets after getting accustomed to the euphoria of growth and a rising internal standard of living.

More than ever, universities are embattled institutions, pressing claims on society that, in many countries, society is reluctant to honor. An air of pessimism pervades the higher education scene as the turn of the century approaches, exemplified only too clearly by the titles of Clark Kerr's important books: *Higher Education Cannot Escape History: Issues for the Twenty-first Century;* and *Troubled Times for American Higher Education: The 1990s and Beyond* (both 1994). The problems of funding, scope, and mission are held to be severe, both in the United States and in many other countries, and the topic of university management thus gains additional urgency.

Inescapably, the focus of this book is on the allocation of scarce resources in universities, and on the analytics of choice about organization, effectiveness, priority, and decision. This management perspective was perhaps more novel in 1974, when the first edition of *Managing Today's University* appeared, than it is in 1995. But the need for explicit and systematic management is, if anything, greater.

As a teacher, administrator, and true believer in the university and what it seeks to do, I am only too aware of the paradox of this book: systematic approaches to management run counter to the university tradition. To some important academic audiences, "management" is a term conveying insult and provocation. And management is indeed a risk, for some of its systematic techniques could deliver the university to its enemies or could damage its capacity to evoke the imagination, the stamina, and the free commitment that are essential for original learning. Thus, the obligation is to create, explain, and use approaches to management that will enhance the university's viability and effectiveness and sensitively serve—and not impair—the work of the scholar and student. Such approaches must be applied with wisdom in the particular case, and their exposition must show that they take into account the elements of motivation and commitment without which the quality—and quantity—of work in the academy could not be sustained.

Processes, Mechanisms, and Consequences

Everyone involved in university management should give equal attention to *processes*, *mechanisms*, and *consequences*.

The most crucial—and mysterious—of the processes are those of learning, seasoning of character, creativity at the edges of knowledge and imagination, and responsible advocacy of values. These are supported by many other processes, such as communication, the delivery of intricate combinations of services, the tracking and evaluation of ideas, people, and resources, and decision making.

The mechanisms and structures of the university—its organization and physical facilities—are the means by which the processes operate. Both structures and mechanisms are largely given at any particular time. Their sizes, shapes, and condition are endowments of capability and also barriers to easy and rapid change. Change is costly and requires both design and investment.

Universities are more attuned to their processes and their mechanisms than they are to consequences. They customarily have much more exact measures of activity or size than of results. It is easier to find out how many students a university has than what the students have learned or how they have changed. The number of books a university has published is more readily determined than the relative merits of those books. Even the moral commitments of a university are largely to processes and mechanisms—for example, the process of free inquiry and exchange of ideas, the mechanisms for fair assessment and for conflict resolution—rather than to consequences or agreed goals. But as to philosophical ends, universities are designed to house enduring disagreements without breaking apart.

Universities may be a prototype of the postindustrial organization. Partly, this is because they live on and for knowledge, and knowledge—its creation, dissemination, and application—is crucial. But it may be, also, that the university at its best offers an interesting and sensitive balance between individuality and collective interdependence; between felt commitment and formal authority; between creativity and production; and even between the frivolous and the serious, the sacred and the profane. Other organizations, if they are to advance the human condition, may in the future have to become more like universities than the other way around. The topics covered here, then, may be of some interest for comparative organization.

We have said that the processes, mechanisms, and consequences of university operations require equal attention. Where, then, are the foci of decision making and of management in this intricate institutional context?

Constraints on Resources

University resources are scarce relative to hopes and needs, and it must be anticipated that this condition will dominate decision making in the 1990s, and beyond. In most instances, explicit institutional decisions are made about the use of resources; but sometimes the pattern of usage is implicitly determined as hundreds or thousands of individuals press their claims on each other and on the institution. Whatever the mode of resource allocation, universities will have to operate in a regime of scarcity for the foreseeable future. Efforts toward more effective use of resources and a fine instinct for the inevitable trade-offs will be important and will even tend to dominate the institutional scene. Therefore, increasing weight is now given to explicit decisions about the allocation of resources, and the good sense with which these decisions can be made is one significant issue to which this book is addressed.

Complexity and Bureaucratization

Universities are complex and bureaucratic; yet in many matters, they are voluntaristic and consultative. We cannot, therefore, examine the issues as if there were one decision maker or one manager. Rather, proposals and counterproposals, weighing of possibilities, and consultation with those who legally or functionally have a role in the decision—all these contribute to the important official determinations. In short, we deal with the operation and design of a managerial process and not the question of coaching a particular executive to do the right thing.

This perspective draws directly from the work of Barnard (1938), Simon (1947), Cyert and March (1963), and their successors in the modern theory of the properties and behavior of formal organizations. According to that theory, authority does not necessarily proceed from the top down but to the extent that one person is willing to have his span of actions limited or directed by another, is conferred by subordinates on their superiors (Barnard). Goals are worked out through numerous accommodations in the organization rather than, as may appear, being adopted and announced from on high. The survival of the organization requires a rough equilibrium between what its participants of all types deliver to it and what they get from it (Barnard, 1938; Simon, 1947). Thus, the boundaries of the organization are not limited by its legal definition but by the functional ways in which various classes of participants are involved in it. In the executive parlance of the 1990s, managers must often deal with a "boundaryless corporation," embracing its suppliers and customers as well as its internal units. (See, for example, Smart, Engardio, and Smith, 1993; Hirschhorn and Gilmore, 1992.)

Within every organization, an informal organization is intertwined with the formal structure (Barnard, 1938; Simon, 1947). The informal organization is a strikingly powerful phenomenon in the university (Pfeffer and Salancik, 1974). Decision makers strive for effective participation and are activated by their identification with the organization, as well as by the desire for pay and status. But they are limited by incomplete information and by difficulties in calculating how to be rational. They function according to concepts of "bounded rationality" (Simon, 1947). The direction of an organization, according to the theory, is imparted by the efforts of its executives to adjust and focus its procedures and mechanisms, by their interest in the selection of key personnel, and by their success in locating the strategic kernel of the often ill-defined choices affecting the organization's long-range future (Barnard, 1938).

This management-as-process approach fits the university. Because we do not accept titles and positions at face value but are interested in the functioning of the managerial process, we shall have to accept that there are many contributors to this process, some with administrative titles and others without. And we must understand how to organize the process; we cannot simply create titles and choose individuals for them. Perhaps it is not a forlorn hope that this functional view will soften the antagonism of the academic reader toward the notion of managing a university, for it will be shown that the skilled and active participation of students and faculty, as individuals and as groups, is crucial to the effective conduct of the institution. Managing can no more be left to administrators than—as the famous aphorism has it—war can be left to the generals.

It is, however, true—and it will be shown, as each topic is

treated, why it increasingly has to be true—that the trend is toward processes of decision that are explicit and systematic, not implicit, diffuse, and atomistic. In the past, many important questions were buried by attempts to build collegial consensus or were left to happenstance. Such questions require us to examine goals, clarify information, consider elements that are difficult to reconcile, and make courageous choices between alternatives.

The Demand for Greater Accountability

All the institutions of contemporary American society face new pressures to "show cause" and to engage in explicit reexamination of what they are doing and of the consequences of their actions. Corporations are required to respond to new legal standards related to environmental concerns. Employers and trade unions must show affirmative action as well as nondiscrimination in employment. Charitable foundations must demonstrate that they are following explicit standards of deportment. Courts and law enforcement agencies must conform to explicit standards of individual justice. Even political organizations and politicians must observe a heightened sensitivity to certain community expectations.

Contemporary society has an increased awareness of interdependence, and all types of organizations are now obliged to deal with additional dimensions of their behavior and its consequences and to function in a more explicit and justifiable manner. Universities cannot expect to be an exception.

University Management and Political Skills

Several important political dimensions and pressures affect both the internal operation and the external relations of universities. Coalition building and bargaining have emerged as important features of the internal workings of universities, and the distribution of power—and its retention—becomes crucial to university presidents and academic leaders. Universities face many novel changes in modes of operation, and the management of change requires high political skills.

Political pressures have also become more powerful at all levels in the external environments of universities—national, state, and local. As resources for all public sector needs become increasingly constrained, universities compete with insistent, politically powerful, and meritorious claimants for public support. Universities must occasionally fight these battles in the highly public arenas of elections and legislative hearings, but more usually they deal with political representatives and government agency personnel who make myriad demands for information and justification of university actions and requests. The university must be able to function in this political arena, and its representatives need to have stamina and an appropriate political perspective to absorb and overcome the inevitable tensions and hostilities. These representatives need to make a positive case for support that will be persuasive to political leaders; doing so is much easier if broader public attitudes toward the universities are favorable, or at least neutral. Vulnerable as they are in the political environment, universities may be greatly damaged by adverse publicity of any kind: a president's perquisites or peccadilloes; a faculty member's alleged falsification of research data; a student protest that gets out of hand.

Universities also feel increasing pressure from formal superstructures of several kinds, including superboards and coordinating agencies, interinstitutional agreements, and complex relationships with agencies at various levels of government. The management of relations with these superstructures occupies an increasingly important place in the university administrator's agenda. This book will show how universities can fulfill their missions more effectively than before by responding in creative ways to the new pressures for explicitness. Ironically, the greater accountability demanded of universities does not necessarily result in greater acceptance and credibility. However, opinion surveys apparently do show mild but positive public confidence in academic institutions and their professors (Prewitt, 1993, pp. 90–93).

The university is only one of many institutions in higher—or, more fashionably, postsecondary—education. But it is the oldest, the most visible, and the most complicated in organization and function. Thus, analysis of university management will also offer many clues to the management of educational institutions having a narrower scope and mission.

Elements of University Management

The first task in developing an appreciation of the managerial process is to examine the main features of university operations and determine the degree of complexity inherent in these and the connections between them. There are several essential domains of analysis: funding (the acquisition of financial balances with which to defray the costs of resource inputs); resource inputs (personnel, raw materials and supplies, and the services of capital goods); processes or activities (which use resource inputs to produce outputs); and goals (indicators of achievement or welfare of the institution).

Each of these domains is composed of numerous elements. Thus, one must speak of multiple sources of funding, multiple resource inputs, multiple activities and outputs, and multiple goals. Furthermore, the linkages between funding elements, resource inputs, activities, and goals involve combinations and interdependencies. It will be necessary to examine the aspects of complementarity, independence, and substitution. These relationships are important to the decision maker. For example, if two types of resources are substitutes for each other in a given process, it may be possible to economize by using more of one resource and less of the other to keep the process operating at the same level as before; but if two resources are strictly complementary, a decrease in the use of one cannot be offset by an increase in the use of the other. Considerations of complementarity, independence, and substitution are discussed here in connection with funding, resource inputs, activities or programs, and purposes. These relationships can be tested by looking backward from purposes to programs to resources to funding.

Suppose that to hire a work-study student, it is necessary to pay 50 percent of the wages from institutional funds, while special federal funds pay the rest. The two sources of funds are complementary, for the university cannot get the federal money without putting up institutional funds of its own. An alumnus who gives money for a guest lectureship, with the restriction that it can be used only for that purpose, illustrates an independence relationship. But two funds are substitutes if they may be used in varying proportions to pay for the same resource.

By looking *forward* from funding toward purposes, we detect other aspects of interdependence. It is noteworthy that the categories of funding come first, and that a particular set of resource inputs and activities may draw its funding entirely from one source, or from multiple sources. An activity supported by a restricted fund (such as an extramurally funded research grant) is conditional on its funding; if that lapses, the research project must be discontinued, unless the university steps in with replacement dollars from discretionary, general funds. The 1990s environment of scarcity guarantees that funding for most resource inputs and activities will be heavily competitive at the margin. The highest marginal value will attach to discretionary university funds. The greatest protection for a particular activity will occur when it has restricted funding that is wholly earmarked to support that activity, and when that funding enables the activity to be self-sustaining—that is, the funding is adequate to support the activity without need of any other support.

Multiple uses of a resource can be easily illustrated. A particular resource such as faculty may be allocated in part to the activity of supervising dissertation research, which produces contributions to two goals (educated people and new knowledge). In this example, each unit of the faculty resource that is used up has inherent joint consequences. If a particular constituency favors the goal of educating people but not the goal of contributing to new knowledge, the fact that both goals receive a contribution leaves that constituency dissatisfied with the employment of the resource. Instances of this kind of interdependence, or "jointness," are widespread in universities. As we shall see in subsequent chapters, jointness complicates considerably the tasks of cost analysis and cost management.

Guiding the affairs of a university would not be an onerous task if the fundamentals of the structure were simple: one funding source providing for the purchase of one type of resource input (bought and sold in a perfect market); and a single productive activity with a single output that contributed to a single, well-defined goal—the achievement of which would induce the sponsors of the activity to provide continued or expanded funding. But the actual situation is not simple. The general goals of a university are shrouded in vagueness. By common consent, there are several goals, but there is no consensus among those concerned with universities about the relative importance of the goals, the interdependencies among them, or ways of measuring attainment of them.

A university contains a great array of processes and activities, each of which produces one or more types of result or output. Some outputs contribute to a single goal and others to the attainment of two or more goals. Classification and analysis of the processes and identification of the ways in which one process is needed for the performance of another are technical tasks in which some progress has been made. But choosing priorities among these processes, assigning responsibilities for them to units of organization, and adding or dropping academic programs involve decisions that arouse questions of institutional purpose, power, and function.

Processes and activities absorb resources. We now have better ways to trace resource use and impute costs to ongoing programs and activities. But in the short run, the capital plant of a university (its buildings, land, library collection, and major equipment) and its roster of professors and senior administrative personnel are fixed in supply and are heterogeneous and specialized resources. One task of management is to finance and allocate variable inputs and supplies so that the plant and faculty can function well. Another is to foster improvements in the quality of plant and faculty and find financing. A further and much more difficult task is to arrange reassignments of the largely fixed resources from lower-priority needs to expanding ones. And finally, management must supervise new investment in capital facilities and approve long-term employment commitments of academic and administrative staff, thereby shaping future patterns of change in institutional programs and mission.

A university has multiple sources and types of funding. For all major universities, the most important source is government. However, this is not a single source, and funding is not in a single, undifferentiated bloc without conditions on use or purpose. (Money is fungible, but funding is not!) Several levels of government and numerous agencies may be sources of financing, each willing to supply funds only for specific uses and under defined conditions. Government (in the United States, state governments; in most of Europe, the national ministries of education) allocates operating support to public universities under stated conditions of use in specific resource input or program categories. American private universities assemble their general university funds from a combination of endowment income (to the extent that it is not earmarked for special purposes), student tuitions, and current gifts from alumni and other donors. Both public and private universities depend heavily on federally funded research grants and contracts.

General university funds are the most precious funding source because they can be applied to a wide range of uses. But there is an important class of funding cases in which increments of funding are strictly tied to one subset of processes or activities contributing to a specific part of the goal domain; the funds may not be used to serve any others. This earmarked, or restricted, funding is independent of general funds. The client—the funding source—is supporting the resource inputs and the subset of activities because of the client's interest in a specific output or goal of the university. In this case, an increase in general university funds has no positive effect—and a decrease may have no negative effect—either on the willingness of the client to supply earmarked funds or on the results obtained from the activities supported with such funds.

Acquisition of funds is a complicated institutional task involving a great many actors and, for the different types of funds, differing sequences of negotiations and decisions. The stewardship function, which ensures that financial resources are accounted for and that legal and other conditions on their use are met, involves additional personnel and decision sequences. Still another group of people and procedures may determine the allocation of funds among activities, units of organization, and uses. (This is true only in cases where such decisions can be made within the university.) And still another group, using its own procedures of decision, monitors the use of funds to ensure that desired effects are achieved from the processes and activities supported.

In dealing with these relationships between funds, resources, activities and their outputs, and goals, the central administration guides and monitors a series of decision sequences and operations. It is no wonder that the crazy-quilt pattern is baffling to outside observers; its inherent complexity is usually not well understood even by those whose professional lives are at stake.

Some universities live in absolute poverty, facing a constant threat of closure because their funds are insufficient to deal with the immediate consequences of fixed commitments. But no university is absolutely rich, in the sense that some source of funds is freely available, without conditions, for every conceivable activity or recommended change of commitments. A university can be well-off only in relation to its commitments and mission.

Mission and Scope

The mission of the university is traditionally defined as "teaching, research, and public service." The full-scale university offers curricula leading to the most advanced degrees in a variety of fields, and in these areas it faces direct competition, as well as some complementary relationships, with other types of institutions. Universities may also offer nondegree instruction, such as short courses, certificate programs, and informal education for specialized, often very advanced clienteles. Frequently classified under the head of *public service* because they do not lead to formal academic degrees, these courses compete with many alternative methods (varying greatly among nations, institutions, and fields) of upgrading professional knowledge or providing intellectual stimulus not related to occupation.

Faculty members in all types of degree-granting institutions may engage in research and original scholarship as well as in teaching. But the obligation to do research is built into the faculty member's role at a university. The proportion of faculty time devoted to research is highest in the research universities, which tend to emphasize basic, rather than applied, research. Systematic inquiry by individuals or groups of scholars, leading to new findings in each field represented at the institution, is a function having a proper claim on a university's resources—a claim that the institution presses on its sponsors. The processes of instruction and the processes of research are in some ways distinct, and they compete for space, personnel, and other resources. Universities, and particularly their academic spokespersons, claim that strong complementary linkages exist between instruction and research. Few people argue that the functions of teaching and research must always be closely coupled. The able high school teacher of mathematics or history should certainly have ample background in the discipline, skills in organization and exposition, and empathy with students. But he or she is not obliged to publish as an original scholar. Industrial or governmental chemists are expected to perform research tasks, and they may publish in the technical literature, but they are not expected to teach. The link between teaching and research is, however, an article of faith in the universities.

Public service—beyond the provision of education to students for their useful lives and of the results of scholarly inquiry to the world generally—is arguably an element of university mission. Public service contributions of a university assist local, regional, or national constituencies by providing them with information, enlightenment, or amusement. In the United States, the Morrill Act of 1863 (establishing land-grant institutions) added public service to the university agenda. The university may have programs of applied research and problem solving for public agencies and other significant clienteles. It may disseminate information to professional and lay clienteles, operate educational radio stations, sponsor cultural events for the university community and a wider public, operate hospitals and clinics, maintain park space and museums, and offer harmless amusements and ritual gatherings.

Some of these activities are spin-offs from teaching and research commitments, others are important to the community and to various clienteles, and still others are part of the university's marketing effort and its attempt to preserve relations with supporting constituencies. These activities add to administrative and organizational complexity, and many of them come into question if they do not make a contribution to the university's resources or at least appear to break even.

A most important task of university management is to guide the institution's definition of its mission and scope, determining changes in the array of programs and in their scale and quality. For institutions that are affected by state or national schemes of planning, coordination, and control, the guidance includes negotiation with the superstructure.

The campus administration, like Janus, must look in two directions at once: to the relations of the university with its external environments (for sources of students, resource markets, clients, and funds) and to its internal relations with the ongoing institutional processes and constituencies. (Thus, the frequently heard accusation that a college president is two-faced is functionally accurate!)

Image and Reputation

When interpreting a university's mission, the administration must look to two levels: the global image of the campus, and the valuation of particular degree programs and their impact on the occupational and academic marketplaces.

The global image of a campus conveys indications of its quality and distinctiveness. Its academic programs and departments contribute to this positively if they are of recognized quality and negatively if they are perceived to be poor. They add to the distinctiveness of the campus if they support an image of specialized strengths (for example, Massachusetts Institute of Technology's programs in physics, computer science, and electrical engineering) or convey independent distinction (for example, Cornell University's medical school, which is separated both geographically and functionally from the Ithaca campus).

Doctoral and professional degree recipients go to distinct and diverse career destinations. They are hired for specialized jobs for which their advanced training is essential. Certain specialists, such as biophysicists, may be needed by only a few employers. A law degree, however, may serve as background for many jobs other than those in a law firm. Executives and administrators who make hiring decisions evaluate a campus mainly as a source for the specialties in which they are hiring. The general reputation of the campus may, however, create a positive or negative halo effect in areas other than those from which graduates are being recruited.

Academic Programs

The design of academic programs is determined by what the bodies of knowledge are held to be, by how the professions are defined, and by the educational selections the university and its sponsors are willing to provide. Any university, at a given time, contains only a sampling of the known span of academic programs.

The bodies of knowledge, thought by the Encyclopedists of the eighteenth century to be capable of definitive classification and integrated mastery, expand in number over time and subdivide into specialties and subspecialties as far as ingenuity and the search for differentiation of the intellectual product can take them. To be a useful point of definition for an academic program, a body of knowledge has to be institutionalized, with an identifiable company of scholars sharing interests and findings in it, an apparatus of publication, agreed standards of scholarship, and some basis for recognizing who the scholars are and what they have to know. Intellectual and academic history gives the broad groupings: humane letters, fine arts, languages, mathematics, philosophy, history; the social sciences; the life sciences; and the physical sciences. Within each of these, subdivision and specialization continue, and hybrids develop.

Intellectual and academic history also provide the list of the traditional learned professions: law, medicine, and theology. Modern professions for which systematic education is all or part of the process of licensing have followed: dentistry; engineering (and its subdivisions); architecture and urban planning; and education. In fields such as business and public administration, librarianship, and social work, systematic education has been developed to improve and standardize training in these fields and to give the trained professional the opportunity to compete advantageously with those who have learned what they know through on-the-job experience; licensing may or may not be a general condition of employment.

The ministries of education in the European countries and the National Center for Education Statistics of the U.S. Department of Education, publish statistics of enrollment and degrees granted. To do this, they adopt descriptive classifications of disciplines and professions. State coordinating agencies and such organizations as the National Center for Higher Education Management Systems (NCHEMS) have developed academic program classifications for use in planning and costing. The most detailed of these classification schemes define the range of programs that a university may offer. As new fields emerge from the research process or from the development of newly defined professions, the classification schemes must include them. In the United States, many disciplines and professions serve as accrediting bodies. Each professional organization develops, for its own purposes, specifications of the educational content and the staffing and resource standards that must be met by an institution seeking certification. Academic institutions in the United States are to a great extent in business for themselves (although state coordinating agencies are now increasingly constraining them), and accrediting organizations provide a means of enforcing some conventions of respectability and quality control. (In other nations, where the ministry of education has power to approve initiation of academic programs and monitor their conduct, and is usually the main or sole source of funding, the ministry does the accrediting.) A university typically has internal mechanisms for approval of each degree program. These enable it to control certification of students' achievements and to identify officially approved programs to which institutional resources may properly be committed.

The decision to have a particular degree program is distinct from the question of how to organize and manage it. Each program leading to a degree is, crudely put, a product, and each student who completes that program is a unit of product. Responsibility for each program may be assigned to any of a great variety of organizations: schools and colleges, departments within colleges, and committees that administer degrees. The design of such structures and assignment of responsibilities within them are discussed in subsequent chapters.

Types of Institutions

A university is defined by the span of academic programs it offers. Some of these programs should lead to academic degrees at the most advanced level of scholarship or graduate professional learning, with concomitant research commitments. If very few fields are represented, the institution has insufficient variety to be thought of as a university, even though it may have high academic distinction. Some of the institutes of technology in the United States have broadened their offerings to include management studies, social sciences, and other fields and professions. Some, such as Carnegie-Mellon University (formerly the Carnegie Institute of Technology) have changed to the university name, while others cling to the old title.

Handelshögskolan in Stockholm, Sweden (the Stockholm School of Economics) continues in the continental tradition of the independent higher technical school. In 1972, the well-known Nederlandse Economische Hogeschool in Rotterdam became part of the new Erasmus University, which also has a new medical faculty and is developing additional faculties. In France, l'École Polytechnique and other *grandes écoles* operate entirely outside the traditional French universities, training the most elite cadres for French government and industry. These independent technical schools, and some remaining independent medical colleges and professional schools in the United States, have the advantage of simplicity of institutional design, but they may be isolated from the wider intellectual developments in academia. Art institutes and conservatories of music offer highly focused curricula and emphasize apprenticeship-like training in performance rather than offering a mainly intellectual and scholarly appreciation of the field. At a major university, such a specialized entity might well have difficulties in meeting general university standards for faculty appointment and advancement.

I have discussed the functions and programs of the university. The name *university* conveys academic status, too, and an implicit mandate to claim more functions. Northern Illinois University and Portland State University in Oregon are examples of state-sponsored colleges that got both the name and the university mandate during the expansion of the 1960s. In 1972, the California legislature changed the name of the California State College system to the California State University and Colleges, and, in 1982, to the California State University. Most of the state colleges, such as San Francisco State (twenty-nine thousand students in 1992) and San Jose State (thirty thousand students), became universities in 1972. For these large and diversified institutions with strong faculties in many areas, that was undoubtedly a welcome step. In other states and in better academic times, renaming has gone in tandem with the initiation of doctoral degrees, programs in the prestigious graduate professions, and a substantial research program.

Programs and Institutional Goals

A university is located in the markets for reputation, faculty, and students. It may be visible or obscure, strong in all fields or variable in reputation from field to field. The same institutionalizing forces that define each body of knowledge—existence of a corps of scholars, standards of evaluation and accreditation, and a system of scholarly publication and communication—serve as the main source of judgment of a university's prestige in each field, largely via the visibility and reputations of its senior faculty.

Changes in the reputation of a department are noted first by the cognoscenti and then, with successive time lags, by the wider groups of academics, graduate students, impinging professional clienteles, and other publics.

The academic administrators of a campus are also interested in how successfully the graduates from each degree program are placed and how well each program is regarded at the career destinations and by those who are knowledgeable about program quality at other institutions. Thus, each degree program contributes in two ways to the institution's image: through its direct, department-specific impact on a clientele community; and through a (generally mild) impact on the reputation of the campus. Although degree programs compete with each other for budgetary support, each degree program is seen by the campus-level administrator as independent of the others or as complementary to them in programmatic and reputational terms. Only if a program actively detracts from the perceived acceptability of the campus and its other degree programs (because, for example, of a very much lower perceived quality than the average on the campus) will the administrator draw the inference that reduction or elimination of that program would improve the status of the campus. (Eliminating a weak program would also save resources, though not right away.)

There are other reasons a given program might be viewed as incompatible with the intentions and market locus of a campus: (1) the program might violate an image of highly defined specialization in degree markets that the campus is seeking to build; (2) the program might require a student clientele that is seen as incompatible with the students normally enrolled on the campus.

A university that has a reasonably wide range of degree programs and deals with both undergraduate and graduate students is unlikely to perceive incompatibility of either of the above types. Thus, in the evaluation of what happens to degree recipients and how well they are regarded, degree programs are generally either independent of or complementary to one another; they are unlikely to be competitors. New degree programs, too, are likely to satisfy the criterion of nonsubstitution with respect to existing ones. Thus, from the standpoint of relations with degree-recipient markets, a campus that is already comprehensive has no incentives to avoid additional programs (the case of independence) and may have positive incentives to initiate them (to achieve complementarity).

A university administration typically has no direct incentives to reduce or eliminate an existing program because of negative impacts on general goals. In principle, a university has an incentive to expand—to offer new programs that will add new elements to its goal performance but will not adversely affect the valuations placed on its existing programs and their size and quality. Only as we focus attention on the strategic advantages of concentrating resources and attention *selectively* is there a check against the proliferation of programs.

The Role of Research in the University

A faculty's high reputation for basic research in a particular discipline has several consequences. First, it adds to the global eminence of the institution. Second, it increases the value of those receiving advanced professional and scholarly degrees in that discipline and enhances their prospects for placement. This is due, in part, to the fact that faculty members who are eminent in research are influential among their peers, nationally and internationally. Third, a good reputation attracts better students, from a wider market, and these students are more likely to become distinguished graduates. Fourth, outstanding researchers in a field with an active funding market will more easily attract funds for their individual research activities and may even act as nucleating agents in attracting funds for the support of junior faculty and graduate students. Finally, an eminent research faculty is, by definition, at the most important frontiers of its field. It thus contributes to an atmosphere of intellectual striving and excitement in its own specialty and on the campus in general.

The university administration views applied research and service activity somewhat differently from the way it views basic research. The former provide a service or problem-solving capability for a clientele group. In scholarly fields where basic research determines reputation and prestige, applied research and service activity are not likely to add to the attracting power of the institution in the eyes of scholars or outstanding students. However, the attitude of the university administration to a proposed new program in one of these categories is likely to be "Why not?" if the client organization is willing to provide full funding. Such funding is considered to be independent of any other funding and not available unless the applied program or service activity is undertaken. Furthermore, an additional external clientele is pleased and (it is hoped) no other clientele is offended. Finally, the added resources brought with the earmarked funding may contribute to other purposes if used in joint-output processes, and the overhead of the institution can be spread over the additional activity.

Nevertheless, problems may arise from the accumulation of applied research and service functions. Within the institution, those committed to basic scholarship may complain that too much energy is devoted to applied research, and may seek control over funding and resources in order to reserve them for "higher-level" purposes. The consequent conflict with the faculty and research cadres who are devoted to the applied research or service activity may become an administrative problem. Furthermore, if the proponents of basic scholarship are successful, the external clientele may be disappointed by the diversion of attention from its perceived needs and interests. The external constituency may impose conditions—tight control of the earmarked funds or security classification of research results and clearance for the personnel involved—that conflict with the policy standards of the institution. Those devoted to basic scholarship may also argue that the applied activity diminishes prestige and thus devalues other areas of goal performance. Finally, although the applied activity may have been thought to be manageable with no increase in overhead, its growth expands the burdens on support administrators and adds to the complexity of the institution's management tasks.

Reputation and Student Enrollment

The charter, origins, and specific history of a university affect the numbers and qualifications of the students it attracts. Some institutions have wide latitude in managing their location in the markets for students. Others must accept enrollment according to rules set by governmental sponsors: neither the amount of enrollment nor the standards of eligibility for admission are within the institution's control.

A private university or college expects to make money on its undergraduates and to use the surplus for its graduate programs. For this reason, it has an interest in pursuing a selective admissions policy. The correlations between the high school achievement level of a student and the educational level, income, and assets of his or her parents are well-known. Less qualified students therefore cost the institution money in financial aid that offsets tuition income. They also make a greater call on academic resources and have less prospect of success in graduate school or in occupational placement. Yet private colleges and universities have devoted increased resources to the education of minority members and economically disadvantaged students. Often, this has been stimulated by the liberal social views of faculty and middle-class students. In the perspective of general public policy, it is a good thing that many private universities and colleges have broadened their admissions policies. But, for the top administrators, this has caused problems of varying acuteness. Internal stresses have been temporarily heightened by the presence of a new student constituency, and many conservative alumni and donor clienteles have become disgruntled.

Admissions policy in a state-supported university must take cues from the political context and the state superstructure of regulation. The link between admissions policy and tuition income is historically weak, although the rapid rise of public university tuition beginning toward the end of the 1980s has forced the state institutions closer to their private competitors.

Selective admission still enhances institutional prestige and the academic performance and career success of graduates. But state institutions must be able to justify denial of admission to a resident of the state, and the standards must be explicit and public. Admissions policy has to be supported by political bargains. If a public university is to exercise some selectivity in admissions policy, it must do so under the shelter of such negotiated arrangements. Political bargains call for budgetary support of each state institution, in return for which the institution provides its share of access to educational opportunity. These shares are variously allocated to the state university, the comprehensive colleges, and the community colleges by means of admissions eligibility rules. Even while it vaunts its academic prestige and tries to demonstrate the worth of that prestige to the political power structure and general citizenry of the state, the administrative leadership of a high-quality state university has to pursue a less selective admissions policy than its counterparts among private universities. And it seeks in various ways to avoid the elitist label. Politically, the greatest enemy of the high-quality public university is the right-wing populist politician, who attracts away the support of the conservative establishment while, at the same time, denying the university support on egalitarian grounds! (For example, in the 1960s then-governor Ronald Reagan sometimes argued that community colleges and master's-granting institutions could deliver mass higher education at less expense than could the University of California, yet also said that the elite functions of doctoral education and research could be the province of the privately supported universities.) The administration of a high-quality public university may also face significant problems in the domain of goals, where it may have to justify graduate programs that fail to meet the workforce needs of the state or that have high loss rates because mobile graduates take jobs outside the state.

We have now completed an examination of the multiplicity inherent in funding, processes and outputs, and institutional goals.

The links between these, in the form of complementarity, independence, and substitution, provide an initial perspective on the managerial process. Next, in Chapter Two, we examine the values or norms of behavior that impress themselves on the members of a university community and give a university its special character. This is a different dimensional view of normative issues from the one just discussed, but it is no less essential, for it is concerned with the individual and group values that make possible a university's scheme of largely voluntaristic learning and determine the atmosphere of the institution.

Chapter Two

Values of the University

The informing values of a university are drawn from the surrounding society and from academic traditions. These values condition important aspects of individuals' behavior in the university community, stimulating them toward the hard effort of learning, and binding them together in subtle ways. Differing interpretations of these values—for example, with respect to "political correctness" and the limits of "hate speech"—may also heighten tensions in the academy and present its leaders with very difficult choices.

Gatherings and Their Protection

Members of a university find themselves together on many different kinds of occasions, sometimes as performers, sometimes as audience. Their expected behavior varies, depending on whether they are at a course lecture, an official exercise, a tutorial session, a political rally, a seminar, or a football game. Each type of occasion reflects a facet of the essential institution. Mass spectator sports are not unique, of course, to universities; but athletic events are a traditional indulgence of Anglo-American universities. Often, these and other large-scale entertainments serve as the one common ground for very different constituencies, from the sentimental alumnus to the undergraduate.

Cultural events also claim large audiences. Universities are justified in serving as patrons of concerts, museums and their exhibitions, plays, films, and public lectures. These stimulate the aesthetic appreciation of students, and they generally yield significant psychic income to the kinds of people who collect in and around universities. They are worthwhile for their own sake, and they promote shared interest in a civilized life.

The university makes specific moral demands of both the performer and the scholarly audience at scheduled academic occasions—such as public lectures, colloquia, or course meetings—where a scholar presents findings and ideas. The presenter is obligated to state findings and views fairly and fully, to give credit to sources, and, as an advocate, to accept fair questions and critique. (It also helps if the speaker is interesting.) The audience has an obligation to hear the speaker out and to distinguish between the courtesy it owes the presenter and the critical response it should make to the ideas presented.

Underlying all of this are presumptions of the lecturer's competence to speak and the audience's openness to being instructed (although not necessarily persuaded) by what is said. The purpose fails if the audience is put to sleep, and it also fails if the speaker is a demagogic success. If the occasion breaks down and the audience will not permit the speaker to go on, this is not merely a discourtesy to the speaker but an affront to the standards of academic life. In periods of heightened political and moral passions, such breakdowns have sometimes occurred, both in sponsored public lectures and—very occasionally—in academic courses offered for credit, when the speaker was an object of rage or when part of the audience was determined to take over the occasion to provoke a confrontation with the university. Prudent presidents have sometimes canceled commencement exercises or have decided not to invite certain lecturers when there were risks of such disruptions.

Universities rediscovered, in the 1960s, that they were vulnerable institutions. The disintegration of the moral consent to let ideas take their chances was a frightening experience, and it demonstrated clearly how dependent a university is on felt restraints, as opposed to mere bureaucratic authority. As the police are well aware, a few policemen at a big gathering can control the aberrant behavior of a few individuals only if the crowd is over-whelmingly interested in allowing them to do so. And, of course, increasing the number of police or the amount of force deployed may be no solution at all.

In the conduct of academic occasions, the university lives by a different and more subtle standard than that guaranteed by the First Amendment. Members of the audience are obligated to restrain or at least postpone their free speech rights so that the purpose of the occasion can be served. The speaker is obligated to conform to stan-dards of academic conduct, in both content and manner of speech. Failure to do so, on the part of either speaker or audience, breaches the academic code, even if the behavior is completely within the scope of First Amendment rights.

When civility fell off in the universities, administrators had to develop explicit distinctions between varieties of academic occa-sion, kinds of speaker, categories of eligible sponsoring organization, and types of eligible participant in the audience. They had to do this not only in the interest of elementary physical control (which was sometimes impossible to guarantee anyhow) but in order to pre-serve the moral imperatives of academic conduct and to make these credible and enforceable in the university community. Adminis-trators faced two other problems not unique to universities: they had to defend their institutions from external intervention and from internal misappropriation.

One distinction that could be drawn fairly easily was between a scheduled meeting of an academic course for credit and any other campus gathering. The administrators increasingly limited their regulation of general meetings to the "time, place, and man-ner" of conducting the particular occasion. There was no longer any institutional guarantee that speakers had academic endorse-ment or that audiences would be respectful. The only remaining restraint—eligibility of the sponsoring organization to use uni-versity facilities—was confined to a few requirements concerning the public responsibility of the sponsoring organization and to questions of scheduling.

This very limited regulation of public political and ideological events was, paradoxically, both a retreat and a liberating change for American universities. Previously, they had tried to stand in loco parentis with respect to the character and content of events and the behavior of those who attended them; they had guaranteed the academic responsibility and respectability of gatherings. If the event was to be politically partisan or ideological, a tax-supported university might have had to deny permission to hold it, because the institution was supposed (often required, by then-prevailing interpretations of constitution or statute) to hold itself separate from partisan or religious influence. Once it became established that there ought to be other kinds of public events and that these should not be held to academic standards, the university could more easily permit them, and it no longer took responsibility for the qualifications of the speaker or the content of speech.

Freedom to Teach and Freedom to Learn

As the university abandoned most forms of institutional control over general public events, it had to regulate more specifically the character of formal instruction. Traditionally, the university has controlled the appointment of instructors and the assignment of their academic duties. It has also had control of the admission of students and their access to facilities, courses, and activities. A person unconnected with the university could properly be barred from an academic event, and attendance at the meetings of a course could be restricted to enrolled students and to other students, staff, and academic visitors having the instructor's specific permission. These restraints could be invoked to protect the academic freedom of the instructor and to establish eligibility based on the competence of the participant as one present to learn. A test of these academic principles came when, in the turmoil of the 1960s and 1970s, groups of students sought the right to initiate courses and choose their own instructors, and when some regularly appointed instructors gave over the meetings of their courses to guest lecturers.

A student-proposed course can be a good thing, but universities had to assert institutional control. They could not escape from institutional responsibility for the content and character of instruction—or for the certification of what is learned and the academic credits awarded. Therefore, universities generally prescribed how a student-initiated course was to be supervised by a competent instructor.

The guest lecturer in a course with a regular instructor, however, is a more delicate matter, because denial of permission to lecture might be construed as denial of the instructor's freedom to choose how to present ideas. Doctors teach medical students by having them look at and talk with hospital patients. Why should law professors not teach law students by introducing them to a celebrated revolutionary?

When this problem arose at the University of California, in 1969–70, institutional control was asserted on three points:

1. The regular instructor was to retain the right and obligation to certify the content of the academic offering and the performance of the students.

2. The guest lecturer (if not academically qualified) was to be present only as an incidental, illustrative case in point for the students, and nothing more.

3. The topic presented, with the guest lecturer serving as illustrative material, was to be pertinent to the purposes of the course.

These distinctions were drawn both to justify the university to the world external to it and to preserve it from internal manipulation. If the university was to resist the efforts of politicians to make or veto academic appointments on political criteria irrelevant to academic qualification, then it had to show that it applied criteria of its own to control such appointments and duties, whether for pay or not. And if the university was to draw a distinction between the strictly scholarly occasion and the nonacademic event, and to insist, on the grounds of preserving free speech, that it ought to permit criticized public events on campus while disclaiming responsibility for their content, then it also had to show that academic occasions followed rules of competence, qualification, and pertinence to academic purposes.

Because judgments of content and teaching competence are so difficult and dangerous to make, universities surround them with institutional procedures and mechanisms instead of embodying them in institutional policy. Responsibility for the design of instructional offerings is lodged in colleges and departments, and the assignment of teaching responsibilities is generally made as an administrative act within these groups. The individual instructor, therefore, has assurance that the main reviewing body for his or her work as a teacher is a group of similarly trained academic specialists who have institutional responsibility for the conduct of the relevant area of specialization.

Should the teacher's freedom to teach be questioned within such a group of specialists, recourse may be had to the university's formal avenues of appeal, in which a broader group of academics sorts out the elements of the controversy and makes recommendations. The university administration, by both of these devices, seeks to ensure that conflicts are channeled through institutional mechanisms, not made into contests that pit academics against administrators.

The old case of William Shockley at Stanford University illustrates another way in which the freedom to teach can be a controversial issue. Shockley, a scientist and cowinner of the Nobel Prize for his work on the transistor, became publicly outspoken concerning the genetic (and inferentially, the racial) basis of intelligence. He announced that he wanted to teach a course on the subject. The response of the Stanford administration was that it would seek the advice of a faculty panel on the question of his academic competence to do so, because the subject was outside the field of his past scholarly work. Shockley's request was in due course denied.

Then there was the 1993 case of Leonard Jeffries, who had

served for twenty years as chair of the Department of Black Studies at the City University of New York. When the administration and trustees sought to remove him from his chairmanship because he had made inflammatory speeches that were construed to be anti-Semitic, he brought a court action for reinstatement and won. Apparently, the university's historic lack of senior administrative oversight with respect to potentially inappropriate academic behavior influenced the court to rule mainly on grounds of free speech and academic freedom.

Academic Freedom and Tenure

The all-but-sacred text on academic freedom is the 1940 statement by the American Association of University Professors (AAUP) on academic freedom and tenure (reprinted in Van Alstyne, 1993, pp. 407–409; see also Metzger's analysis of that statement in Van Alstyne, 1993, pp. 3–77).

Controversies in the United States have also stimulated the effort to define general codes of faculty conduct. The Carnegie Commission on Higher Education, in its report *Dissent and Disruption* (1971), discussed the need for codes of both faculty and student conduct and provided a model faculty code. Numerous individual universities have struggled to define explicit standards. These are intended to serve as a credible guide for academic conduct in general, while the particular obligations and hazards of proper performance in each field are spelled out case by case in the decisions of specialist peer groups.

"Political Correctness"

Universities have long been targets of leftist critics who have charged that they are tools of the Establishment. Herbert Marcuse (1969) and his followers inveighed against intellectual freedom because a tolerance of radical dissent (they referred to it as "repressive tolerance") might prevent the buildup of effective revolutionary fervor.

In *God and Man at Yale* (1951), the young William F. Buckley earlier found another devil—softminded and irreligious liberalism—and so launched his career as a sophisticated conservative curmudgeon. Universities (and the intellectuals who are just outside them but are easily hit by the same brickbats) should by now be used to attacks on their fairness, morality, and balance.

Academic conservatives of the National Association of Scholars have led the most recent effort to save the virtue of the academy. They utilized the concept of "political correctness" (PC) and attacked the academic Establishment for becoming enslaved to it. A prominent spokesman for these views, Dinesh D'Souza, gained his spurs in the ideological wars as an undergraduate at Dartmouth College, where he wrote for the *Dartmouth Review*. This publication, backed by politically ultraconservative alumni, engaged in a sustained verbal assault on the college's administration and faculty. Later, assisted by an affiliation with the Heritage Foundation, D'Souza wrote *Illiberal Education* (1991) and a string of promotional essays on the same theme.

What is the bill of indictment? Academic people are said to engage in a collective (even, perhaps, unconscious) conspiracy to require their fellow faculty members and their students to follow a prescribed, leftist philosophical line: the "politically correct" one. The prescriptions and proscriptions include:

- In curriculum, demanding an antimarket orthodoxy in the social sciences and preventing honest discussion of differences among the races and between the sexes

- In faculty selection, screening for acceptance of politically correct doctrine in each field, and also tipping the scales to favor appointment of minorities and women regardless of whether they are well-qualified or best-qualified

- In institutional oversight, stifling conservative views and criticism of the university itself and of the surrounding society

President Harold Shapiro of Princeton University focused on the pluralistic society and the challenges and advantages of diversity in his 1992 commencement address (Shapiro, 1992)—clearly, politically correct. Incoming president George E. Rupp of Columbia University struck a similar chord (Rupp, 1993).

The Department of Sociology at Berkeley, having experienced the departure of an assistant professor who was a minority member, searched for a replacement. It recommended appointment of Loic Wacquant. He had been a Harvard junior fellow and is French by origin. His specialty is the study of ethnic inequality and racial conflict in New Caledonia and in Chicago's African-American ghettos. He has also coauthored a major book in sociological theory.

Reacting against the department's recommendation of appointment of a nonminority person for a "minority slot," graduate students in the department organized a boycott of classes in spring 1992. Berkeley's provost and dean of letters and science then denied the appointment on procedural grounds: the application for the appointment had been filed after the published deadline (Rodarmor, 1992).

There is a curious epilogue to this story. In 1993, the appointment was again offered to Wacquant; he accepted and joined the department, with little apparent objection from any quarter. The entire episode nicely combines two areas of value-loaded conflict: faculty and student diversity, and alleged political correctness.

Faculty Diversity

Major university faculties have historically had very low percentages of the identified minorities—African American, Chicano/Latino, and Asian American—and, in most fields, low percentages of women faculty. One immediate reason for this is that each field's "eligibility pool"—the population of Ph.D.'s available for consideration as faculty candidates—has historically contained few minority and female members. The percentages vary greatly among disciplines but in most are growing fairly rapidly.

University administrators feel the challenge of demonstrating affirmative action in faculty appointment and advancement, but academic departments, where new appointments originate, often do not put high priority on locating a female or minority candidate when, as many see it, the issue is to appoint the best-qualified person. In its most categorical form, the academic conservative view favors a "race-blind, gender-blind" policy of appointment and promotion. Efforts to bring about greater diversity are seen to be in conflict with this view. Critics of the status quo also question the procedures for defining the academic qualifications and specialization that are sought in a new appointee, and they point out that traditional ways of searching for qualified candidates often involve reliance on the "old boy" network that operates among major universities and ignores potentially qualified minority and women candidates from less well-known institutions. At Berkeley, a special task force on faculty diversity was assigned to review procedures of recruitment, selection, appointment, and advancement and to recommend any changes that might be needed in the interest of greater fairness and inclusiveness. It recommended numerous changes, of which more than half were adopted by the Academic Senate committees. (See Academic Senate of the University of California, Berkeley, 1991, appendix V.)

Smelser (1993) points out that all parties to such controversies over diversity exhibit ambivalence: the academic leaders—most of them liberal and moderate—who find themselves cast as reactionary defenders of the status quo; and the various blocs (women, minorities, and others) who demand change and recompense for past and present evils committed against them but at the same time are sensitive to meritocratic, universalistic academic values.

As the percentages of minority and women students have increased at both undergraduate and graduate levels in most fields, these students have often campaigned for the recruitment of additional minority and women professors. They argue that topics of special interest to them have been scanted in the curriculum, and they express the need to have women and minority faculty members available to them as mentors and role models.

Administrators necessarily become involved in diversity issues whenever asserted definitions of competence to teach differ from conventional, specialized, academic judgments. As African-American students became more numerous and more assertively self-conscious on university campuses, demands were made to provide courses in African-American literature, history, and other areas of special interest. In addition, the argument was often advanced that these should be staffed by African-American instructors. Asian Americans and Chicano/Latino Americans have enunciated parallel claims. In response, many universities have created departments of ethnic studies, but these have been less than satisfying to the most active leaders of the minority student constituencies.

The same issue has arisen in connection with women's history, the psychology of women, and similar courses.

Three distinct claims are made:

- The subject ought to be taught.
- The teacher must be qualified by categorical condition (race or sex) and not merely by academic background.
- Student admission to the course ought to be based on categorical condition, not merely on curricular eligibility or interest. (This claim is made only in some cases.)

The first claim necessitates a decision with respect to resource priorities. It also raises questions about whether a valid body of knowledge is available. Those who have a strong interest are not content to leave the judgment on this to the academic specialists normally concerned with the curricular area in question; the advocates want the offering whether or not the specialists say that there is something valid to be taught.

The second claim raises the question of whether academic preparation is as relevant as outlook and personal experience. If it becomes an issue between the academic department that would normally pass on teacher qualifications and the administrators who are trying to cope with pressure from interest groups, there is an ideal resolution: to find a prospective appointee who meets both the criterion of academic competence and background and the criterion of category. But this ideal solution, or a compromise approximation to it, may fail if the specialists balk or if the proponents of the new course demand exclusive control over the nominations for appointment. The proponents may sometimes make such demands to secure patronage control of employment or to enforce an ideological orientation. Because American university faculties are mostly white and mostly male, the denial of the demands can lead to charges of institutional racism or institutional sexism.

The third issue—occasional demands for restricted admission to the course based on a categorical criterion—raises another painful problem. Universities are accustomed to invoking criteria of academic eligibility for course enrollment. They may also use rationing, not only of the total number of students on a campus at each degree level, but in each major, school, or college. The rationing may extend to a limitation on enrollment in a particular course because the institution or, with its consent, the instructor wants to ensure a particular style of learning in that course. But here is a request, or a demand, for self-segregation of students by race or sex and for the exclusion of those not meeting the criterion. Not only is this an additional form of rationing; it is one that collides with principles (and probably with laws) of nondiscrimination. Once again, the prudent administrator can resort to a mechanism that will avoid the risks of a purely administrative determination, but the outcome cannot, for reasons both of law and of general university policy, be de jure recognition of a discriminatory criterion of eligibility to attend a course.

Diversity and the Scholarly Research Agenda

There is a positive philosophical case for increased faculty diversity and for concomitant efforts to develop course offerings for previously unexplored topics that will challenge students to serious intellectual probing. The literatures and cultures of minority communities are now much more systematically studied than before. (This, in turn, has provoked a counterrevolution by those who deplore the dilution of the classical canon with what they regard as faddish contemporary material. See Bloom, 1987.)

Provost Jonathan Cole of Columbia University argues convincingly that these and other clashes of academic perspectives arise as contests for "control of the null [hypothesis]" (Cole, 1993). For example, the issue of gender discrimination in a university's appointments can be cast as a presumption that there is none. In the terminology of statistical hypothesis testing, the null hypothesis here is: there is no sex discrimination. Those who claim that there is or might be are thus forced to bear the burden of proof. Suppose, however, that "everybody knows there is sex discrimination," and this is the null hypothesis; then those who do not believe that there is sex discrimination have the burden of proof. As Cole points out, university curricula and collective expectations have behind them the inertia of tradition, and the defenders of the tradition have usually had control of the null in significant areas of concern. This compels the reformers and the incoming new factions—for example, women faculty and minority students and faculty—to find evidence to overcome status quo presumptions against much that they seek to do.

Issues of gender in science, medicine, law, and economics are high on the social as well as the intellectual agenda of the 1990s. In 1992, Bernadine Healy, then director of the National Institutes of Health, announced that heart attack, which had previously been studied only among male subjects as a predominantly "male" disease, would now be investigated as an illness of women. Leaders of women's organizations have insisted on higher priorities for other medical research topics, such as breast cancer, that bear directly on female health. Research on the law, based in challenges to traditional assumptions concerning the status of women, encompasses employment rights, family law, and questions of violence and abuse.

Some academic leaders point out that a "women's topic" need not necessarily be studied by a woman, or a topic relating to a minority by a member of that minority. To this, the frequent contemporary rejoinder is that a decided change in the de facto research agenda does come about as more of the previously underrepresented gain places in university faculties. (See Academic Senate, University of California, 1991.)

If the university can demonstrate a sympathetic responsiveness to novel demands, and if its processes show a capacity to critically examine whether a valid area of study has been overlooked, then it will be better able—depending on circumstances—to experiment with promising possibilities, to explain why budgetary difficulties prevent an ideal response, or to deny the academic validity of the proposals or demands.

The existing units of organization may not be adaptable to new areas of curricular interest, yet may oppose the independent development of particular offerings or of entire new programs or academic departments. By disciplinary and professional definitions, units of organization emerge rather slowly and in an evolutionary manner, with boundaries that are in accord with the definition of the discipline. It is fitting that they do, for a unit of academic organization can be adequately defined and developed only after a significant period of systematic scholarly work and the emergence of a body of knowledge and some criteria of competence. Many universities, however, were cautious and slow in adopting curricula and academic organization for women's studies and ethnic studies.

But student and public interest in areas of study may also rise in an unexpected and even faddish fashion. Witness the interest in the study of ecology and environmental quality, the rapid growth (and now incipient decline) of specialties in space science, the swings of interest in Zen, and the attempts to develop the integrated study of the language, culture, social structure, and politics of particular areas of the world. In these situations, university administration becomes an exercise in balancing the following risks:

- Very long-term resource commitment
- Incomplete specification of the course or program as a field of proper academic interest
- Insistent but possibly temporary bursts of enrollment demand
- In some cases, temporary external funding—enough to start a new area of study but not enough to sustain it

Political Accountability and the Intrusions of Politics

One striking episode provides an American example of the broad problem of conflict between academic freedom and political accountability. In May 1970, at the time of the United States invasion of Cambodia, large numbers of students and faculty were greatly disturbed. Several universities closed down altogether or waived the requirements for final examinations. Most remained open, and there were movements for "reconstitution" of the university—putting aside academic business-as-usual in all academic courses and institutional process so that (it was urged) the university could devote itself as an institution to opposing the war.

If, at that time of crisis, universities had acceded to a test of moral or ideological relevance among their academic offerings, how could they have successfully resisted the ideological and political intrusions of outside interest groups on other, even less welcome, occasions? Thus, universities struggled to draw boundary distinctions that would make it possible for students and staff to express their concerns as citizens, yet without drawing the institutions into endorsement of particular positions and without exposing them to the accusation that academic facilities and operations had been given over wholesale to a partisan cause.

Over the centuries, universities in many societies have faced such crises of purpose and character. Sometimes, they have collapsed from within. More frequently, if the surrounding society goes through a major convulsion, the universities are overwhelmed—physically destroyed or converted into barracks for revolutionary cadres or made symbols of the victor's interests. The German universities during the rise of Hitler, the Cuban universities subjected to *Fidelista* zeal, the Czech universities after the Prague Spring of 1968, the Chilean universities under Pinochet—all became chattels of the state and objects of control and "purification."

After the Czechs' great Velvet Revolution of 1989, Czech universities had to confront the consequences of a generation of heavy-handed Stalinist control of academic appointments and curricula. The Czech parliament, against the public opposition of President Vaclav Havel, passed laws requiring "screening" of all those in governmental positions to determine who had acted improperly or illegally (for example, as a paid informer) under the former communist regime. University instructors and officials, because of their civil-servant status, fall under this screening requirement. For many years, party-affiliated functionaries had made faculty appointment conditional on "reliability," and they punished those who would not bend the neck.

One must now anticipate a number of years of painful adjustment within these universities, as the old injustices are gradually corrected. Also, curricula are reformed by replacing Marxist orthodoxies with subjects that are in the worldwide intellectual mainstream and that students now want to learn. In economics, for example, Marxist treatments are replaced by standard market-based analysis. Instructors in the old material have little or nothing to do unless they can become competent in the new.

Even during calmer times, when no convulsive social movement threatens to penetrate every area of academic discourse, inflaming issues can arise as test cases in almost any field and are not by any means confined to the social sciences, where questions of values are endemic. Nuclear chemists and engineers become embroiled in controversies over reactor safety. Biologists and agronomists make farmers angry about pesticides, genetically engineered products, and environmental quality. English professors lock horns with official doctrine about obscenity. Educational psychologists, anthropologists, and statisticians arouse passions over the question of racial and genetic versus environmental sources of difference in human intelligence. Gynecologists unsettle the church and traditional morality over questions of contraception and abortion.

In the best of circumstances, universities are constitutionally protected from external pressures, while internal regulation protects them from the harassment of those among their members who take intellectual positions unpopular with the academic community. But a university's academic and administrative leadership is hard put to deal wisely with the ad hoc crisis, which is often a confusing mixture of personalities, factions, interest groups, and principles. The private university does not have to face the bludgeon of budget cuts in such controversies; this gives it more time to cope or to let controversy burn out—but time is not immunity.

"Hate Speech" Dilemmas

Today, a university has to cope with the sensibilities and sensitivities of a large, increasingly diverse, and occasionally volatile student population. It therefore has a compelling interest in promoting harmony and mutual respect among members of different groups—different as to race, ethnicity, religion, gender, sexual preference, or ideology. "Hate speech," construed as an attack on the dignity and humanity of a targeted group, may shatter civility. Acts of violence by those inflamed against the targeted group may ensue, and acts of violence by the targeted group, in self-defense or retaliation, may also result. How far do—and should—First Amendment protections extend on the campus? For a comprehensive legal analysis of "hate speech" and academic freedom, see Smolla (1993).

At the University of Pennsylvania, a white student shouted the epithet "Water buffalo!" at minority students who were making a loud racket; he was brought up on disciplinary charges. At the same university, African-American students confiscated and destroyed thousands of copies of *The Daily Pennsylvanian* in protest against an editorial they felt was humiliating to them. The student who shouted was disciplined; those who confiscated the newspaper were not.

Law professor Catherine McKinnon has attacked pornographic photographs and literature, saying that they are not only an insult to women but that they incite acts of humiliation and violence against them. This theme forms the dramatic backbone of David Mamet's play *Oleanna* (1992). The male professor and the female undergraduate exhibit traditional frailties in Act One: she is dependent and uncertain of herself, and he is overbearing and aggressively comforting. In Act Two, she offers to withdraw a report that she has filed charging sexual harassment if he will agree to stop assigning a number of books that she and her group consider offensive to women—including one book that he himself has written. The male professor loses control and some rather ineffectual acts of physical violence ensue. The professor's behavior thus proves the student's point.

Freedom to Inquire

A university exists, in large measure, to support, facilitate, and give recognition to new scholarship. As an institution, it does not endorse the product, even though it is morally bound to defend the responsible process that gave rise to that product, the scholar whose work it is, and the full publication of the results.

Traditionally, academic scholarship has been an individualistic activity: a topic is chosen by the scholar, pursued by him or her alone, and the results eventually published in the author's name, with praise or blame directed solely to the author. Although universities did not become the major locus of original scholarship until the nineteenth century, their libraries, laboratories, and ability to underwrite groups of specialists have now become indispensable to systematic scholarship.

Recognition of the merit of the work comes from the scholar's professional peers, partly within but even more outside the university where the appointment is held. The university uses these signals to gauge the worth and originality of the work. It is one of the paradoxes of academic life that the scholar's judges are also competitors, colleagues, and personal friends.

Productive scholars drive themselves hard, make heavy demands for personal autonomy, and would probably not be able to gain remotely comparable satisfaction from any other career. Thus, it is easy to see why the scholar needs the university as patron and facilitator. But why does the university need the research scholar? Three reasons are often given:

1. Research and the researcher are necessary for good teaching.
2. Society needs new knowledge.
3. The university gains prominence through the reputations of its research scholars.

The student, if he or she is to become acquainted with a subject in its most current state, must have access to the knowledge that is emerging from the frontiers of the field. As scientific knowledge accumulates and as societies change, educational materials and the ideas to be taught need continually to be refreshed. This obligation to remain current imposes a major demand on the scholar as teacher, and it is easier to meet if the teacher is stretching his or her own intellectual bounds, is in a group of colleagues whose joint command of their field is current, and is part of the wider network of scholarship in that discipline. Further, advanced students become socialized to the scholarly role and need apprenticeship in research in order to gain facility for later original work of their own. (Teachers of less advanced students need to be skilled in the systematic exposition of the settled concepts and techniques of the field. They must be able to reach into the mental set and motivation of the student. For these aspects of the teacher's work, however, it is not so clear that scholarly originality is a crucial factor.)

Universities assert that society needs new knowledge, and make their claims for institutional resources partly on this basis. As the tempo of new discovery and accretion of knowledge has increased during the last two or three generations, large-scale commitments have become more necessary for good fundamental scholarship, not just in the laboratory sciences and science-based professions, but in most fields. Many scholars believe that freedom to inquire means, among other things, adequate financial and psychic support. Societies, for their part, need applied research conducted on a large scale and have become dependent on organized expertise to support a changing technology and to solve a plethora of old and new problems.

The process of inquiry is guided by explicit and implicit standards of scholarly behavior (for the most part, self-enforced) that are important aspects of university policy. Each field of academic interest develops its own canons of method, rigor, and style of reporting, to which the scholar generally has to conform. The scholar participates in the field in two ways: as part of the receptive and critical audience for new work, wherever and by whomever it is done; and by contributing to the flow of new findings.

Each field has understood standards of care and competence for the assembling of data or the investigation of sources and for the construction of theory or interpretation. The scholar is bound to fair disclosure of sources and methods. Once a piece of work is completed, the scholar is also obliged to report it to an audience of peers, and in this capacity is an advocate for the truth as he or she sees it. In many areas of science, promptness is important in the announcement of results; this pressure creates temptations to publish prematurely or to overclaim results, and it is a duty to resist these temptations.

Unfortunately, the temptations are not always resisted. A number of gaudy cases of overstatement of scientific results, and even falsification of data in the interest of speedy publication, have come to light in recent years. This has been a particular issue in medical research, where senior professors and institute heads have signed as principal authors of studies, yet have not exercised adequate responsibility in guiding the quality of the work done in their large teams. Disclosure of faulty work has led to a number of prominent resignations, including that of David Baltimore as president of Rockefeller University, New York, in 1991.

These incidents (often involving research supported by federal funds) have damaged the credibility of academic science and cast doubt on the capacity of the university to exercise adequate oversight. In two areas of research, universities are bound by stringent regulatory requirements: programs involving human subjects must be based on informed consent and provide proper protection of the subject; and research on animal subjects requires maintenance of the animals at a high standard of health and humane treatment in research procedures.

Other classic academic sins are plagiarism and misappropriation of the ideas of others. It is incumbent on faculty leaders to hold the perpetrator to account, and the university as an institution must provide adequate backing for the sanctions that are necessary.

The crucial interaction among scholars is exploratory dialogue, in which ideas are searchingly tested for their merit but the opposing scholar is not under ad hominem attack. Many scholars are tough controversialists, and in every field there have been bitter disputes and personal feuds—natural enough because scholars care about their work and have their share of human failings, but deplorable nonetheless when they poison the atmosphere of inquiry.

Even though scholars are often affiliated with a particular school of thought within their field, this should not lead them to judge a like-minded friend's work too kindly or an opponent's too harshly. They must also avoid judgments that are biased by chauvinism, irrelevant loyalties or enmities, or considerations of rank or prestige.

Time is usually the scholar's scarcest resource, yet there is a positive obligation to offer criticism, referee others' work in progress, and share ongoing work with other scholars who are, at the same time, competitors.

Like any statements of an ideal, these add up to a counsel of perfection, and the men and women in a scholarly field may have their occasions of missing the mark.

In the short run, visibility and good reputation among peers matter a great deal, not only to nourish the scholar's ego but also to advance the personal case for pay, rank, and resources. Yet the moral satisfactions of doing work of enduring quality and serving the company of scholars can be enjoyed by those of quite modest achievement as well as by the outstanding scholars of a discipline.

The moral authority of scholarship flows from the engagement of student and scholar in the process of learning. This is different from politics and different from bureaucratic organization. It has to be voluntary.

These observations may help to indicate why a good university is a moral community, and they may convey why the creative scholar is a character model as well as an intellectual resource to students.

The guiding principles outlined above operate in universities in many countries, although the surrounding social and cultural environment may be so hostile to them that their implementation is made very difficult. Universities are organized, operated, and financed in a wide variety of patterns and styles that affect these values. Thus, the essentials of the atmosphere for learning need to be fostered if the university is to work, and certain restraints need to be observed in its design and manner of operation.

There are those who deny, because they believe so strongly in collegiality and consent, that a university can or should be tended and managed as an organization. Some managerial techniques would indeed damage both individual autonomy and collegial cohesion to the point where the essentials of the university would be lost. But rationing and choices are vital because time, money, and other resources are never in sufficient supply to meet all needs. Discerning and sophisticated forms of administration are required.

Enemies of Fundamental Values

Three prime enemies of fundamental academic values are lack of interest, isolation, and intolerant zeal.

Lack of Interest

If, at a university, the number of people who are interested in core academic values is low in relation to the total size of the community, the values that call for great effort are frustrated and the inducements to learn and to be creative become insufficient. This is one reason why universities that have an option to do so are selective in the admission of their students and why all universities select faculty with great care. Universities that cannot be selective in admissions often seek to defend the numerical strength of the interested by early screening or other forms of discouragement of the uninterested. Unless there is great care in organization, sheer numbers can also overwhelm the spirit of learning by giving the student a sense that his or her mind and interests are not significant.

Isolation

A university is a place for judgments—is this a good book, a good paper or thesis, a good idea, a good course, a good student or professor? Making these judgments properly and fairly is hard work and requires both energy and reasonable cohesion in the groups of people who share concern about the judgments to be made. Communication within such groups, and across groups where there are wider concerns, is an essential feature of the university. Communication by the scholar with the wider community of academic peers is equally necessary to good work. Thus, the isolation of one person from another within the university handicaps its internal function, and isolation from the wider community of knowledge throughout the world prevents the sharing and recognition of new work.

There are interesting problems of balance between cohesion and individuality within a university, and between the claims of the university on the energy of its members for its internal needs and the claims on them for interaction with peers in their disciplines elsewhere.

Time and the materials of scholarship have to be rationed. The feeling that there is not enough time to make good on the claims of students and colleagues can drive scholars into isolation, where in the short run they can at least enjoy the satisfactions of creative work. Thus, a precarious feature of the equilibrium of a university is that if its problems of numbers, conflict, or poverty become severe, its members may withdraw from interaction and thus worsen the general plight of the institution.

Intolerant Zeal

The same qualities that enable a university to foster individual autonomy and to preserve numerous arenas of exploration and disagreement make it vulnerable to intolerant zeal or intransigence. The need for easy movement of persons and their fair access to university facilities make police controls and security repugnant—and also increase the exposure to risk if intransigent or even violent behavior erupts. The quickness to defend liberty of ideas makes a university community a convenient arena for some kinds of demagoguery, particularly when the surrounding society has heavy conflicts. The necessity for collegial forums of decision makes their conversion to political misuse a serious hazard. The underlying voluntarism of the institution makes the application of sanctions difficult unless the authoritative basis for them, and their procedural fairness, are widely supported by the university population.

Those who are concerned for the university need to find ways to overcome the hazards of lack of interest, isolation, and intransigence, and also to care for its moral condition and foster an atmosphere for learning. If that atmosphere is good, students and scholars are induced to great effort. If for any reason that atmosphere is seriously weakened or poisoned, the university is reduced to a collection of buildings and paper and meaningless routines.

Chapter Three

University Governance

This chapter focuses on fundamental issues of power and responsibility as dealt with by the university's trustees, the president and senior administration, the legislators or major funders, and those who are or seek to be influencers of the regime of the institution.

Definition of Governance

A general definition of governance refers to the distribution of authority and functions among the units within a larger entity, the modes of communication and control among them, and the conduct of relationships between the entity and the surrounding environment. When that entity is a contemporary U.S. university, the conventional building blocks for governance within the university are its trustees, the executive administration, the faculty, and other groupings and units, such as student government and alumni. The traditional discussion of the basic internal and external relationships of a private university focuses on the ways boards of trustees, presidents, and numerous other actors discharge their institutional responsibilities. In the case of a public university or multicampus university system, however, account must be made of the ties to executive and legislative branches of state government and, typically, to a higher education coordinating agency.

The Association of Governing Boards has published two thorough compendia of good institutional practice, one focusing on independent, the other on public colleges and universities (Ingram and Associates, 1993a, 1993b). Their observations and advice concerning good practice distill much experience and serve as useful guides for the many decision makers and stakeholders within a university system.

The Pyramid of Governance

The authority for governance derives, in principle, from a charter or constitution enacted by a chartering entity. Such a charter may ordinarily be amended by a board of trustees. In practice, however, the fundamental bargains that determine the actual distribution of authority may be tilted by external agencies, such as a state government that supports a public university.

At the level below the constitutional, broad policy decisions are enacted—ordinarily by the governing board but sometimes also by the president and senior administration—which provide for detailed, formal dispositions of authority and obligations throughout the institution. The functions of overseeing the operations of the institution and of enforcing the delegations of authority are established in tandem with such enactments.

Distinct from the level of policy making are the arrangements or bargains that create an interface with the larger societal environment. Because many stakeholders are involved, the president and trustees must undertake the arduous task of extracting a set of compromises that the institution and all other interested parties can live with.

The Governing Board

Governance is formally defined as the responsibility of the governing board of an institution. In U.S. law and practice, every corporation, whether for-profit or nonprofit, must have a board of directors. (The term "trustee" or "regent" may be used by nonprofit corporations.) The board is responsible for safeguarding the assets of the corporation, electing its officers, overseeing its activities, and filing required reports with state and federal agencies. Additional obligations of the board may be specified in the charter and bylaws of the institution, which also state how board members are to be selected and how long they may serve.

The governing board of a university is not in continuous session, as the full-time presidency may be said to be. Rather, it meets periodically, usually with provision for interim actions between meetings. As Kerr and Gade (1989) characterize the role of the trustees, "[It] is above all to serve as guardians" (p. 12). They then list the fundamental decisions and policy domains that are essentials of trustee governance (pp. 12–13).

The governing board may also be seen as the apex of a system of ministerial and advisory bodies parallel to the administration. They may include:

- Boards of directors of alumni organizations
- Boards of foundations linked to the university corporation
- Boards of subsidiary entities
- Formal and informal advisory bodies appointed for various purposes

These bodies—and the governing board—engage in complex patterns of interaction with the administration of the university and with the world outside the university. The governing board itself may be "layered," as is the case in the unusual structure of Harvard University: the Harvard Corporation has seven members, meets at least once a month, and has ultimate power to act on corporate matters; the Board of Overseers has thirty members and meets quarterly to advise on broader policy and governance questions.

The Many Faces of University Governance

The following list of functions that governance comprises may help to define the problem for which governance is said to be the solution:

1. The safeguarding of the institutional mission
2. The provision of a "buffer" between the internal world of the university and its external constituencies
3. Oversight of the financial integrity and viability of the university
4. The enunciation of major policy standards and the initiation of actions of such magnitude that they could affect the viability of the institution
5. Selection of the president and other key figures in the university hierarchy
6. The balancing of interests between the contending stakeholders of the university

The "Players" or Stakeholders of the University

Many groups claim formal power or significant informal influence in the U.S. university and are therefore "players" or stakeholders.

Governments, including both state governments and federal agencies, are sources of funding; they also exercise oversight and auditing functions. The federal agencies include:

- The Department of Education, which administers financial aid programs
- The National Science Foundation and National Institutes of Health, which award research grants
- Several cabinet departments, which award research grants and contracts

Private as well as public universities have to cope with funding and oversight issues involving government. Each public university, typically a land-grant institution, has a charter issued by the state. Some state universities have constitutionally autonomous status; others are subject to statutory control by the governor and legislature.

The *alumni* of the university are its keepers of nostalgia and a major source of donation. Private universities select many trustees from among the alumni; some provide for election of trustees by the alumni from a slate of nominees. Alumni factions may also become pressure groups working for or against a university policy or against the administration. Some, deeply involved in donor financing of intercollegiate athletic programs, may seek to influence university policies concerning athletics.

Non-alumni *donors*, individual and corporate, are important to all private universities, and increasingly to public ones.

The *faculty* is a major stakeholder in a university. In the research universities, public and private, the faculty generally has an influential advisory role, but the mechanisms vary a great deal. Where faculty collective bargaining and union representation have developed, the new adversarial approach has tended to reduce the level of mutual confidence, thereby greatly weakening older concepts of "shared governance."

Students and their organizations are stakeholders. Some universities have recognized student interests symbolically by appointing a student as a voting trustee. Others provide for a nonvoting student representative. Whether at the table or not, students now expect to have a voice in numerous matters of policy. During university crises of the 1960s, student factions invented and exercised a sort of franchise through mass action. By the 1990s, student lobbies at state legislatures had political entree for stating their positions and seeking leverage. In the internal councils of a university, the student government and the student newspaper focus influential attention on the university administration in connection with numerous matters, and through the administration—if not directly—on the governing board.

The *president and senior administration* of a university are stakeholders in several areas of leverage. The president is the main chan-

nel for official materials—information and recommended actions—
to be considered by the governing board at its meetings. He or others in the senior administration also provide a flow of reports to
government agencies and to the public. A major presidential task
is to tend and manage the relationships between the administration
and the governing board. Having selected the president, the board
also has power of removal, and both parties are ever mindful of this.
The president makes recommendations to the board on key officer
appointments in the administration, usually after a public search
process and recommendation of a slate of nominees.

The *administrative staff* of the university as well as its *service
workforce and their organizations* are stakeholders. In many universities, the organizational position of some employee groups is formalized in union recognition and collective bargaining agreements.
Other staff employee groups have different modes of representation.
A university benefits by cultivating good communication and positive organizational commitment; their absence bodes ill for administrative morale and productivity.

Local government and the local community are stakeholders in several direct and significant ways. The university is an employer with
major payrolls and purchasing power. With its own large and complex community that includes thousands of young adults, it has
security and public safety needs that require intensive cooperation
with local police and fire departments. The university is a land-
owner and a possessor of large-scale capital facilities. Territorial
expansion for new buildings and improvements may cause friction
with neighbors and local government bodies. "Town and gown" is
too simple a phrase to convey the contemporary mix of technical,
economic, and politically adversarial and cooperative relationships
that university officials must maintain. Some universities, in fact,
have become involved in extensive urban development in order
to have long-term influence on the quality of their surroundings.
Lawrence A. Kimpton and Edward Levy of the University of
Chicago and Martin Meyerson of the University of Pennsylvania

became leaders in the urban development of Chicago and Philadelphia for this very purpose.

The *general public*, though normally passive and not a direct influence, may become a stakeholder during major crises. For example, voters may press state governors and legislators to enact restrictions on the university or to reduce or augment its budget. Parents may dissuade their sons and daughters from enrolling in an institution that is in crisis. The leading public universities have more than local visibility; the mass of the population is aware of them through media coverage and sports. Some private universities, such as the University of Notre Dame and Harvard University, have exceptional name recognition that, on the whole, is an asset to them.

Linkages with Stakeholders

Spokesmanship and symbolic representation are primarily the duties of the university president, but many people, in both official and informal roles, are involved in maintaining linkages with the various categories of stakeholders. The process is not tidy and is difficult to manage, but it is of great importance. Some stakeholder interests are comprehensive, entailing a wide range of issues, extensive communication, and a high frequency of contacts. Linkages between the president and the governing board reflect this breadth and intensity of interest, as do those between the senior administration and the university faculty. Other linkages are narrower, focusing on a specific agenda or defined set of interests. One such is the linkage between the football boosters' club, the intercollegiate athletics department, and the president's office.

Some linkages are direct, while others are conducted through a mediating communication channel. The chair of the governing board or the head of a major board committee will expect direct communications with the university president. A rank-and-file board member, on the other hand, may have to be content with a phone call from one of the president's subordinates. Linkages with trade unions are maintained by employee relations professionals and attorneys; the president strives to maintain distance from day-to-day problems and from bargaining negotiations.

If a constituency is geographically scattered, face-to-face contacts are infeasible, except when the university convenes large-scale alumni reunions and public events. Responsibility for mass communication lies with public affairs specialists who generate a steady flow of stories for the media. By this means, the university tries to maintain favorable visibility and garner support from targeted groups and a variety of publics.

One of the challenges in the work of linkage is to act at the appropriate point in the spectrum from confidential to public, informal to formal, personal to institutional. When an insistent stakeholder pushes its case on the president and senior administration, however, an ideal mode of interaction may not be available. This puts a premium on quick adaptation to pressure.

External Factors Conditioning Governance

No university can survive without students, faculty, and financial resources. It is no accident, therefore, that the handbooks on trustee responsibilities include substantial chapters on these factors: one on the demographics of the potential student population, and several on finance, tuition, and student financial aid (Ingram, 1993a; Ingram, 1993b).

California's well-known Master Plan for Higher Education, adopted in 1960, set the stage for a vast expansion of the community colleges, the California State University, and the University of California. The Master Plan allocated educational program functions and enrollment-taking obligations to the three public sectors of higher education, and the state succeeded in financing the capital and operating budget needs of each sector, thus guaranteeing growth and program quality.

Kerr (1994a) views the principle of selectivity in enrollment-taking as having been crucial to the success of the University of California since the Master Plan was enacted (pp. 71–75). A private California research policy group argues in a recent report that a series of significant increases in tuition and fees at public institutions in response to the state's very austere budgeting have badly fractured the Master Plan and the social bargain it contained. It is argued that these increases of tuition, together with budget cuts that reduce availability of courses and programs, have all but negated the principle of access for every qualified student to some appropriate part of public higher education (California Higher Education Policy Center, 1994).

Federal research funding also declined in real terms in the early 1990s, and the caps placed on indirect cost recovery have had significant adverse impact on the research universities.

In addition, the legal environment has changed in dramatic ways, constraining the independence of action that universities had come to believe was essential to them. The expanded reach of federal and state regulations on a wide variety of institutional matters compels university administrators to establish and enforce institutional policies regarding human research subjects, animal subjects, access for the disabled, and equal treatment of the sexes in intercollegiate athletics. These changes are expensive financially, and they necessitate greater institutional control in the historically decentralized university environment.

Some Key Tasks in Governance

Of all the tasks of university governance, the one that is fundamental is *the assurance of effective autonomy*. The ability to resist intrusion by political groups or factional interests and the opportunity and obligation to keep the operation of the university self-directed are essential to the integrity of the institution. Public universities are prone to political intrusion, and no more so than when budgetary threats are used as a means of intimidation. Both public and private universities face insistent factional pressures from within the institution and from without. University leaders must be able to anticipate intrusive pressures and be in a position to mobilize a dominant coalition of stakeholders to help resist them. In this effort, the president and governing board, together, are usually the critical players.

The next crucial task is *the definition and implementation of the university's mission and the approval of long-range plans*. A university adrift is not a pretty sight: it tolerates ad hoc decisions about programs and priorities, and it fails to mobilize superior energies toward defined goals, so that its resources and goodwill are wasted. The austere atmosphere of the 1990s and beyond, contrasting with earlier periods of unrestricted expansion, will force universities to be selective in their programs, even though selection runs against the academic grain. The university that is able to identify its special strengths and back those vigorously is likely to prosper better in coming decades than the institution that tries to accommodate all desires.

A prime task of governance is *the achievement of unified support for major university commitments*. The number and variety of stakeholder interests make this a difficult task. If unified support is not achieved, factional elements of the university fight to survive as best they can in the fragmented state that is normal for many institutions. This approach may keep antagonistic coalitions from forming, at least for a time; but it is not a good way to generate support for spirited institutional leadership.

The president and governing board, standing at the apex of governance, are responsible for *the determination of institutionwide policy standards and the delegation of authority*. Universities are highly ramified institutions, and hierarchical regularities are unavoidable—in fact, essential. The discretionary administration found in a simpler setting has to give way to explicit policy standards. These are necessary in many areas of institutional operation, including:

- Financial control
- Human resource management (both faculty and administrative staff)
- Academic programs and degrees, and their approval or discontinuation
- Student fees, financial aid, admissions standards, and guidelines for student conduct

There must also be a determination of what specific authorities the governing board will keep to itself and which it will delegate elsewhere in the institution.

The selection and oversight of faculty and administrators are central to effective governance, so *the determination of procedures and standards for appointment, advancement, and termination of key personnel* is a perennial task. For the most senior administrative and academic positions, the governing board itself may retain the power of direct appointment and evaluation. The institution of academic tenure, however, traditionally prevents termination of a senior faculty member unless an egregious breach of the principles of academic conduct is shown to have occurred or unless the university is compelled to phase out academic programs as a result of financial stringency. (The 1990s have seen much soul-searching in regard to the institution of academic tenure. Its inflexibility and its protection of marginal competence are costs to be weighed against its function as a shield protecting unpopular intellectual views, but to revise this institution would indeed be a major test of the skills of governance.)

A traditional task of a corporate and of a university board is *the approval of budgets and major financial commitments and the exercise of financial oversight*. Delegation makes it possible to avoid infinite detail, but in their major outline, the finances and budgetary posture of a university require governance attention. A budget is in some respects a proposal for the future period, not a totally fixed commitment, for the available revenues depend on negotiations (especially in state universities, for the state's appropriation) and on the realization of revenue forecasts. The president and governing board are the risk takers of last resort, although constituent colleges and professional schools that operate as autonomous financial entities—especially in private universities—face the first layer of risks.

More than occasionally in modern times, a university has confronted a major crisis, calling for *the provision of effective crisis management*. Causes and triggers are numerous. Among them are

Loss of faculty confidence in the president

Student unrest over a political cause or a university action that inflames resentments

Alumni attacks on perceived evils of the institution

Allegations of serious deficiencies in financial control

The final task of governance is *the integration of the mix of financial, academic, and institutional commitments* in the interest of long-term viability. Governing board and president, together, need to answer the question: does the span of commitments add up to a coherent and realistic path of institutional action? This is not a one-year question but an issue of viability in relation to mission and goals. President Harold Shapiro of Princeton (1992) refers to that university's efforts to carry out a universitywide strategic planning exercise, the results of which were expected to guide the fundraising campaigns and academic priorities of the institution for a number of years. Similar planning efforts have guided selective retrenchments at Stanford, the University of Pennsylvania, and other institutions.

Sponsor Control, State Agency, or Self-Directing Institutions

In the founding years of several major U.S. universities, one wealthy patron and that patron's executive designee developed the basic pattern of the institution: at the University of Chicago, for example, John D. Rockefeller and William Rainey Harper; at Leland Stanford, Jr. University, Leland and Jane Lathrop Stanford with David Starr Jordan. Many other U.S. universities evolved slowly toward secular status and large academic scale from small denominational beginnings. As will be discussed, their governance shifted away from the early control by sponsors.

A dream of academic innovators and rebels in the United States is to launch a new type of institution with self-generated leadership and control, independent of wealthy sponsors or meddling governments. Universities are too big to launch as nongovernmental start-ups, but innovators have founded a number of colleges with academic designs and institutional styles that depart from convention. Most are private. One of the few surviving experimental public colleges is Evergreen College in the state of Washington. Entry from an unconventional power base has become a rarity in U.S. higher education. Only in some multicampus state systems has a major new campus been established and attained major-league status in the years since World War II.

In the continental European tradition, the sponsor of a country's universities is the ministry of education, which by the latter part of the nineteenth century had replaced royal patronage or that of the Roman Catholic Church. In the Netherlands, the minister of education and science, and a special deputy—the minister of state for higher education—have authority under parliamentary statutes to set budgets and engineer changes in the programs offered at the public universities. (Three universities affiliated with religious bodies have a slightly different relationship with the state, although the bulk of their budgets also comes from the ministry.) High-level civil servants do detailed preparatory work on budgets, enrollment projections, and leading issues for the ministerial decision makers.

Each public university is administered by its *College van Bestuur*, which consists of five persons including the (elected) university rector and four others appointed by the minister. Each faculty within the university is organized separately in its academic program, admission of students, and allocation of academic staff to tasks. Very few funds come to the Dutch university from sources other than the main governmental allocations, so the university is heavily dependent on the minister of education and the minister of state for higher education. This dependency was illustrated graphically when, in the early 1980s, significant cuts in academic programs were instituted throughout the Dutch university system on the initiative of the minister of state for higher education. (See Acherman, 1984.)

The Parliament of the Netherlands also mandated sweeping changes in the distribution of power within the Dutch universities. Each academic department would be required to have a representative voting body with 50 percent of voting strength allocated to the professors and 50 percent to the students and the staff, thereby weakening greatly the power of the senior professors. Many German Länder mandated similar "democratization" in the early 1970s. Kerr (1994a, p. 74) offers the judgment that increased diversity of the governing board is a more suitable approach to democratization than is a broadening of power lower down the hierarchy, since the ability of senior faculty to uphold academic standards in appointments may otherwise be jeopardized.

Funders, too, can shift the balance of power in their favor and upset traditional roles. The universities in England came under increasingly tight funding control during the government of Prime Minister Margaret Thatcher. In major policy papers and reports, the government expressed dissatisfaction with the traditionally elite university sector and its alleged remoteness from the challenges of new technology and improved productivity in late-twentieth-century Britain.

Martin Trow (1993) describes this background and analyzes its policy consequences: the development of "managerialism" as an ideology as well as a set of techniques for the detailed control of government funding allocations, on which all British universities depend (pp. 1–2). Trow then notes the breakdown of mutual confidence between government and the universities and examines the basis of "hard" managerialism, which is contrasted with the "soft" (more traditional) variety previously exemplified by the University Grants Committee. The chief tools of "hard" managerialism are schemes of assessment that can be used to identify, and withdraw funding from, weak academic programs within a university, and the move to separate the funding of teaching from the funding of research, with separate assessments for each (pp. 7–14). This approach could be labeled "assessment for accountability."

Striking at the budgetary base, these actions have greatly reduced the autonomy of the universities and the academic authority and administrative influence of the professoriate. The long-term consequences of this aggressive restructuring of relationships remain to be understood and evaluated. Meanwhile, the former British polytechnics have experienced substantial growth of funding and enrollment. Ironically, they achieved parity with universities in name (and ostensibly in function) at just the time that standards of the older university sector came under extreme pressure.

Multicampus University Systems and Their Governance Issues

Most multicampus public university systems have a single governing board (regents or trustees). Some states, such as Texas and Illinois, have two or more parallel multicampus systems, each with its own separate governing board and each contending with the other for public resources. Illinois has tried to resolve the competition problem by establishing a superboard over all public higher education. If the two systems in a state are differentiated as to function, as in California, then the different missions are associated with different budgetary standards and, usually, different modes of governance.

An alternative is to have, within one multicampus university system, different designated roles for different campuses. This is the historic pattern in Minnesota, Texas, and Wisconsin, where "flag-ship" campuses have the larger missions and the lion's share of resources. The State University of New York (SUNY) has five cam-puses designated as major research universities and several dozen other campuses of varying types and sizes throughout central and northern New York State. Extensive bureaucratic control is neces-sary in such a ramified system.

Large multicampus systems are so complicated that de facto del-egation of many governance functions to the headquarters admin-istration and thence to campus administrators becomes necessary. The governing board has limited purview over the details of finances, programs, and personnel selection. Governance then devolves for the most part on stakeholders other than the governing board, even though the board has final authority. Gade (1993) points to the useful distinction between a multicampus system in which all campuses have missions at the same educational level (for example, all offering the doctorate and advanced professional degrees) and those comprehensive systems which encompass cam-puses of several different types, from four-year colleges to special technical institutions to research universities.

Gade (1993) also provides a useful distillation of policies and practices applicable to the governance of multicampus systems. She undertook field reviews of three university systems (the University of North Carolina, the Kansas system, and the University of Cali-fornia) and one community college system (Maricopa, in the Phoenix, Arizona, metropolitan area). North Carolina has a note-worthy feature: a board of trustees at each campus, in addition to the systemwide administration and board of governors. Local over-sight and involvement are fostered in this way, yet the system as a whole has so far maintained coherence through strong presidential leadership, intensive communication (including use of consultative panels for ten-year academic reviews) and successful relationships with a traditionally fractious state legislature.

Kansas has a powerful commitment to state support of higher

education, though it is not a wealthy state. The system is bound together, Gade finds, through councils: a Council of Presidents, a Council of Chief Academic Officers, and other councils at functional levels. Benefits are thus derived both from cooperation and coordination and from the natural spur of competition. Designation of a "lead" campus for certain programs helps to reduce duplication (Gade, 1993, p. 38).

Multicampus systems are, however, susceptible to tampering on the part of local legislators and other politicians, to whom campus administrators and factions may appeal if they are losers in internal power struggles. A governing board that fails to resist such tampering invites the disintegration of its system.

Some states with major public universities do not have an explicit governing structure to coordinate budgets and missions of the several institutions. The University of Michigan, Michigan State University, Wayne State University, and an array of other public universities and colleges in Michigan have independent boards and administrations and contend with each other for state support. The result is that determinative leverage becomes lodged in the state's budget office or some other locus of governmental control. While such an arrangement may offer a workable solution to the problems of governing several public universities within a state, it does present a greater risk of severe political contention.

Numerous states have established a coordinating board with certain powers of oversight and extensive responsibilities for data collection and policy analysis on behalf of the executive and legislative branches. Lacking budgetary control, these boards concentrate on more sharply delimited issues, such as: articulation of student flows and transfer credits from high schools into four-year public institutions; review of proposals for new degree programs; and analysis of student tuition and financial aid policies. The executive director of such a board differs in executive responsibility from the chief executive (president or chancellor) of a multicampus system. Examples of coordinating mechanisms are the California Postsecondary Education Commission (CPEC) and the Commission on Higher Education, in Colorado.

The Institutional Boundary for Governance

A contemporary university, whether it is a single-campus university or a multicampus system, whether it is public or private, is usually composed of a number of distinguishable corporate entities. In public universities, a separate alumni foundation is often established to receive, administer, and sequester donated funds. The teaching hospitals connected with a medical school may be separate university corporations, city hospitals with contractual affiliation to the university, or Veterans Administration hospitals. Some major research laboratories are established as subsidiary not-for-profit corporations or as consortium corporations governed in concert with other universities, as Brookhaven and Argonne are. The latest entrant in this array of possibilities is the for-profit industrial park or research-exploiting corporation, controlled by the university as parent and beneficiary.

Each such entity poses its own problems of governance, mission, administration, and financial viability. The governing board and headquarters administration of the parent university may be hard put to maintain even minimal oversight when they are technically responsible for so many, and such different, entities. As a practical matter, specialized cadres within the headquarters administration are established to provide administrative sponsorship and support and to minimize risks of organizational breakdown.

However committed an administration may be to streamlining structures and processes, the proliferation of entities and the widening of institutional boundaries mock any effort at simplification. In the past, universities have sometimes cut loose a particular entity if it became a political or academic liability or if it could be expected to prosper better as an independent corporation. Cornell

University took the latter view of the Cornell Aeronautical Laboratory in Buffalo, New York, and Stanford made a similar evaluation of what is now SRI International, a contract research and consulting organization that is still located in close physical proximity to the Stanford University campus.

Selection of Board Members

When politically feasible, prescreening of qualifications for appointment or nomination to the board is strongly preferred. The process may screen out the occasional rebel or eccentric genius, but it also helps to protect the university from seriously inappropriate appointments. However, state governors typically resist constraints on their appointing power and may accept prescreening only if forced to do so. To reduce the political risks inherent in overconcentration of appointing power, a number of public and private universities entrust board positions to different modes of appointment or election.

In public universities, a purely representative governing board—one seat for agriculture, another for industry, and some for the relevant geographical regions—may devolve into a bargaining arena for interest groups. Single-interest groups press hard for their own board seats as issues of diversity penetrate to the board level.

These representational issues further compromise the "philosopher king" ideal of the perfect regent or trustee. While some gestures to stakeholder representation may be quite tolerable, a board is best able to promote the cause of the institution if it contains a significant number of members who command respect and wield influence over a broad front—some representing the leading professions, others drawn from previous public service, and still others from powerful corporations or public organizations. Such a group, with sufficiently long terms of service to provide deep familiarity with board procedures and with the problems, opportunities, and goals of the university, can make the most of its assignment.

Leadership Among Stakeholder Groups

Stakeholder groups may or may not be willing to offer up spokespersons. Fear of co-optation is typical among employee and student organizations, and to be "too constructive" is often to invite loss of confidence among the rank and file. Furthermore, most internal stakeholder groups, with the exception of the university's faculty and its organizations, have rapid turnover of leadership; this reduces their leverage.

The faculty, through its senate or other representative body, has substantial opportunities to be influential in a major university. To buttress the quality of faculty leadership, the university administration will be wise to provide at least minimal staff support to the faculty organization and its committees and to be visibly committed to consultation and shared governance. If such involvement is seen as a sham, or as inordinately wasteful of faculty members' time, interest will inevitably decline.

Faculty leadership can in fact be nurtured over time with astute guidance from deans and senior administrators. Although the administration and the faculty compete for power in some areas, they need to make common cause on the larger issues of the institution. Particularly during periods of strain, faculty leaders must be able to work cooperatively with the administration while at the same time keeping the confidence of their rank and file—no easy feat on matters prone to misunderstanding, miscommunication, and conflicts based on genuine differences of interest.

Theories of Governance

A series of terms has informed this discussion of university governance: these include *governing board, stakeholders, linkages, external factors,* and *institutional boundary.* This approach has emphasized the development of shared norms and standards and agreement on rules of behavior. The actors, in this case, are constrained by a joint understanding of what is appropriate, which guides their behavior.

In this characterization, the university is an *institution* with its own norms and rules to guide individuals. It becomes important to both the practice and the theory of university governance to explain the sources of the norms and rules. That challenge is what makes our discussion in Chapter Two of the values of a university deeply relevant to the issue of governance. Loss of academic commitment and motivation—for example, in the university's faculty—may disturb or even negate important institutional norms and thereby threaten the stability of governance. (See Kerr, 1994a, pp. 129–156.)

In contrast to this characterization of governance in terms of institutional structures and controls, there is the view that a scheme of organizational governance can be achieved by systematizing transactions or exchanges to mutual benefit, where the only functions at the level of governance are to convey information, set transaction-making rules, and enforce the consequences of transactions (March and Olsen, 1994). The actors, according to this, are presumed to be motivated by self-interest, eager to maximize their personal gains without reference to any larger, collective goals. Their behavior is likely to be "strategic," in the sense that they may put out misleading information and may seek advantage by bluffing, cheating, or making power plays. Yet the organization is bound together by the transactions that its members find advantageous. A university, according to this mode of reasoning, could hire each teacher on a contract contingent upon sufficient student enrollment in the course offered, and the students would pay a fee for the course and expect to earn a degree when they had satisfied the university's requirements. The university would be responsible in this case for assuring instructional quality and the enforcement of passing standards, and it would use part of its fee income to defray infrastructure costs (libraries, computer centers, administration, and facilities). Even some of these might be paid for through specific fees, and the university would seemingly have only the most minimal institutional functions!

In the spirit of this transactional approach to the way economic organizations function, Coase (1988) raised a crucial question: Why do economic organizations really need to exist at all, if markets are competitive and resources to produce, market, and consume can be assembled by contract? This question is of greatest interest to the economic theorist, but it has general significance, for the replacement of sets of pure market transactions with a set of organizational arrangements and administrative transfers pushes economic analysis toward political science, sociology, and law. Other important contributions to this analysis rest upon the work of Williamson (1975, 1985).

For universities, the transactional approach may call into question the use of revenues to support expensive institutional structures and their governance. Universities are not exempt from this sort of reexamination, as we shall discuss in Chapters Fourteen and Fifteen.

The study of governance in general—an effort to explain what forms it may take, and why, in public institutions and corporations—is a hot intellectual topic for the 1990s at a conjuncture of political science, economics, and legal studies. University leaders will need to pay attention to this analytical theme.

Chapter Four

Leadership and
the Presidency

Leadership in a university is partly based on formal authority, but leadership is also exercised without the mantle of authority and title. In the American tradition of the chief executive, institutional bylaws, formal title, and symbolism combine to give the university president great saliency, and it is natural for many to think of the university's president and university leadership as coextensive. This simplified picture of leadership is promoted by trustees, alumni, the press, and by nearly all presidents.

A closer look at the actual conditions of operation of a university discloses great complexity in the underlying patterns of responsibility and initiative. A university is a "loosely coupled organization," and many people work at getting things done. The organization chart usually has the board of trustees at its apex and the president as the delegated agent to manage the organizational hierarchy, but this schema often conceals as much as it reveals.

This chapter will, it is hoped, reveal facets of leadership and of the university presidency that will interest current and potential future presidents and will alert the trustees who hire and fire them to the complexities of the jobs of president and senior administrators. Other stakeholders should also find their leadership contributions placed in context, and they may gain a greater appreciation of the many ways in which leadership is exercised throughout an academic institution.

Functions of University Leadership

Five major functions of leadership are characteristic of organizations generally:

1. Clarification of the mission of the organization and determination of long-range objectives and shorter-range goals
2. Allocation of the organization's resources to priority uses within the terms of objectives and goals
3. Selection and evaluation of key personnel
4. Representation of the organization to external constituencies
5. Strategic management and organizational change

Leadership in the university will be examined in all five of the above areas of concern—first, with respect to the role of the president and the president's official team of immediate associates; then, wherever leadership may appear from other sources.

The University as a "Loosely Coupled Organization"

One challenging view is that a university is simply an "organized anarchy" (Cohen and March, 1974). According to this characterization, no agreement on goals is necessary or feasible; formal authority offers no institutional direction and few constraints on individual choices; and, to the extent that the institution is run, it in effect runs itself. The directly opposite view sees the university as an ultrastable, hierarchical organization.

Kerr and Gade (1986, pp. 125–157) pose not one but an array of five models of institutional operation. These are

- The hierarchical model with administrative authority and responsibility
- The collegial consensus model, with the president as the center of influence and shared governance as the main mechanism

- The polycentric model, in which the president is one center of influence but others also exist in political coalitions
- The "organized anarchy" model
- The atomistic decision-making model

Some institutions lean strongly to one or another of these models in their behavior. At some times, and in some aspects, a university is likely to display symptoms of all of them.

We say that the university is "loosely coupled" in the sense that its academic units and senior faculty members have wide discretion. They choose how to spend their time. They vie for achievement and recognition in their own fields and according to their own chosen reference points, many of which are outside the institution. As investigators on research projects, they control significant resources, and this gives them bargaining strength for command of space and other institutionally supplied items. Most important of all, they have the power to resist what they regard as inappropriate demands on them or intrusions on their freedom to act and think.

In this situation, the administrative heads of departments, colleges, and the institution as a whole find that they have to negotiate and persuade individuals and groups, rather than command. Some decisions are indeed collective ones, such as the adoption or major modification of a program design or curriculum; but proposals pass through numerous iterations of review and consultation among committees and other academic bodies. The senior administration may engage in vigorous nudging of the process, but it does not really control either the process or the outcome. This is the ongoing situation for the president and the president's senior administrative associates. Even when a significant change in the institution's commitments is in the offing, the president has to share initiatives with other sources of power.

Walker (1979) goes further and advises that the president *seek* the important sources of initiative in the faculty and administration and then respond to these, rather than being at the head of the parade. He warns of serious hazards in attempts to lead "from the top down" (p. 107), and the "heroic presidency," which is often adduced as an ideal, strikes him as institutionally counterproductive and at the same time corrupting of the presidential incumbent (pp. 114–116).

Loose coupling, then, works easily when the intent is to continue on a known and accepted path. It sometimes works extraordinarily well when initiatives are taken to define and implement new directions, but this requires a great deal of time for consensus building—and many sources of leadership must be counted on to propose and carry forward the desired changes. Loose coupling is likely to fail as an organizational form when quick and decisive action must be taken to preserve the institution. It is also likely to fail when there are factions that resist cooperation and coordination.

Cornford's famous and witty *Microcosmographia Academica* (1923) remains the classic treatment of styles of leadership action—and inaction—in the faculty-led institution. His argument is in the form of a primer for the (distressingly) ambitious faculty politician who aspires to institutional leadership. Many of the gambits Cornford discusses can be seen in action at committee tables and discreet luncheons at any university, and the members present often show allegiance to Cornford's wisdom even if they have never heard of him. One of his memorable passages is a commentary on the phrase (almost bound to come up in an academic committee) that "the time is not ripe." Cornford's musings on the ripeness of time remind us that those concerned with the university as their life are likely to be unmoved by arguments of urgency or threat.

Walker (1979, pp. 36–84) views the university as embodying political forces, pressures, and dominant realities. If this characterization is accepted, the president (and all of the other significant actors, too) can function well only by practicing the political arts: persuasive advocacy, continual communication, negotiation, and coalition building. In effect, the exercise of leadership is an exercise in process rather than a matter of achieving preset goals.

The Role of the University President

The circumstances and traditions of universities vary enormously. A few defining elements, however, are the same whether the university is public or private, a single-campus or a multicampus system, wealthy or financially distressed, urban or rural. The president has a large role as symbol and spokesperson, looked to by external and internal constituencies. The role therefore contains significant ritual content.

This symbolic role is perhaps in its finest feather when a new president makes his or her inaugural address to the institutional community. For example, President George Rupp, when he was inaugurated at Columbia University, argued that Columbia both had and needed a great emphasis on community (Rupp, 1993). With many large, strong, and autonomous professional schools and the distinguished and small-scale undergraduate program of Columbia College, Columbia has not been thought of as a cohesive academic institution but rather as the archetypal urban university.

Rupp discussed Columbia's effort to embrace several polarities. The first of these, "diversity/quality," promotes intensive interactions within a heterogeneous academic community, with latitude for free utterance, equally free critique, and efforts to include high-potential students from all communities. "Liberal/professional" is Rupp's second polarity. Rupp advocates intensive, mutually enriching contacts between the graduate professional schools and liberal education.

Rupp's third polarity, or tension, is "global/local"—not only in the spirit of intellectual exploration but in the university's sense of place. The formal name of the institution is "Columbia University in the City of New York," and this uniquely demanding location cannot be forgotten. With his emphasis on these polarities, Rupp sought to set a helpful intellectual and moral tone for the early part of his presidency, which would also involve, inevitably, all of the usual struggles with budgets, money raising, and high and low politics.

At Yale University, Richard Levin assumed office against the backdrop of bitter controversy over his predecessor's proposals for severe budget cuts and program eliminations. An economist, Levin assured the Yale community that while further savings needed to be achieved, nothing so draconian as the cuts proposed by former president Benno Schmidt would be needed ("Yale Installs Dean as Its 22nd President," 1993). (Schmidt's record as president of Yale is portrayed by Bernstein, 1992.)

Levin referred to Yale's massive program of renovation of its physical plant, whittling down an accumulation of deferred maintenance that was the legacy of decades of preoccupation with other uses of financial resources. He endorsed this as a necessary productivity-enhancing program, but he went on to say: "[I]f you think of students as our output, the only way you can produce more students per faculty member is to change the nature of education. I'm not for that. I don't want to substitute machines for teachers." Levin praised Yale's tradition of faculty attention to undergraduate teaching and said that while new presidents at Stanford and Harvard had proclaimed a need for a greater emphasis on teaching, Yale would not need to. (He thereby struck an ingratiating note of praise for his constituency and at the same time struck the competition at least a glancing blow!)

The university president maintains intensive relationships with the institution's governing board and is responsible to the board for the administration of board-level policies. The board regards the president as the manager of the institution's budget and the guardian of its financial health. In some ways, also, institutional and academic administrators, faculty leaders, and student leaders expect the president to respond to their problems and requests. But the nature of these relationships does vary substantially, depending on the university's structure and its internal and external conditions.

Birnbaum (1992) undertakes extensive analysis based on the Institutional Leadership Program (ILP), a five-year longitudinal study conducted at a purposive sample of thirty-two cooperating institutions. About one-fourth of the presidents were identified as "exemplary," one-half as "modal" (not roaring successes, but not failures either), and one-fourth as "failures." Of the three strategic constituencies of the president—the trustees, the administrators, and the faculty—the trustees and administrators tended to be pro-president most securely. A new president typically started with faculty endorsement and support, especially if the search and selection process involved faculty leaders and was trusted (pp. 74–76). The withdrawal of faculty support over time was fatal for the failed presidents, because the other strategic constituencies sooner or later accepted negative faculty sentiment as an important factor. Mixed or low faculty support was a source of stress for the modal presidents (pp. 89–103).

Birnbaum also finds that shared leadership was the dominant mode in these institutions (see especially, figure 1, p. 107). The exemplary presidents were able to emphasize important features of the institution's values and tradition (pp. 158–159). They embraced an approach of "cognitive complexity," displaying an ability to shift between bureaucratic, problem-solving and consultative styles (p. 180). They performed well in both instrumental and interpretive leadership, whereas failed presidents "lose the ability to constructively influence either institutional processes or symbolic interpretations" (p. 159).

Walker (1979, pp. 55–56), too, emphasizes the duality of administrative actions and interpretive efforts, and he offers interesting comments concerning the phenomenon of "interpretive drift."

According to Birnbaum, failed presidents "act preemptively or in an authoritarian manner" (p. 169). He concludes, however, that institutions are not fatally damaged by less than stellar presidential performance, because a university has many sources of initiative and it benefits from its historical momentum. A major cost is lost opportunity for strengthening and improvement (p. 170). Walker

(1979) maintains that a democratic style is the most productive one in the American setting.

Kerr (1994b) identifies three models of the university president: the organized anarchy model of Cohen and March, which in essence denies that the president matters; the "faculty opinion" model, in which the faculty perception is often one of the president as autocratic and at the same time poor in performance; and the "president makes a difference" model. Kerr, of course, prefers the third (pp. 38–40).

The Chief Executive in a Multicampus University System

The multicampus university system, almost always a public university system, is fundamentally different from the single-campus institution in the definition of the chief executive's role. Each campus has its own chief campus officer who is typically responsible, under broad delegations of authority, for academic and administrative affairs within that campus. (Unfortunately, the nomenclature is nonstandard: some multicampus executive heads are called "president," with "chancellor" used for chief campus officers; others reverse the title designations.) The chief system officer has primary responsibility both for board relationships and for budgetary and political representation of the system to the state government.

Within the system, this office is responsible for the promulgation and oversight of general university policies, for ministerial functions of the university as a nonprofit corporation, and for oversight of the performance of the chief campus officers. The system head may also take occasional educational initiatives, but the position is generally remote from the processes of instruction and research, which take place entirely on the campuses.

The Chief Executive Officer of a Campus in a Multicampus University System

When delegations of broad authority provide ample scope for the chief campus officer in a multicampus system, the role approximates that of the single-campus university president in many respects. However, board relationships and official representation of the university system to the state government typically remain with the chief system officer. In fact, if a chief campus officer makes independent approaches to legislative and other politicians, for budgetary or other purposes, such an action may create confusion and undercut the position of the system executive.

Internal administrative and academic responsibilities approximate those of the single-campus chief executive. Typically, the chief campus officer speaks for an expansive mission:

- To enhance the reputation and visibility of existing academic programs and research centers
- To emphasize the attractive power of its undergraduate as well as graduate instruction, so that it can justify additional faculty positions and other resources
- To develop the ambience and attractiveness of the campus for the benefit of students, alumni, and external supporters
- To obtain approval and mandates for new academic programs that will broaden and strengthen the campus
- To press for capital project funding and for operating budget support

Crucial to all of this is the recruitment and retention of outstanding faculty, deans, and skillful administrators. The chief officer's most important legacies to the future of the campus are the quality of faculty members, their visible achievements, and the dedication of the students who pass through the institution and become its representatives in the community and its loyal alumni.

In external relationships, including alumni and community affairs, advocacy of new programs, and fund-raising, the chief campus officer has wide scope. In fact, the chief system executive has little fund-raising responsibility, as this is typically a campus function. The chief campus officer is regarded as the advocate for program approvals and budgetary support when allocations of resources among campuses and programs are being decided within the university system.

In some multicampus systems, a sharp distinction in program breadth and resource support is made between a "flagship campus" and the smaller campuses. The University of Wisconsin's Madison campus, the Twin Cities (Minneapolis and St. Paul) campus of the University of Minnesota, and the College Park campus of the University of Maryland are flagships. The chief campus officer of each of these defends the preferred status of the campus. The chief officers of lesser campuses are typically pressed by their campus constituencies to obtain a broader range of programs, stronger academic support, and opportunities for expanded visibility.

An interesting feature of the multicampus system is that its chief campus officers generally have longer tenure than do the chief executives of single-campus institutions. Perhaps the relative shelter from often hostile pressures of political and budgetary representation increases the effective length of term in the job.

The Chief Executive in a Private Single-Campus University

Board relationships and the orchestration of public approval and internal morale are crucial functions of the private university president. Getting the money is all-important, and this never-ending struggle to raise private and corporate funds cannot be won without both board support and a good campus face. Support-raising tasks and the management of external visibility are so time-consuming that many chief executives are "outside presidents," leaving most internal academic policy and administration to the provost or academic vice president and most financial administration to a senior vice president for administration. Rosovsky (1990) gives an engaging portrayal of the wide duties of his role as Harvard's Dean of Faculty (although he had purview only over the arts and sciences and not the professional schools) and its relationship to the president.

Control of the university's budget cannot be left to subordinates, however, as the university's financial viability is the president's responsibility. The board will not forgive a serious slippage of financial position. Furthermore, the budget and the fiscal projections that go with it embody in the most tangible form the priorities of the institution. The president's leadership on priorities can be expressed forcefully in the budget and fiscal plans; alternatively, a status quo budget implies that the university will rock along on the present path.

Academic reputation is critical to the private university. Its viability depends on its capacity to attract undergraduate students and keep tuition revenue flowing, and on the solidity of its relationships with sources of funding support—corporations, foundations, private donors, and research funding agencies. The perceived attractiveness of the undergraduate student experience depends on the strength of the academic program (a sensible curriculum and famous scholars, at least some of whom are outstanding teachers and lecturers accessible to undergraduate students) and on a positive "quality of life" aura. Research faculty must be able to attract substantial extramural funds, for this fund flow is a critical component of the faculty compensation budget and the support base for graduate programs, as well as contributing through indirect cost recovery to the overhead costs of the institution as a whole.

No university can be visibly excellent in every conceivable academic specialty. Given the central importance of quality, the president and provost are challenged to place risky bets on people and programs. Private universities are more likely than public ones to partition some of their risks by using the "every tub on its own bottom" rule for the array of more or less freestanding professional schools and specialized programs. Each dean of a professional school then has the entrepreneurial duty of seeing to its survival and prosperity, and the school may indeed be required to make some net contribution to the general overhead of the institution. The responsibility includes both operating solvency and the raising of permanent endowments for professorships and programs. If the dean and faculty of the school cannot "produce," they will not be able to call on more than short-term subsidy assistance from general university funds. In this regime of decentralized responsibility, the president and provost are obligated to make good choices of deans and monitor the progress of each school.

The basic scholarly disciplines in the humanities, social sciences, and laboratory sciences, on the other hand, are typically organized together in a College of Arts and Sciences or Letters and Science. Some departments and fields of research lend themselves to entrepreneurial effort and acquisition of extramural research grants and other funds, but letters and science as a whole are so central to the academic mission and health of the institution that it can claim substantial support from general institutional funds.

The Office of the President or "Presidency"

The president is one individual. The conduct of the Office of the President, or "Presidency," requires allocation of responsibility among several very senior administrators, who then function as a team. Kerr and Gade (1986) concentrate their attention on the selection, role, conduct, and length of tenure of the president. To a minor extent, they consider the role of the provost as "inside president."

The contemporary management literature, however, emphasizes the significance of the Top Management Team (TMT), of whom the CEO is the most important individual (Hambrick, 1987). Despite the saliency of the person of the university president, it is worthwhile to examine the concept of the TMT and apply it, as far as possible, to the Office of the President, or "Presidency."

The Top Management Team embodies the several kinds of expertise that are required for general management of the enterprise. Internal communication patterns and sense of mutual confidence must be strong if the team is to function well. Similar length of tenure in the same organization and intimate personal acquaintance promote communication and trust, and there is evidence of significant positive effects on the firm's performance (O'Reilly and Flatt, 1989; O'Reilly, Snyder and Boothe, forthcoming). The ability to foster organizational change is also linked to the extent of homogeneity of the TMT. The prime conditions of homogeneity are same length of tenure within the organization and similarity of outlook. The payoffs of homogeneity are ease of communication and a greater prospect of mutual trust. If a corporation is sliding toward bankruptcy, deterioration of the Top Management Team is held to be both a cause and an effect of the downward spiral (Hambrick and D'Aveni, 1992). The size of the team, the composition of functional capabilities, and the executive quality of the members (signaled by compensation) are important factors. So is the extent of CEO dominance (excessive dominance implies lack of team contributions). Hambrick and D'Aveni show that in matched samples, the Top Management Teams of deteriorating firms diverged farther and farther from the TMT attributes of successful firms, *at an accelerating rate* as bankruptcy loomed.

Possible lessons for the Office of the President of a university are

1. The president, provost, and a few other very senior positions should be assessed to assure that they constitute a balanced team in types of functional expertise.

2. High mutual confidence and ease of internal communication are essential. (This, in turn, implies that the president, as team leader, should recommend choices to the board of trustees that will promote these qualities.) A substantial degree of homogeneity of organizational experience will probably be conducive to achieving confidence and smooth communication.

3. The board and the president should be on their guard against any tendencies to split off portions of the administration and

make them beholden either to a board faction or to a constituency faction, internal or external. Disunity has a high price.

While these may seem to be straightforward lessons from management analysis for an Office of the President, it is doubtful whether the advice can be implemented fully in many universities. The president and the provost almost invariably have academic backgrounds, although in the case of the president, this may be a "once upon a time" academic appointment before administrative entanglements dominated the presidential career. The senior vice president for administration, or finance and budget, may sometimes come from academic origins, as did Stanford vice president for finance William F. Massy; at least as frequently, however, the long-serving finance, accounting, and budget professionals produce a strong candidate who is the natural choice for the most senior post. Similarly, the critical areas of fund-raising, public affairs, and legal counsel are likely to have their own separate ladders of advancement, although an academic person (especially a very devoted alumnus or alumna) may often qualify in the public affairs or development areas. The legal counsel, of course, must be assumed to come from a tribal culture sharply different from everybody else in the executive ranks.

As a result of the separateness of these streams of competence, it is not likely that a desirable homogeneity of outlook and ease of communication will come naturally. Worse yet, universities are unlike corporate organizations in having a generally low level of confidence in the promotability of their long-service midlevel professionals. The search process—often a formal committee assisted by an executive search firm ("headhunter")—frequently exhibits a bias toward filling a key position other than president or provost by locating an outside candidate whose weak points are not sufficiently identified to disable his or her candidacy. Thus, the university's Top Management Team is likely to be more heterogeneous in the critical dimensions of educational and professional background, length of service in the university, and mutuality of experience, than is true of the successful corporate TMT.

Fostering Innovation and Change

As was stated in the introduction to this book, universities expect to live forever, and they make very long-term commitments accordingly; yet they keep their budgets and meet their revenue needs one precarious year at a time. The expectation of permanence imparts more deliberateness to the university's attitude toward change than is true of many other organizations, for which the rule is: change or die. Nevertheless, despite the weight of tradition and the presumption of permanence, the university displays extraordinary rates of change in some areas.

In all fields of scholarly work, the excitement and the fame come from discovery. In the major universities, this bias toward novelty makes its way into the informal faculty seminars and advanced research topics and papers, then into graduate courses, and finally into undergraduate studies. The penetration of the new is, however, episodic and piecemeal; only rarely does an entire curriculum become reorganized from top to bottom as a result of novel scholarship. The genius of the course and seminar system is that it can assimilate change rapidly without causing overt political and philosophical strife.

The physical and biological sciences and the engineering disciplines experience the additional pulses of academic change that come from generation after generation of new equipment and instrumentation, without which many systematic advances in these fields could not occur. Academic change here requires capital as well as brains.

Gross structural change in a university is quite infrequent—the initiation of a major new degree program or professional school, for example, or the anointing of a cross-disciplinary research area (biophysics, bioengineering, women's studies) as a distinct, official focus for the curriculum and for departmental faculty organization and careers. It is change of this kind that requires provostial and even presidential and board attention. The incremental innovations that occur routinely do not need to receive much official notice and do not raise governance questions.

A university that loses momentum and approaches a moribund state does so first through the slowing or lapsing of the incremental changes that are essential to academic vitality. The provost, president, and board need to be very sensitive in their monitoring to register this phenomenon.

In administrative services and the organization of student life, change more frequently takes the form of overhaul to improve efficiency or to respond to a change of institutional (and market) tastes. Some universities are good at promoting effective change in these areas. Others spend few resources and no high-level political capital to push through such changes against the usual bureaucratic resistances.

As is discussed in Chapters Fourteen and Fifteen, the early 1990s have seen an upsurge of interest in radical decentralization and empowerment, supported by strong investment in information technology and other infrastructure. How widespread will be the adoption of this brand of administrative reform is difficult to predict. The contemporaneous trend toward downsizing and retrenchment militates against it.

Localized and Volunteered Leadership

Piecemeal academic changes and innovations can appear anywhere in the academic structure. Initiatives and sponsorship by individual faculty members and small teams are in fact essential, for their expertise, imagination, and credibility are required both to try out a research approach or instructional innovation and to validate it. It is true that the wise risk taking of a provost, dean, or department chair may be important in the approval of a new battery of courses or a new academic position. They may also play a role by providing "seed money," releasing faculty time for developmental efforts, supplying necessary initial equipment, or even designating a special academic task force. But the higher level is rarely as effective as the grassroots in promoting piecemeal academic improvements.

Rosovsky (1990) discusses at length the special problems, and the high front-end costs, of attracting a "star" professor to initiate a new academic effort.

Institutional innovations, as opposed to the purely academic and disciplinary ones, more often need initiatives and leadership from the senior levels of administration. Even here, however, it may be necessary to establish a task force or experimental administrative group to provide the senior administrator with a tangibly promising proposal for implementation. Major capital projects— especially for academic buildings—display this feature, because they have to involve the main users directly in the process of planning and design. Given the swift advances in information technology and the changing patterns of organization of academic fields, the planning of a new building offers an academic organization an important and very taxing opportunity: to look ahead to the ten- or twenty-year horizon of the field and to plan for the future instead of continually struggling to bring up to date the configurations and equipment inherited from the past.

Emergencies and Crises

Any university may be caught up in an emergency or crisis. Many of these arise from an unexpected source, bursting over the institution with little or no warning. Some low-probability natural events such as earthquake, fire, and hurricane justify an investment in institutional preparation through an Emergency Preparedness Program, which would, among other things, ensure the safety of buildings and the robustness of infrastructure systems.

Riot, social upheaval, or political crisis is another matter. As Kerr and Gade (1986) point out, student unrest and other campus conflicts of the 1960s and 1970s shortened the tenure of many university presidents. They discuss the president who becomes the institution's lightning rod and then scapegoat (pp. 73–74), and follow with a quote from John Gardner's speech at the inauguration of a president in 1968: "We have now proven beyond reasonable argument that a university community can make life unlivable for a president. We make him a scapegoat for every failure of society . . . We can fight so savagely among ourselves that he is clawed to ribbons in the process" (p. 74).

In the 1980s, some presidents came under siege from the right rather than from the left or the counterculture of the young. President James O. Freedman of Dartmouth College faced drumfire criticism from the *Dartmouth Review*, a student publication financed from off-campus by ultraconservative Dartmouth alumni. Having learned his trade from the *Review*, Dinesh D'Souza went on to write *Illiberal Education* (1991) and became a spokesman for conservative ideology, backed by the Heritage Foundation and by allies such as former secretary of education William Bennett.

Numerous other zealous forces can precipitate campus crises. Animal rights groups have sometimes moved from argumentation to confrontation and laboratory sabotage. Academic controversies over appointment or denial of appointment of a favored female or minority faculty member can boil up into pressure-group tactics and sit-ins. The campus is, after all, an assemblage of energetic young people whose days and hours are not wholly constrained, and some faculty members, for their part, may see in even a minor incident a cause worth pursuing.

The institution faces little threat to its stability, however, unless unwisdom or bad luck brings about a steep escalation. John Searle (1971) provides a trenchant analysis of this escalation process, of which the ultimate goal and consequence is a full-scale police intervention and a parade of broken heads (see especially, chap. 1). To keep trouble below the point of explosion, the campus administration needs to have in place a variety of preventive and ameliorative mechanisms: student affairs professionals who understand and appreciate the bases of student indignation or angst; a sophisticated and self-restrained uniformed campus police force; and the support of moderates in the student community and the faculty. The chief campus officer needs (but does not always have) some mechanism for mobilizing quickly the all-important moderate support on campus. He or she is inevitably a player in the game, just as a city mayor can be found close to the center of the cyclone when a riot occurs. Even the exercise of courage and finesse cannot always head off the worst, and if the worst happens, the chief officer may get the blame for the community's disaster.

The "Overreaching" President

Corporate and political life are replete with instances of the fall following the ascent of a powerful leader. Ross Johnson maneuvered successfully, as merger succeeded merger, from an insignificant corporate position to the office of CEO of RJR-Nabisco. (See Pfeffer, 1992, for a discussion of Johnson's mobilization of personal power.) But Johnson's subsequent attempt to take the corporation private through a leveraged buyout—at outrageous profit to himself—was derailed by outside directors of the corporation, who managed to deliver control to another contender (Burrough and Helyar, 1990). Epic struggles among egos brought about the eventual collapse of two major Wall Street firms in the 1980s: E. F. Hutton and Lehman Brothers (Pfeffer, 1992, pp. 315, 322–323). Political leaders from Xerxes to Ceausescu have overestimated their power and paid the price.

The U.S. presidency is notorious for placing the incumbent in a cocoon of protection and shelter from unwelcome information. University presidents, commencing with the intention of open communication with their external constituencies and with the campus, have often become isolated by the protective actions of personal staff and by their own fatigue with public exposure. Isolation and the belief that one is very special are dysfunctional in the conduct of the executive role, and on occasion they can lead to personal disaster.

Presidents need to keep an open door to healthy criticism of their office and of their personal actions. They should assume that any action concerning terms and conditions of executive employment will soon become public, because it is impossible to maintain confidentiality on such matters in a public institution. The course of wisdom is to release the facts of any decision on executive compensation at the time the board of the institution makes the decision. If any measure is contemplated that could not stand public scrutiny, it should be abandoned. It is a grave mistake for either trustees or presidents to see the position and powers of the university president as analogous to the presidency of a for-profit corporation. Such a view is contrary to the fundamental values of an academic institution. In addition, any president who is perceived to be earning an excessively high salary and to have fringe benefits which are far beyond those of senior faculty is likely to arouse academic suspicion and envy.

Episodes of self-aggrandizement are object lessons for the conduct of the presidency, whether in business corporations or in universities. Tighter laws and security regulations are now likely to constrain boards of for-profit corporations from providing excessive and undisclosed compensation to their CEOs and other senior executives. University boards and presidents are held to a still higher standard of self-restraint. Incoming president Jack Peltason of the University of California canceled a number of special top-management fringe benefits in his first official actions after taking office in October 1992.

Even the essential requirements of special housing and staff for institutional representation (including money raising) are likely to provoke envy and antagonism. While the setting for official duties needs to be appropriate (and often, it is expensive), the president has to balance these needs against the potential political costs. Needless to say, a chief officer who is already unpopular is likely to find that special perquisites attract intense criticism and may even jeopardize his or her tenure in office.

Learning and Strategic Change

We have discussed the fact that piecemeal innovations in academic programs percolate through the university and help it to maintain freshness and vitality in instruction and research. Other types of institutional change—in some aspects of academic structure and operations, in administrative organization, and in the provision of essential services—are much slower to come about.

There are few incentives to repair inefficiencies and weaknesses in the academic structure and in academic operations. The provost and deans of a major university serve on the sufferance of the faculty. Exploration of the possible need to close a weak program or to increase teaching load will arouse strong resistance unless an appropriate mechanism for studying the need for change and recommending an acceptable new policy can be found.

In Chapter Fourteen, we point to the relative lack of interest in substitution of capital for labor in the instructional process, particularly through the use of computer-based, self-paced instruction. Though institutional learning does occur in this area, it occurs slowly and grudgingly. Also typical are very low levels of developmental investment out of institutional funds.

Leadership from the grass roots—that is, from faculty and department chairs—is needed to set in motion the experiments that would enable the university to learn what improvements are worth adopting on a wider scale. So far, library systems have been more progressive in this respect than departments of instruction and research.

Kerr and Gade (1986) point to the growing number of requirements for consultation and consent in university decision making.
Two of their models of the presidency emphasize this feature: the
"collegial consensus model and shared governance" and the model
of "the president as one center of power and influence—the polycentric model and political coalitions" (pp. 133–148). The most
senior administrators in a major university must typically operate
in one or other of these veto-ridden frameworks. Autocratic,
strongly top-down administration is unworkable. How, then, can
orderly, smooth, and timely change be promoted? The answer seems
to be to mobilize problem-solving efforts, invest in experiments for
change, and continuously communicate what is learned as well as
what needs to be done. Birnbaum, too, discusses ways of promoting
campus renewal (1992, pp. 124–147).

Even with strenuous effort, of course, the reform of many
aspects of university operation proceeds at a slower pace than would
make sense in the abstract. This is part of the price—and it can be
a very high price—for administration through consensus building
and consent. The administration and the faculty do need to attend
to the incentives for students, faculty, and staff to become partners
in the planning of reform. If the university invests little of its
resources in such activity and offers scant reward to individuals who
involve themselves in the work of innovation, those interested in
change are likely to infer, correctly, that the institutional leadership
is not serious about promoting it.

Chapter Five

Academic Organization

Having examined in earlier chapters the topics of management-as-process, institutional values, governance, and leadership, we now turn to the academic organization of the university.

A "Macro" View of the Academic Span of the University

An institution's mission is expressed mainly—though not entirely—in the breadth of its educational programs and in the range of degrees that it offers. The 1994 edition of *A Classification of Institutions of Higher Education* (Carnegie Foundation for the Advancement of Teaching) contains eleven categories. By degree level, 1,480 Associate of Arts Colleges—community and technical colleges—are the "base" of the taxonomy. At the doctoral level are 88 Research Universities I and 37 Research Universities II. Closely following are 111 Doctoral Universities, which offer doctorates in fewer fields and in smaller numbers. While this book focuses mainly on the challenges facing the doctorate-granting institutions, it may also be useful to those concerned with institutions that offer programs up to the master's degree. In the 1994 Carnegie classification, these are called Master's (Comprehensive) Universities and Colleges I (439 institutions) and II (93 institutions).

Aspirations toward higher academic program status are reflected in upward shifts in the classification. From 1987 to 1994, for example, sixteen Research Universities II shifted into the Research Universities I category, and sixteen Doctoral Universities I shifted to

Research University II (Evangelauf, 1994). These shifts reflect the powerful ambitions of institutional leaders and faculty to attain the status and significance of a university that emphasizes research and advanced graduate education. The expansion occurred during a period when academic placement of new doctorates was in the doldrums. Thus, it was not a response to urgent short-term signals from the job market, although projections of academic supply and demand for new doctorates into the late 1990s and beyond did show demand sufficient for some net expansion. Inevitably, these efforts to reach into doctoral education and to establish research university status do leave unsettled the question of the academic quality of so many new programs. Small-enrollment doctoral programs do appear to show higher completion rates for the Ph.D. and shorter times to complete the degree than do large-enrollment programs (Bowen and Rudenstine, 1992, p. 12), but the highly rated and larger programs experienced no decline in quality of entering doctoral students (p. 24).

The strenuous efforts of numerous institutions to upgrade also imply that the mission definition and institutional role of the comprehensive college was ambiguous or unsatisfactory to many academic participants.

Parallel with the Carnegie classification is a series of efforts to assess the quality of doctoral and professional degree education. These studies give indications of the competitive positioning of each institution. The most comprehensive study was a 1982 national assessment of the quality of doctoral programs (Jones, Lindzey, and Coggeshall), which was undergoing a major follow-up in 1994. Assessment or ranking imposes a kind of discipline on the institutions, although assessments differ greatly in the care and skill with which they are designed, administered, and interpreted. Chapter Thirteen covers issues of quality and assessment.

Competitive positioning of a university's programs implies the necessity to match the academic salary ranges of similar institutions, as well as their laboratory and other facilities, their research support arrangements, and their teaching loads. This leads us to consideration of the internal functioning of the university's academic organization—the "micro" view.

"Micro" Perspectives on Academic Organization

The formal hierarchy of the university, from the governing board down, is curiously constrained in its impact on the most fundamental processes of learning—those that take place between scholars and scholars, scholars and students, and students and students. Most of the operating apparatus of formal authority sets frameworks, establishes schedules, allocates enabling resources, records (fragments of) results, and monitors the general trend of performance. The actual conduct of learning is, of course, indirectly affected by all this. But there is so much latitude between minimum and maximum performance that the individuals at a university retain significant autonomy. This gives them many vetoes over the official intentions of authority in the most important aspects of the university.

Decentralized Learning Processes

The formal apparatus of the institution does bear on the selection of those who will come into the academic process. But once these choices are made, the largest differences in results arise not from the enabling framework but from the capacities, motivations, and incentives of individual scholars and students. They have the ultimate authority in a university, because they determine whether or not great things will happen in the process of learning.

The criteria for results are imperfectly formulated, and the gauges of quality entail highly specialized and very personal academic judgments. The processes of learning are not well understood. But it may also be true that university administrators are reluctant to move toward systematic measures of accountability for what is discovered and learned because they have so little immediate power to affect the outcomes of these processes.

Academic Organization According to Specializations

A university is not a tight, integrated entity: it is a loosely coupled organization of academic units that are differentiated from one another and that operate with significant, though varying, degrees of decentralization. The European universities are organized according to "faculties," such as the faculty of law and the faculty of natural science. Each faculty is academically autonomous, to the point that a student who decides to shift from one faculty to another may not have transferability of credits and may have to go back to the starting post (Clark, 1983, chap. 2, especially p. 70).

In the United States, the two basic units of operating academic organization are the school or college and within the school or college, its divisions and/or academic departments. A professor is said to hold appointment "in the department of biochemistry" or "the law school," implying (correctly) that for budget, personnel administration, and academic duties, this is the professor's main point of institutional reference and locus of activity. In the areas of professional education such as law, engineering, or business management, an alternative to departments may be an organization of divisions or committee groups within a single academic department that includes all academic personnel of the school and has the powers and duties of a department as specified in university regulations. These divisions or committees do not have the formal powers of budget allocation and personnel supervision that an academic department has.

In a campus organized according to classically defined scholarly disciplines, each academic department is a collectivity of faculty expertise with (in the pure case) an exclusive mandate to control what is offered to any student on the campus in that field. No department can poach on another's territory. Even though students' choices of majors and electives determine the enrollment distribution, the departments are not permitted to duplicate others' course offerings and thereby become direct substitutes of one another.

Departments are all independent or complementary in the supply of course offerings. The pure case of exclusive mandate for each disciplinary department avoids duplications of faculty positions and course offerings. It would be a violation of this principle, for example, to have two departments of mathematics competing with each other and offering identical courses. (However, because of nuances of difference within a field and because of unresolved disagreements over academic matters, some universities do permit competing departments and doctoral programs in essentially the same field. This is an expensive way to resolve academic policy conflicts!)

There are also important cross-relationships between fields, for students majoring in one field may be required or expected to take courses in another. Then, an increase in the number of majors in one field leads to an enrollment increase in the related field. Correspondingly, the elimination of a department or a required course results in indirect as well as direct dislocations.

Alternative Designs: The Professional School and the Decentralized College System

In the U.S. university, there are two important dimensional alternatives to the disciplinary specialization principle: the professional schools and the decentralized collegiate organization.

The professional schools often claim their expertise not in a scholarly discipline but in the design of a curriculum to fit students for a professional vocation and in the inculcation of the mores and perspective of that profession. Some of the intellectual content may overlap with one or another of the basic scholarly disciplines. In that case, the faculty of the professional school may then have to decide whether to send its students to the academic discipline departments for background courses or to create specially designed courses within the school, taught by the school's own faculty.

Organization of a campus into decentralized colleges strikes even more deeply at the fundamental principle of complementarity, because each college may seek a faculty and offer a set of courses or seminars chosen to be consistent with its style and mission. Course offerings in one college on the campus may then overlap with those in another, yet remain totally independent. College-initiated courses also compete with those offered by disciplinary specialists to the campus as a whole.

The alternative of organization in residential colleges was made famous by Oxford and Cambridge. At Oxford, the university administers examinations and confers degrees. There are some university lecturers, but most members of the academic staff have traditionally been appointed as fellows of colleges. The student receives formal education, and a great deal of other guidance, through the tutorial system of each college.

Academic Departments in the Research University

Each academic department is the university's vehicle for work in a given discipline or professional specialty. Faculty in the department have in common a great many elements of training, interest, and outlook, even though they may work in different subfields, use different research methods, and (on occasion) disagree vehemently about professional and institutional matters.

The array of discipline departments in the university's faculty of arts and sciences or letters and science reflects the conventional taxonomy of scholarly knowledge. However, the departmental organization in a particular university may contain seeming irrationalities, which can be accounted for by specific institutional history. There may, for example, be a finer breakdown into small departmental units, or even partially parallel and competing departments if there is a history of ideological schism or a conflict of leadership personalities. A nationwide assessment of the quality of doctoral programs in U.S. universities found numerous instances of duplicative degree programs at a single campus (Jones, Lindzey, and Coggeshall, 1982).

There is also a problem of scale. Academic departments, measured by the number of faculty positions, can vary within one campus from one professor (a distinguished isolate or a tenured survivor of a past phaseout decision) to more than one hundred. Very large academic departments cannot operate internally by the consensual and collegial styles that are traditional to academic life. They have to develop internal committee systems and bureaucratic structures for the large mass of work entailed in personnel administration, scheduling, and student contact.

In a study of Ph.D. programs at the University of California, Berkeley, David Breneman (1970, 1971a, 1971b) developed the concept of the academic department as a *prestige-maximizing firm* and sought to explain, in these terms, differences between departments in rates of persistence to the degree, aspirations for eminence, and other factors. From this point of view, the faculty members of a department gain reputation in two ways: through the recognition accorded their individual research by peers in the discipline, and by sharing the collective reputation and visibility of the department.

Graduate students who attain the Ph.D. are the protégés of one or two individual faculty members, who vouch for them at the time of job placement, and of the departmental Ph.D. program. Conventionally prestige-increasing Ph.D. placements include those in university academic departments of high reputation or prized postdoctoral research appointments. There are also prestige-neutral appointments (in middling institutions and in most industrial or government jobs) and prestige-reducing appointments (in teaching or professional posts at institutions low in their respective "pecking orders"). Breneman's hypothesis, generally confirmed through systematic interviews and other qualitative evidence, includes the inference that a department interested in maximizing prestige tightens its passing standard for Ph.D.'s if it fears that, on completion, some candidates could be placed only in prestige-reducing positions.

In these aspects of a department's operation, its faculty members are bound together in a calculus of mutuality in which the good of one contributes to the good of all, and all have incentives to enforce on themselves and on their advanced graduate students the highest (conventionally defined) academic standards, both for research and for graduate teaching. At the same time, inevitable personal rivalries and competition for departmental space and other resources can endanger collegiality.

In any university, an academic department has many duties and responsibilities, and these must be shared by its members. Unless there are separate graduate and undergraduate faculties—which in American universities is rare—a department administers a program for undergraduate degree majors and often one for terminal master's degree candidates who will go into pure teaching jobs or into professional employment. The department's roster of courses is partly for these students and partly for students who are not in its stream of majors but take its courses as requirements, electives, or prerequisites for other work.

In ways ranging from the general and qualitative to the precisely quantitative, the number of students enrolled in a department's courses and graduate programs serves as a major determinant of the operating budget it receives—particularly for operating support, temporary faculty lecturers and graduate assistant positions, and additional positions for career faculty appointment in the following year. The stronger these budgetary factors are, the greater is the departmental incentive to register large and increasing enrollment. Once again, there is a calculus of mutuality; in particular, the members of the department have strong incentives to value the additional faculty positions that will add to collective reputation. Those teaching responsibilities that require heavy work are shared in a more or less equitable fashion. The faculty member can hope to gain professional satisfactions (and many indeed do) from these teaching responsibilities. But teaching assignments that are distant from the faculty member's research interests and from work with advanced graduate students are regarded as burdensome.

The Role of Department Head

The department chair, who represents the department to the several levels of the administration and is responsible for assigning course duties and budgetary resources as well as for personnel administration, is subject to the classic "linking pin" stresses. The higher levels of university administration regard the chair as a first-line supervisor, responsible for interpreting and enforcing university policies and regulations and for making sensible allocations of the department's budgeted resources. Department members regard the chair as a colleague and as their agent in bringing to the department what it needs from the university administration. In situations of conflict and scarcity, the chair cannot satisfy both forces all of the time.

Universities and even departments within a university differ in the extent of discretionary power accorded the department chair and in the expected length of service in that position. In occasional instances, the chair serves for a very long time—decades, rather than years. If this is known to be likely, the chair can use the power of budget allocation, teaching assignment, and personnel recommendations as sanctions over rank-and-file members of the department. (In some medical schools, the department head has substantial control over the allocation to individuals of the collective "patient income pool," and this confers greater power, and usually greater length of term, to the job.) Most professors have lifetime tenure, and this and other factors limit the amount of top-down control. The chair must secure mostly voluntary cooperation from departmental colleagues, who have avenues of redress if they feel abused.

Much more usual is frequent rotation of the chair position among senior members of a department, each taking the duty for two or three years, with reduced responsibilities in course teaching and at some cost to individual research and work with graduate students.

This procedure has several consequences. It emphasizes collegiality and consensus methods of operation. The incumbent is aware that next year, or the year after, the colleague with whom it is necessary to disagree, or on whom an unwelcome duty is foisted, may be the chair. Rotation also produces quite a variance in administrative skill over time, because capacity for administration is unevenly distributed in a typical group of faculty members. This amateur and uneven capacity results in the devolution of substantial, effective power on skilled, long-service (and usually female) administrative assistants who are noncompetitive in role with the academics of the department. Rotation also results in greater emphasis on the internal needs of the department than on the wider concerns and administrative pressures emanating from the higher levels of the university administration. (See also Pfeffer and Moore, 1980.)

Increased complexity of administration—particularly personnel administration—and pressures for skill in budgeting and planning and for initiatives in extramural funding are changing the departmental chair's role. Tenure in the position may have to lengthen and the very small administrative stipends for duties performed will have to improve as the job becomes more demanding.

Program and Process Relationships:
Departmental View

When a campus is organized according to academic specializations or scholarly disciplines, with a distinct budgetary unit for each, the faculty and chair of each department face both complementary and competitive relationships with other departments: academic process and operating interactions; relationships in the design of curriculum; competition within departments for priorities; and budgetary relationships between departments.

Faculty in two fields are sometimes strongly dependent on one another. Historian and linguist, chemist and physicist, lawyer and political scientist may trade mutually helpful knowledge and techniques and may share in the training of students who are, in effect, hybrid products of the respective specialties.

Academic departments may also rely on each other in a milder form of complementarity, any given department sending students to another that has the expertise and the jurisdictional mandate to provide essential background. Service courses offer institutional efficiencies through economies of scale. But the students arrive from a variety of majors, and the design of a service course is often, necessarily, a compromise that does not quite fit any one of the student constituencies attending.

Thus, at many universities, the mandate of exclusive jurisdiction partly breaks down. An example is the proliferation of introductory statistics courses. The mathematical statisticians may offer to majors in the mathematics and statistics departments an introductory statistics course that presumes mathematical background and ability. They may also offer an introductory service course for nonmajors with less mathematics training. A large university is also likely to have courses in educational statistics, engineering statistics, psychological statistics, business statistics, biostatistics—each offered in the respective department and each tailored to the most important applications in the particular field and to the department's passing standard. A single, large-scale offering in introductory statistics might be considerably cheaper than this menu of specially tailored courses (and it might be better statistics), but it would entail compromises of course design and administration. These compromises have to be evaluated as a loss. Students taking the large-scale service course may be dissatisfied with it. Too many of them may do badly in it from the point of view of their home departments. And the course may not contain enough of the special topics and applications desired by each department.

If the campus budgetary mechanism is an internal market driven by the volume of instructional activity, an academic department can maximize its resources by making its major fields as attractive as possible, thereby boosting its student enrollments; by retaining the course elections or requirements of its major students to the extent of its discretionary power over curriculum; and by having other departments specify its offerings as required courses or preferred electives, making its courses attractive as free electives to students over the whole campus.

Pfeffer and Salancik (1974) approach departmental budgeting and resource allocation as a political process. They point to many political factors that, taken together, outweigh economic logic in resource allocation.

Budgetary Standards

The budgetary standards written into the resource allocation mechanism also exert profound influence. For example, the laboratory sciences typically cannot conduct instruction properly unless they have a large amount of building space, equipment, and operating support per faculty member and per student. Standards are then derived from institutional experience and, sometimes, from inter-institutional comparisons.

Once adopted, standards are not easy to reopen as an explicit issue of resource allocation, even when the allocation fails to approximate the standard (either exceeding it temporarily if the department's enrollment falls subsequent to a large allocation of space or equipment, or falling below it if enrollment rises too quickly to allow the allocation to catch up.) A significant change in the preferred style of work in an academic field, leading to a demand for a raising of the budgetary standard, is likely to arouse acute controversy between the department and the campus administration.

The Tendency to Proliferate Versus Competitive Constraint

An academic department is responsible for the design and provision of graduate and undergraduate degree programs, and sometimes for specialties within the field. Each subgroup of the departmental faculty is, of course, most interested in the courses, students, and research activities in its specialty.

Elements of both competition and complementarity appear in the struggle to define programs, evaluate their worth to the department and the campus, set priorities, and make budgetary allocations. There is a resultant clash here between two well-recognized principles. On the one hand, the forces of complementarity and independence trigger the action of the Law of Indefinite Augmentation, which identifies a tendency to add new sources of funding, new units of organization and program commitments, and even new elements of purpose to an institution if they do not appear to conflict with what is already being done and may bring complementary strengths. But the Law of Competition at the Margin warns that resources drawn in to support new or augmented activities in one department may, at the margin, have to be financed by cutting back in other departments or by making allocations from small amounts of discretionary funds and reserves.

If a department must justify resources according to student workload, it will need to consider whether a proposed additional program will attract additional net enrollment. If so, the new program can be financed by budget augmentation; but if not, the potential losing factions within the department may oppose the change.

The department may also assert priorities that run counter to wider interests perceived by the campus administration. For example, during the period when doctoral programs were being expanded, many academic departments saw their interests best served by a sharp increase in doctoral-level instruction. If faculty wanted to pursue this before all the needed additional resources (faculty positions, support budget, and so forth) could be made available, they often did so by reducing the resources allocated to undergraduate teaching and by allowing undergraduate class sizes to increase while assigning academic staff to new doctoral-level courses and tutorial instruction. Only an assertion of counterpressure by college deans or campus-level administrators could prevent this shift in emphasis. Also, many departments had been admitting graduate students as master's degree candidates. Some of these students might eventually enter doctoral programs, but many were not interested in doing so. A large number of academic departments de-emphasized or eliminated these terminal master's programs, consolidating their attention on doctoral students. Unless the administrators at a higher level saw some harm to institutional interests, they tended to ignore such departmental actions. Only when the Ph.D. hiring market turned sour did many departments begin to wonder whether their cutoff of terminal master's degree candidates had been wise.

Academic Plans and the Funding of Academic Units

The campus administration typically requires each academic unit—the school or college, and each academic department within a college—to submit a multiyear academic plan that will inform the administration of the department's desired direction of development and its rationale for growth. Colleges, schools, and departments almost never choose voluntarily to curtail their activities; planning guidelines have to instruct them explicitly to provide scenarios for zero growth or reductions if that is the necessary direction for the campus. The departmental planning process may be guided by campus enrollment forecasts and by standard expectations of faculty replacement and future expansion. The campus assembles these unit-level plans into a comprehensive campus academic plan that can guide budgetary development, space planning, and academic coordination.

When negotiating its budget with the campuswide administration, a department is likely to win ready acceptance of any proposal it might make for reduction of budgeted resources, but it can expect an uphill fight to obtain an increase. A department's proposed reallocation of effort can be separated into two distinct components: reductions of activity in area A, and increases of activity in area B.

The latter must be scrutinized carefully. In conditions of significant resource constraint, the campus administration has a negative bias about such expansions. The only safe departmental strategy is to avoid showing the possibility of any budgetary reductions, and to press for budgetary expansion to support desired growth. The campus administration is likely to insist on some trade-offs to help finance growth.

Training grants and research support from foundations and federal research agencies have provided a seeming escape from the dilemmas of resource allocation in existing academic units. If a vigorous faculty group can find outside funding for what it wants to do, and if its plans are academically respectable or innovative, it is not likely to be opposed, either by the department or by the higher administration. Once obtained, such funds result in demands for additional enrollment and for space to house the expanded program. Some farsighted administrators have cautioned about the institutional liabilities that would arise if such outside funding were discontinued. But, in the short run, enthusiasm for expansion has muffled arguments about future risks.

Some argue that the faculty of the university is inherently in the best position to decide to initiate, expand, reduce, or eliminate academic programs and that peer review of research proposals also ensures preservation of academic quality. (See especially, Stigler, 1993, for a strong defense of this viewpoint.) Indeed, most research universities have, in one form or another, a joint faculty-administration mechanism that allows for such involvement. But to claim that the faculty is best situated to make serious academic judgments and that it will invariably do so to enhance academic quality and protect the university's viability is to claim too much. Academic ambitions may result in willingness to continue a weak program rather than give up the charter represented by previous approvals. Higher-level institutional review mechanisms may or may not be strong enough to withstand such pressures.

Public universities must in most states submit proposals for new schools, colleges, or advanced degree programs to the coordinating board, which oversees the state's public higher education and provides advice on academic priorities. In periods of severe budgetary stringency, this requirement of higher-level review and approval is an obstacle to program growth.

A departmental faculty has many expansionary incentives and few ways to cope with reductions. Also, the faculty—whether departmental or universitywide—does not usually have a good basis for judging effects of such decisions on the short-term and long-term viability of the institution. Those questions are dominantly in the purview of the president, the provost, and the trustees.

Organizational Issues of Departmental Structure

Conventional departmentalization presents three typical problems of organization:

1. Inconsistencies and gaps in assigning academic program responsibilities to the departmental and school (or college) units
2. Inadequate internal cohesion and clarity of objectives
3. Rigidity

Each of these is discussed as an analytical issue.

A curricular example of gaps in program responsibilities is the interdisciplinary degree program. Each student in such a program gets part of the work toward the degree from each of several departments. An interdisciplinary faculty committee typically oversees the program and the progress of students, but these faculty members have many other responsibilities. It is not unusual for such interdisciplinary programs to starve for lack of attention, because no formal unit of organization sees its welfare as depending on the performance of students in the program or on the program's survival.

Research units have been created at many American universities as responses to another kind of incomplete mapping of program responsibilities: the existence of a significant multidisciplinary research area that no one departmental faculty can serve. This type of organizational unit is discussed later in the present chapter and in Chapter Twelve.

The analytical problem—which becomes a practical issue of academic management—is that an incomplete mapping of academic program responsibilities leaves some significant areas of academic concern unmanaged and unbudgeted (so that if they are absorbing resources, this is not identified). There is never a definitive cure for this problem, because there are many dimensionally different ways to design curricula and areas of academic study. Several of these dimensional approaches to curriculum have already been mentioned: area studies programs, in which the language, literature, history, and social science topics of a geographical area are grouped together so that the student can study them all in a single department; theme colleges; social problems curricula, such as social ecology and women's studies; and most important in size and scope, the various professional school curricula.

A university administration cannot foreclose all of these options, which fill gaps in the existing pattern of organization. Indeed, the interests of scholarly flexibility and experiment are often served by such departures from conventional programs. Yet the monitoring of faculty time and other resources and the evaluation of student and faculty performance remains a challenging task.

The second problem of departmentalization is that of cohesion and clarity of objectives. At some universities there is little contact—whether official or informal—between department members. This is especially true in an urban university where faculty members work at home on several days of the week and come to the campus only for course meetings and other specific obligations. In these circumstances, it is difficult to sustain the consensual style of decision making and administration that is preferred by academic people. Information filters slowly and uncertainly, and low frequency of contact prevents the building and maintenance of mutual confidence. The chair and administrative hierarchy of the department may, by default, become the only points of reference for students, for faculty members from other fields, and for the campus administration.

An academic department that functions with low internal cohesion but according to a theory of consensual decision making is unable to go beyond minimal routines and may function badly even with respect to those. Questions of objectives and priorities—difficult enough to resolve even when people of good will are highly informed and have a strong sense of mutual trust—are left unexamined and unresolved. And the social pressure to perform, so important to a voluntaristic scheme of organization, is missing.

The alternative to a consensual style is increased bureaucratization and a larger managerial role for the chair, who may be encouraged or compelled to assume such a role if pressed for decisions and tidy results by higher levels of administration. But when there is a low level of cohesion, department members resist bureaucratic pressures.

Rigidity in academic organization is proverbial. One contributing factor is lifetime tenure, which commits the university to members of an academic group for a long period. Individuals in an academic department have few personal incentives to work toward change. The composition of the group changes only slowly, except in unusual circumstances of rapid growth (with flexibility only during the growth interval and long-persistent rigidity thereafter) or academic reorganization. The latter may be triggered by a revolution in the discipline—as occurred in the biological sciences in the 1980s and early 1990s—or by the necessity to overhaul a field that shows serious weaknesses in quality. (Quality assessment is discussed in Chapter Thirteen.)

The higher levels of administration at a university approach such reorganization with understandable caution. A proposal to consolidate or merge two departments arouses questions of philosophical intent and reach. It also raises issues of power and prerogative, which, in the routines of normal departmental operation, are either dealt with by compromise or suppressed. In order to be on the soundest possible ground for a reorganization decision, the administrators have to negotiate a solution agreeable to all—which may not be possible or may have high costs in money and institutional commitments—or they have to obtain expert academic judgments on a reasonable plan of consolidation, because on academic matters their judgments as administrators lack credibility with the relevant academic constituencies. Strategies for consolidation and phaseout are discussed in detail in Chapter Fifteen. The process is intricate, time consuming, expensive of administrative and academic energy, and risky.

The governing board and administration of a university do not permit the casual establishment of an academic department, school, or college. They ordinarily require a showing that there is a sound academic basis for the creation of a new unit, with its long-term consequences. At the point of initiation, attention must be given to questions that may have been scanted during previous periods of euphoric expansion:

1. Given a sound academic case for establishing the new unit, what is the specific rationale for it in this particular university? How will it add to the strengths and distinction of the institution?

2. Can the university find a nucleus of exceptionally able and entrepreneurial faculty to start the new unit? The characteristics of this nucleus will set the course of the department for at least thirty years.

3. Is the new academic unit sustainable over time? The starting nucleus of staff and facilities is usually much smaller than the

number needed for steady-state viability. What is the best judgment of that steady-state size? Are there favorable forecasts of available research resources and extramural funding? Will the university be able to provide resources and commitments, not merely for the start-up nucleus but for the path toward steady-state size?

Schools and Colleges

The school or college is the next level of academic organization beyond the department. The dean of a professional school or college is in a linking-pin position similar to the department chair, but the role of spokesperson to external constituencies is greater. The professional school dean is a member of a council of deans or some similar body with whom the chief campus officer consults. The administrative tasks are usually numerous and burdensome. The dean is generally appointed for a longer period of expected service than a department chair: five to seven years, with review for continuation.

In radical contrast to this is the dean of letters and science. In many American research universities, the college of letters and science consists of all departments in the basic scholarly disciplines, making it the largest college in the university. Traditionally, the college served as the administrative frame for approving all curricula leading to the bachelor of arts degree and all bachelor of science degrees except those in professional schools, and for monitoring the flow of students through them. We have noted Rosovsky's extensive account (1990) of the role of dean of the faculty of arts and sciences at Harvard.

Over time, academic departments have expanded in number and size, and many have developed both master's degree and doctoral programs. Sometimes a dean with a strong personality and exceptional administrative skills has developed ways to cope with increasing scale and specialization, multiplying program levels, and growing demands for his or her judgments on budgets and personnel matters. More often, because the letters and science portion of the campus accounts for a major part of the total budget, the president and senior administration have developed a campuswide budgetary mechanism to which the larger departments have direct appeal, and they have assigned functional responsibilities to other officials, weakening the position of the dean of letters and science to the point that it does not go beyond routine duties.

The graduate dean has ultimate responsibility for the content and quality of graduate instructional programs, often receiving advisory assistance from a graduate council of senior faculty from the various disciplines. He or she also oversees the administration of graduate admissions, fellowship support, the status of graduate students, and the mechanisms for examinations and awarding of graduate degrees. With the advent of large-scale, extramurally funded research, the graduate dean has sometimes assumed responsibility for research policy, for monitoring the work of organized research units, and for contract and grant administration. But these last have become complex bureaucratic functions, requiring both accounting and regulatory expertise, and are now often handled by a specialized technical branch of the campus administration.

In some universities, academic departments are gathered not under an umbrella college of letters and science but into specialized divisions, each with its own dean: physical and biological sciences, social sciences, humanities, and possibly others. This design was adopted at the start for the Irvine campus of the University of California and was achieved, after great internal struggle, at the university's Riverside campus. The dean of each division is responsible for most important budgetary, personnel, and organizational matters. He or she can thus exert effective leadership and control over department chairs in that division. The role is most effective if there is no strong ideological commitment to the notion that all fundamental scholarship is interdependent and that the liberal arts curriculum (which is therefore, in principle, integral) must be controlled within a single academic organization.

In some fields, the undergraduate major is now designed as an essential preparation, gateway, and screening device for graduate study in that discipline, not as the deeper part of a program of liberal education. Both students and faculty then gauge success in the undergraduate major in terms of admission to graduate study in the field. Some universities have also reduced or abandoned general education requirements in undergraduate letters and science. Both of these developments weaken the case for continuing a single college of letters and science. However, renewed interest in liberal arts curricula and the reform of general education, which began to arise toward the end of the 1980s, may in due course reverse the earlier trend toward fragmentation.

Federations and Consortia of Colleges

In the early 1920s, the Claremont Colleges in California established a blueprint of confederation and intercollege cooperation; now there are five colleges, plus the Claremont University Center. The student is officially enrolled in one college but may take courses and have access to academic and other facilities at other colleges. Each faculty member is appointed to one college, but often with an eye to the appointment needs of the discipline in other colleges as well. The central administration provides some common administrative services to all of the colleges and has developed, on their joint behalf, a computer center and a central library.

The Five Colleges (Amherst, Smith, Mt. Holyoke, and Hampshire, together with the larger, state-supported University of Massachusetts) created an intercollege coordinating office to foster cooperative, academically enriching, and cost-reducing relationships between them. The student is officially enrolled in one college and receives a degree from that college. Faculty appointments are made by the separate colleges, but with prior consultation.

A campus, too, can be organized as a set of colleges. The University of California campus at Santa Cruz was established in the early 1960s and was organized from the beginning into largely residential colleges. Each student enrolled at Santa Cruz is a member of a college. With a few exceptions, each faculty member holds appointment as both a fellow of a college and a member of a disciplinary board of studies, and his salary and duties are split between the two. Inevitable tensions were created by these dual appointments. It was originally expected that each student would take a significant portion—perhaps one-fourth—of academic work in courses and seminars offered by the college. Though the colleges proved to be important in student life and informal learning, they did not develop strong curriculum offerings. The investment in course development and administration in the boards of studies (academic departments) was much greater. The faculty member faced insistent pressures from the board, reflecting the conventional expectations with respect to disciplinary interests, research initiatives, scholarly competence, and responsibility to teach assigned courses. Growth of enrollment in the disciplines' doctoral programs reinforced the boards of studies and weakened the institutional and academic importance of the colleges.

Other Academic Units

The most important supporting units of a university are its library system and computer center. The general library contributes significantly to the global image of the university's quality and distinctiveness. A library justifies its existence mainly by supporting teaching and research, although in a public university it also has public service obligations.

The university library is central to the academic operation of the university. It is discussed in detail in Chapter Ten.

Compared with the library, the computer center is a newcomer. University computing emerged after World War II as an increasingly significant handmaiden to research in high-energy physics, chemistry, and engineering. University computing centers are also discussed in Chapter Ten.

Libraries and computer centers are but two of many academic support facilities. Also important are some types of multidisciplinary research stations, as well as museums, botanical gardens, and other major installations. These often get their start with a major act of academic entrepreneurship, allied with the interest of a donor or a granting agency, when the university administration and key faculty negotiate the financing of programs and facilities. After a time, the university administration finds that the ongoing costs of maintenance of the installation become general obligations and that the installation, like the library and the computer center, has become important to substantial academic clienteles. These long-term obligations should be faced when the installation is first proposed; once built, it becomes a respectable and insistent client for subsidy support from university general funds.

Organized Research Units

Every faculty member is appointed to an academic department and does some research. Why, then, have universities established separate organized research units (ORUs) for the administration of research, rather than using the departmental units of academic organization for this purpose? The answer to this question comes in several parts.

First, an area of research interest may extend beyond the boundaries of one academic department, causing concerned faculty members to propose an administrative entity compatible with the multidisciplinary or problem-centered (as distinct from discipline-centered) definition of their joint interest. An institute of international studies may attract not only political scientists but economists, sociologists, historians, environmental scientists, and anthropologists.

Second, when the need arises for intricate research administration or entrepreneurial efforts to obtain extramural funding, specialized expertise must either be grafted onto the administrative apparatus of a department, school, or college—which is generally not organized for it—or be developed independently. The administration of substantial research activities also entails decisions on research personnel, some of whom are highly paid and on a professional par with faculty but are not members of the department. If these personnel matters are dealt with through the largely consensual mode of department decision making, conflicts of focus and policy may become significant.

Third, when a university as an institution takes on the role of administering certain research programs sponsored by a federal agency, a state government, or a major foundation, it is effectively operating as a long-term partner of the sponsor. Therefore, the sponsor tries to ensure that the special program of research meets its needs, and the university maintains oversight of its academic quality and its financial viability.

Management of the university's research enterprise is of such importance that a separate chapter, Chapter Twelve, is devoted to it.

Chapter Six

Administrative and Coordinating Functions

Analysis of university organizational structure is completed in this chapter with a discussion of nonacademic administrative units and representational entities that provide communication and oversight within the institution.

Students and faculty are ambivalent about administrative units and structures, which they often regard as constraining, harassing, and bureaucratic. Yet they expect the institution to work smoothly, and they want a great variety of facilitating services that can be provided only by means of elaborate procedures and organization. Participation, communication, and consultation are also essential, yet these functions require another layer of mechanisms and draw off the attention and energy of many members of the university from their primary duties. Harmonizing and humanizing these administrative and communicative aspects of the university is an important task.

The Case for Growth of Administration— and the Importance of Resisting It

Administrative functions and services of universities have grown in scope and cost, in great part as a response to mandated governmental requirements (state and federal) in numerous areas. In personnel and human resource management, universities are, like other substantial employers, obliged to report how they meet the Equal Employment Opportunities Commission's procedural requirements. Universities must make adequate provision, again by federal regulation, for the care of animal subjects for biological and biomedical research, and they must meet parallel requirements of informed consent and other safeguards for human subjects in experimentation. Financial aid administration has ballooned in overhead requirements and costs, partly because federal grants and loans are involved, with their elaborate reporting obligations, and partly because the preparation and administration of each eligible student's "aid package" are arduous and complicated tasks.

Demand for improved services in public universities—for example, better student services and amenities, comparable to those that private universities provide—results in more elaborate service functions and consequent cost increases, the justification for these being improved ability to attract able students. A safe campus environment, needed for all members of the community, is critically necessary to allay the fears of parents.

Task shifting also increases administrative service costs. For example, faculty members used to advise undergraduate students on choice of courses and were responsible for approving the student's class program each term, but in many universities this function is now performed by administrators in the departmental office. Faculty members also ask for more extensive support, and universities sometimes provide it in order to keep up with the competition in professional amenities.

Preventing a ratchet-like accumulation of administrative overhead is also critically important in the constrained environment of the 1990s. (See Massy, 1990, on the "ratchet.") The problem is that each administrative service activity sees unmet needs, and its managers have the usual bureaucratic incentives to grow. Finding strategies to contract is discussed in Chapter Fifteen. More fundamental ways of addressing issues of efficiency and productivity are discussed in Chapter Fourteen. In this chapter, we discuss the growing complexity of administrative services, organizations, and systems. Learning how to cope with this increase of complexity while continuing to pursue the objectives of modernization and responsiveness *within constant budgets* is a challenge indeed.

Administrative Services

The administrative services of a major university include student services, support services, maintenance and operation of capital plant, auxiliary enterprises, and general administrative and business services. Within each of these, there may be a large array of specialized departments. These services and enterprises facilitate the academic business of the university and in other ways cater to members of the university community. Some activities develop significant constituency support. For example, the intercollegiate athletics program may be as important for alumni relations and institutional publicity as it is for campus morale. A teaching hospital provides patient care services for the immediately surrounding community and is a regional resource for the treatment of difficult and exotic illnesses.

Before a university takes on a service or function in response to a request from within the institution, a number of questions should be asked:

1. Should the request for service be opposed or ignored?
2. If the service is to be provided, should it be bought from the outside market or supplied by a unit of the university?
3. If it is to be undertaken by a unit of the university, how should it be organized and funded?
4. Should the service be "free," or should the users pay a fee that partly or fully covers costs?

Each of these questions calls for an explicit and carefully examined decision.

Student Services

The student's academic business includes admission procedures, payment of tuition and fees, maintenance of grade records and transcripts, resolution of delinquency and discipline problems, counseling and advising, administration of financial aid and student work-study or other part-time work (where the university is the employer), and, at the end of the line, assistance in job placement.

Some of these functions are performed centrally by one administrative unit. Others are performed by academic departments, schools, and colleges on a decentralized basis. The level of cost, intensity, and skill with which these functions are performed varies among universities, affecting not only the ease with which students can get their business done but also their morale and even their academic performance.

Students have many other problems, needs, and interests besides the purely academic: housing, physical and mental health, transportation, recreation, and involvement with political and community life. For many students, and for the university as an institution, there is no easy or clear point of division between education and the way of life represented by being a student. Partly depending on whether a university is located in isolation or in an urban area with a broad span of community services, and depending also on its history and its definition of mission, it may be involved in all dimensions of student living (as the elite liberal arts colleges are), or it may provide nothing beyond instructional service, relying on local private markets, public services, and parents. The distribution of student needs and the demands for university services are also not uniform for each type of service. Nearly all students at University of California campuses, for example, use the student health service, but only 20 to 25 percent on most campuses live in university-provided housing. At Williams College, on the other hand, the great majority of students live in the college's residence halls. Only a fraction of a university's student body (the numbers vary considerably) uses athletic facilities. Only a small percentage wants child-care centers.

The university administration may be under pressure to provide a service even though only an insignificant fraction of the students uses it. One possible solution is to declare the service unit to be "self-financing" and charge each user a price that will, ostensibly at least, cover the cost. This approach avoids implicit subsidy to only a portion of the student population. But the university may also face intense pressure to provide some services at a subsidized price. When it does this from general institutional resources, the money is diverted from other purposes. When services are provided to some students but are funded from fees paid uniformly by all students, a student-to-student subsidy is involved. Faced with a variety of demands and with the consequences of a series of ad hoc responses to them, a university administration needs to establish policies and procedures for determining what student services it will provide, how they will be paid for, how to alter services offered as new needs arise, and how to assess the contribution that student services make to the vitality of the university community and the academic progress of students.

In many public universities, compulsory student fees are the main source of funding for widely used student services. Determination of what is to be funded and what special user fees may be charged becomes partly a political issue. Often, the allocations are recommended by a committee or board with heavy student representation and with student affairs administrators as its guiding leadership.

Child-care services (for students, staff, and faculty) promise to be a frontline issue at many universities in the 1990s, as more women with children become enrolled students and as more single parents are in the workforce. Universities, like other employers, face complicated issues of institutional policy, personnel administration, and community responsibility in connection with the issue of child care. Partial subsidies may be available from state governments, but these are typically not sufficient to meet the needs.

Maintenance and Operation of Capital Plant and Equipment

Typically, two types of administrative units deal with problems of capital plant. One controls the planning, design, construction, and financing of additions to capital plant. The other manages the maintenance and upkeep of existing buildings and capital equipment and the land owned by the institution. If the university has a substantial capital program, it must centralize most of these functions, which require many different kinds of technical and managerial expertise. At the same time, each building project, from its design phase on, needs to be developed in cooperation with the units that will use it.

Capital plant and equipment are key resources analyzed in Chapter Ten.

Auxiliary Enterprises

American universities have operated bookstores, dairy farms, conference centers, electricity-generating plants, forests, student dormitories and apartments, staff and faculty residences, automobile and bus fleets, printing plants, glassblowing shops, and large hospitals. Each of these auxiliary enterprises rests on a presumption that the university should take responsibility for providing a service for a campus constituency or academic organization and that it would be better not to buy the service on the open market.

Many auxiliary enterprises operate on the break-even principle, charging their individual or organizational clients enough to defray operating costs, and sometimes enough to cover depreciation and capital charges as well. But this does not guarantee that the service will be produced and delivered at an (unsubsidized) price that is as low as the open market price, because the university's service unit may not be operating on the most efficient scale or with management incentives that maximize efficiency. Also, university policy often accords an internal monopoly to the service unit, and this reduces the pressure for cost minimization.

Some auxiliary enterprises have a customer mix that includes purchasers outside the university. If net income from such external customers is appreciable, it may be taxable as unrelated business income and complicate the tax-exempt status of a university cor-poration under state and federal tax laws. This hazard is worth avoiding by tailoring auxiliary enterprises to serve a customer mix dominated by students, faculty, and staff of the university. But most institutions worry more about losing money in auxiliary enterprises than making it.

University teaching hospitals, for example, often charge rates that are at or above those of neighboring community hospitals. But they must still be subsidized, because they attract patients with espe-cially costly treatment needs and because some costly state-of-the-art tests and procedures are ordered as part of the education of medical students and medical residents who are involved with clin-ical treatment and research. It is sometimes difficult to separate expenses incurred for these reasons from expenses that would be incurred anyway for prudent and normal patient care.

General Administrative and Business Services

As a large-scale organization, the contemporary university has had to develop many specialized cadres of personnel for the various tasks of general administration—accounting, budgeting, personnel administration, procurement, contract and grant administration, law enforcement and safety, public relations, and fund-raising. These functions may be departmentalized in various ways for effec-tive supervision and interaction.

The contemporary university must face the need for adminis-trative modernization and efficiency (for many universities have traditionally underinvested in administration, as compared with industrial and financial corporations). Among the decisions to be made are those bearing on centralization and decentralization. If administrative functions are heavily centralized, they may operate in a tidy, professional manner, but without sufficient understanding of the administrative needs of individual academic units. If the functions are decentralized, they tend to be duplicative of central processing, they may not be staffed by sufficiently qualified professionals, and they may develop inconsistent procedures and techniques. However, if the institution builds up administrative capability both at a central point and in the operating academic units, the total cost of such duplications is enormous. Avoiding the worst of all three evils requires careful managerial design and effective administrative coordination.

For example, extramurally funded research requires a great deal of accounting work. Task areas that must be attended to include: the recording of transactions; payroll and personnel records; control of grant budgets so that the principal investigator, the institution, and the granting agency are all informed in appropriate and timely ways about the status of each grant; and the enforcement of conformity with institutional and funding-agency policies and regulations. At the extreme of centralization, all this could be done in the offices of the central campus administration. In a more decentralized arrangement, basic financial accounting would continue to be taken care of in the central accounting office, but some decentralized grant accounting and the other functions would be arranged through the administrative offices of schools and colleges. And in a still more decentralized pattern, individual departments or specially authorized research units would do a major share of the work.

Decentralized budgetary responsibility for academic operations—known as "every tub on its own bottom"—is an interesting example of decentralization and is discussed in Chapters Five and Seven.

Universities, like other large-scale organizations, must judge whether each overhead service is organized to deliver an appropriate amount and quality of service. Service quality is partly a function of organizational design and standards, but it also depends heavily on personnel competence and morale. Historically, universities have often tried to get by with lower salary ranges for middle- and higher-level administrative jobs than would be paid for comparable responsibilities in industry and finance. They have counted

on the dedication of university staff and a sense of secure employment to counterbalance the effects of unequal pay, or have settled
for a lower level of qualification and training than considered necessary in industry. The former produces feelings of inequity, and the
latter is usually false economy.

Stresses Between Academic and Administrative Value Systems

The university faces another personnel problem. Faculty and research personnel share a value system and the attitudes about academic status that such a value system induces. Administrative staff
members, including those at professional and senior levels, cannot
share directly in this status system and are, worse yet, sometimes the
victims of academic snobbery and academic contempt for bureaucracy. Most universities need to increase understanding between
the two worlds if they are to avoid the retreat into bureaucratic
rigidity that is an all too natural defensive reaction of administrators. Clark (1983, p. 89) points to the relative isolation of faculty
members and administrative professionals from each other and the
separate outlooks or cultures that this brings about.

Each category of administrative professionals develops its own
reference group and organization, with annual meetings, member-
ships, and ways of promoting professionalization and greater recognition. (See Clark, p. 90, for an extensive quotation of the findings
of Terry Lunsford on this theme.)

The line of advancement in the purely administrative hierarchy ends in such top positions as director of budget, treasurer, controller, or vice president (or vice chancellor) for administration.
These are positions of large responsibility and often of substantial
discretionary power, and universities now pay respectable salaries
to incumbents of recognized ability. But the crucial positions of president, executive vice president, and provost are, with rare exceptions, reserved for those who came into academic administration

through the faculty ranks. There are positive reasons for this policy, the chief being that faculty often require academically qualified spokespersons; there is likely to be mistrust of a president not having an academic background.

Ineligibility for the top posts, however, inevitably conveys implications of second-class status to even the most gifted of nonacademic administrators and thus blunts career aspirations all the way down the line. The rewards of service and a sense of professionalism are some compensation for these disadvantages. It is a tribute to the strength of these values and to the institutional loyalty of career administrators that many able men and women do make a career commitment to their university and will not leave it—except possibly for improved pay and position at another university.

The heads of administrative service units and their staffs are primarily concerned with operations—often involving large numbers of personnel, large budgets, and large populations of intractable students and faculty. Senior administrators participate in policy formulation and planning, but in roles secondary to those of the senior academic administrators who speak to the dominant academic content of many institutional policies and plans. Perhaps this is why the enormous range of operating information that is hidden in the accounting system and administrative records of a university is not better shaped and focused toward policy making and planning. The academic administrators, in turn, may have tastes and styles that prevent them from making systematic demands for accounting and other information that could contribute greatly to policy deliberations.

There is a set of institutional consultative devices—dimensionally different from the academic organization of the university discussed in Chapter Five and from the units of administration—in which managers of auxiliary enterprises and heads of administrative service units are involved together with students, faculty, and academic administrators. We now turn to these.

Units of Communication and Representation

Quite different in design and character from the units of academic organization or administration are the many units of communication, representation, and oversight at a university. These include student organizations, faculty organizations, administrative committees, advisory panels, task forces, multipartite bodies and committees, and now, labor unions.

Both the student government and the faculty government in a U.S. university have official status. They are recognized and approved by the governing board, they often have specific powers delegated to them by the governing board or the top administration, and they almost always have some official budget. For student government, the funds often come in part from compulsory student fees collected by the administration and spent by the agencies of the student government under conditions set by the administration.

Faculty Government

The faculty government usually has modest institutional funds for office and running expenses. Additional organizations such as faculty clubs usually charge dues and may have institutional subsidy as well, in recognition of the importance of a common point of institutional contact. The official status and financial subsidies of both student and faculty organizations establish a role for them within the institution and, correspondingly, limit their adversary capacity when disputes arise.

Gilmour (1991) reported on a 1989 national survey of participative governance bodies; the sample was stratified to include two-year colleges and comprehensive colleges as well as universities. All had full-time faculty representation, a majority included administrators, and a relatively small percentage included students (Gilmour, table 1, p. 29).

Traditionally, faculty government—whether a senate composed of all regular faculty from assistant professors up or a more limited representational body elected by eligible faculty—has specific delegated powers to supervise courses and curricula and has strong advisory influence in matters of academic freedom, academic personnel selection, and educational policy.

Generally, these powers are exercised to some degree by legislative deliberation and action that are expressed in faculty regulations and recommendations to the administration and the governing board. But the main work is done through faculty committees that report either to the faculty government, for recommended legislative action, or to the administration, with recommendations and findings on particular issues. Faculty members in each college, school, and department generally are empowered to adopt academic regulations by faculty vote and also to make personnel and other recommendations to the administration. But much of their ongoing work is also done by college-level or departmental committees. The great majority of governance arrangements that Gilmour studied had standing committees on curriculum, degree requirements, and course approvals; in most, there were committees on faculty affairs and student affairs, and on planning and budget (Gilmour, 1991, table 3, p. 31).

Multicampus university systems must determine the desired extent of universitywide—as distinct from campuswide—faculty government and the powers and structure this should have.

Faculty Collective Bargaining

Faculty unions became a growing factor in U.S. higher education during the 1960s; as of 1989, 21 percent of all types of institutions in a national survey had faculty unions, and 35 percent of large-enrollment institutions (ten to twenty thousand students) had unions (Gilmour, 1991, p. 32). At this upper range, most of the institutions concerned would be public colleges and universities.

Collective bargaining, Gilmour reported, "was also more likely at research II, comprehensive I, and two-year institutions and less likely at research I, doctorate-granting I, and liberal arts I institutions" (p. 33).

Research universities have prided themselves on elaborate forms of "shared governance," and perhaps this has inhibited acceptance of unionization, even though many states now specifically permit public employees to form unions and qualify as collective bargaining units. Garbarino (1974a, 1974b, 1975) analyzed faculty collective bargaining and its relationship to faculty senates and similar governance mechanisms, pointing out the potential for conflict between the union organization and the faculty governance structure (1974b, pp. 1–2). Gilmour's survey, however, reported that the relationship was supportive or complementary 74 percent of the time, and it was adversarial only 4 percent of the time (Gilmour, 1991, p. 33).

Whether union protections will become more attractive to faculty members in the context of retrenchment in the 1990s is an interesting issue.

Faculty Involvement in Representational Boards and Committees

Faculty members and administrators also serve on boards and committees appointed by the campus administration. Such committees may investigate ways of dealing with a pending policy issue, or they may be standing advisory committees for oversight of a particular function or unit of activity—for example, the Advisory Committee of the Harvard Institute for International Development. Beyond these formalized involvements in faculty government and administrative committees, a university faculty possesses great informal influence on the operation of the institution and the conduct of administration. These contributions are made by individual faculty members and working groups, through their academic departments and research organizations, in the normal course of teaching and research.

One is tempted to say that the better the university, the more conclusive and complete is the institutional influence of the faculty in "shared governance." But many of the best universities in the United States—the older, private institutions—have customarily operated on a basis of more or less benign autocracy. A distinguished faculty trusted an unobtrusive and deft administration, and faculty time was reserved for academic duties. However, as these same universities have become more complicated, as some of the state-supported universities have emerged in the front ranks of academia, and as many problems have emerged that call for the combined attention of the academic and the administrative structures, the formal and informal involvement of faculty in institutional policies and managerial questions has increased.

This involvement creates several problems. First, the activities consume valuable time. Studies of the distribution of faculty time and effort show that, out of a quite long work week, faculty members (other than those with specific administrative appointments) spend an average of about 10 percent of their time on administrative and institutional duties. A commitment of this kind has an opportunity cost, for the time could instead be devoted to other duties. Yet the faculty government and the administrators who call on faculty for committee duties often disregard the marginal cost of a faculty member's time.

A second issue is the use of committees for work that could and should be done by one responsible person. Committees are endemic in all government agencies and large business firms; often there is no substitute for them, for reasons of communication, coordination, representational bargaining, or the need to pool specialized judgments. But the committee style is carried much too far in some universities, absorbing great energy for small results.

The third problem is amateurism and rapid turnover of committee membership. If a committee has a long-term advisory or coordinating responsibility, each member must usually spend some months acquiring enough background to be effective. But typically, because of research leaves or regular rotation, committee members are replaced soon after they become valuable, and the cycle is repeated over again.

Despite these drawbacks, faculty involvement in university affairs is vitally necessary, and committee structures are the main vehicle for it, aside from the recruitment of full-time academic administrators from faculty ranks (who then become somewhat tainted as academics in the eyes of the faculty rank and file). The need to obtain judgments from a wide variety of institutional and representative sources, the need for communication, and the need to build consensus (or at least acquiescence) are all reasons for the use of committees.

Student Representation on Boards and Committees

Student government has historically been far less strong and politically assertive in U.S. than in European universities, although extracurricular activities—from athletics to cultural organizations to student politics—have been important to student life since late in the nineteenth century. Rising student consciousness in the 1960s led to condemnation of "sandbox" student government and to a growing agenda of protest on university and community issues. In the aftermath of those disturbed times, the voting age was lowered from twenty-one to eighteen and long residence requirements for voting were struck down, propelling the most politically active students into local electoral politics in university towns.

Many universities responded to student demands by including student representatives on administrative and academic committees and by giving student spokespersons regular access to top administration and to the governing board. In addition, the student governments in some state universities began to lobby in state capitals, causing a new level of nervousness in the university administration.

Student representatives on university and college committees suffer from the same disabilities—time constraints, amateurism, and rapid turnover—as do faculty members, and are likely to be even more seriously inhibited by them. But the most serious difficulties arise if student representatives are strongly politicized and regard the committee, whatever its stated agenda, as an arena of contest with the institution and with society. A student role in departmental committees, especially affecting questions of academic personnel, may be challenged when confidentiality or faculty competence is an issue. There is often dispute on how student views can be taken into account. Students and faculty may have deeply opposing views on matters of academic policy, curriculum, passing standards, and academic personnel. It is not clear how student participation in deliberations on these matters can be maintained without severe periodic conflict.

Multipartite Government and Policy Control

A few U.S. and Canadian universities, and numerous European ones, have recently developed multipartite structures of representation at the highest, or almost the highest, level of internal government. Each Dutch university, according to the law of governance passed by the Netherlands parliament in 1971, has a university council (*Universitatsraad*) composed of eleven elected faculty representatives, eleven elected nonacademic staff representatives, eleven elected student representatives, and seven members appointed by the minister of education. The council has general responsibility for policy setting at the university, and a board of administration (*College van Bestuur*) consisting of five full-time members, including the rector, has executive authority. The consequences of this democratization of governance are difficult to predict; the changes may turn out to have a highly constructive influence on the operation of the Dutch universities, or they may prove to be unworkable.

The multipartite structure is a parliamentary body, or a large-scale committee, with representation of each of the significant estates of the university. When it is consultative and advisory, it can be valuable as a source of insights and a channel of communication. If it has determinative power over legislated standards, appointments, and budgets, its multipartite character and its parliamentary form can result in a politicized treatment of many issues that, to the believer in underlying academic values of the sort discussed in Chapter Two, bodes ill for the university. That this hazard is real, not imaginary, is indicated by the experience of some of the German universities under the political pressures of democratization in the 1960s.

Even though the national parliaments of European countries legislated democratization, there is no assurance that they will provide substantial funding support or restrain themselves from administrative interventions if they are disappointed by the institutional and academic consequences of democratized governance. In U.S. higher education, which has a very different tradition, the moves toward democratization were much more cautious than in Europe, and one can guess that the funding and supporting constituencies in the general community would be impatient with a university that lost the capacity for executive leadership and effective external representation.

The Joint Big Decision Committee (JBDC) has been proposed as a device to facilitate intensive high-level consultation for speedy response to major administrative and resource policy concerns (Keller, 1983). Yamada (1991) conducted follow-up interviews in 1987 at four institutions cited by Keller, and she found that the JBDC had quite limited influence on major decisions at these institutions, although it did stimulate the development of more open and systematic budgeting processes (p. 84).

Relation of Administrative Structure
to the Presidency

We have discussed leadership and the presidency in Chapter Four. The many units and mechanisms examined in this chapter are a response to the diversified workload that devolves on the institution and compels the development of specialized administrative hierarchies. Even in the immediate circle of the presidency, the senior administration needs an effective internal division of labor to handle the several major areas of functional responsibility. All of these require data background (now, computerized databases), communication flow, management of decision sequences, effective policy formulation, and spokesmanship. The presidency must also have some means of internal coordination. Problems do not come neatly packaged but often have impacts on several areas, or even on the survival of the institution. The crossover between senior academic administration and the heads of the cadres of the various administrative services becomes important in the resolution of many major problems.

Administrative units are also discussed in Chapters Fourteen and Fifteen. Possible new departures include outsourcing, work simplification, "delayering" (eliminating layers of hierarchy to speed information flow and decisions), and consolidation of functions.

Chapter Seven

Budgets and Budgeting Systems

The budgets of a university are the most reliable indicators of what the institution is committed to—and is stuck with. This is true partly because, underneath the rhetoric of leadership, there is a hard logic in putting funds where institutional necessity points. Budgets are generally good signals of a university's priorities even though not all funds of an institution are counted as budgeted funds (which causes confusion in the analysis of fiscal patterns) and even though some important resources are not dealt with explicitly in the conventional dollar-budgeting process.

Budget Formats: Capital and Operating Budgets

Universities traditionally follow a rigid division between capital funds and operating funds, a convention of their financial accounting that is based on fund-accounting concepts. One reason for this division is that the planning and management of major maintenance, renovations, and expansion of capital plant and major equipment need specialized expertise. Also, many dollars are strictly earmarked by the funding source either for an operating or a capital purpose.

For long-range planning purposes, the capital and operating aspects of a major program commitment (and the trade-offs between them) should be considered together—to see that their full magnitude is understood when the commitment is made, and to ensure that increments of capital funding and of operating funds will be reasonably in phase. Separation between capital budgets and operating budgets tends to make disjoint what should be a joint process and may also cause the university's decision makers to overlook possible trade-offs between capital and operating elements of the decision.

A university's customary treatment of its long-lived (capital) items and its short-term (operating) commitments would baffle the hardheaded business analyst. Universities ordinarily do not do depreciation accounting on their buildings. The reason usually given is that universities do not have to calculate profit and loss, and so they do not have incentives to look at the rate of depreciation of long-lived assets. (An exception is the use of depreciation accounting for hospital plant, because third-party reimbursements in the health care system permit the charging of depreciation.)

Failure to account for depreciation means that universities undervalue, in costing various activities, those services that happen to be supplied by capital plant and equipment rather than being accounted for through operating transactions and payroll. A further problem is that universities often fail to set up reserves for major maintenance and for equipment replacement; these then take on the appearance of one-of-a-kind emergencies, rather than normal features of effective managing through time.

Part of the rationale for the lack of such reserves—probably an enticing one in former times—was that a crisis or potential disaster would rally loyal donors, whereas evidence of prudent accumulation of reserves would tend to discourage them. But this could work well only for institutions that relied on a few wealthy patrons. Nowadays, the private and increasingly the public universities have institutionalized the donor relationship, with organized annual giving and proudly orchestrated capital campaigns. One may now doubt the tactical wisdom of an institution's fooling itself for the sake of creating an "emergency."

Universities also observe the convention of capitalizing only commitments for physical plant and equipment, or for long-term debts and financial arrangements. They have not, for example, customarily regarded as a capitalized commitment the contractual obligations to faculty and other long-term personnel. Yet associated with these commitments are important long-range risks that could be better understood if there were explicit accounting for them.

The operating and capital budgets may have to be separated as to format and preparation, but it is also sensible to develop a consolidated budget showing the interactions of the two.

Budget Horizons: Annual and Multiyear Budgets

The university administration perforce concentrates greatest policy attention on administering and enforcing (and in emergencies, amending) the current-year budget and on preparing the budget for the upcoming fiscal year. But it uses multiyear budget projections for both capital and operating budgets. Long-range budget projection is not universal; some universities do not do it at all. And the horizons considered vary among universities that do undertake such projections. One state university, for example, has periodically published ten-year fiscal plans or projections and has also developed still longer-range fiscal projections for internal, specialized purposes. These are most useful if there is institutional intent to pursue a fixed path of development and the resource implications of this intent need to be examined. Long-range projections have to be based on plausible assumptions, but they are conditional and cannot be read as forecasts. The assumed path of the institution, which the long-range fiscal projection prices out, is almost never a hard and fast commitment. It may have to be adjusted to new environmental events (for example, a change in the expectations for federal research funding) and also to changes in internal policies and priorities. The dollar values of long-range projections in constant dollars must also be restated into current dollars of future years under various assumptions concerning the rate of inflation.

Intermediate-range budget projections extending over a few years can be clearly tied to the existing span of institutional commitments and to enrollment projections. Multiyear budget projections, updated annually, can be built into the process of budget preparation and analysis, and they provide a convenient point of takeoff for the preliminary phases of the following year's budget work.

Multiyear budget projections are indispensable for showing, on the capital outlay side, the estimated costs—distributed over several years—of completing building projects that are currently in a planning phase or an early phase of construction.

The Budgeting Cycle

Although long-range and intermediate-range fiscal projections have important uses for planning, the greatest practical preoccupation of administrators is the annual budgeting cycle. The fiscal year just past provides history and the last actual, measured figures; the current fiscal year has a budget to be administered and held in control; and the upcoming year's budget must be prepared, defended, negotiated, and adopted. Every academic and administrative unit of a university is caught up in this iron cycle. The fiscal year budget, once adopted, contains signals of the most definite of the university's commitments; other projections beyond that adopted budget are subject to change with the availability of new information about resources, costs, and priorities. Thus, the budget is to be read not only for what it authorizes and pledges but for what it implies.

The Budget-Making Process

The annual operating budget consists of: (1) a set of revenue expectations; (2) a set of expenditure commitments; and (3) an indicated method of coping with the gap between the two, if any.

Revenue Projection

The administration's budget office is generally responsible for projecting the components of revenue, sometimes drawing on specialized projections from auxiliary enterprises and other revenue-related departments, such as the contracts and grants office. In a private university (and increasingly, in public ones as well), the forecast of tuition and fees (at current levels) is a crucial revenue component, subject to adjustment if there is a budget gap later in the process. (See later discussion in Chapter Eight.)

Expenditure Budget Preparation: Top-Down and Bottom-Up

The two conceptual extremes of the budget-making process are to go from the top down or to assemble the expenditure budget from the grass roots, beginning with departments and other units. The president and other senior executives of a university have advantages and responsibilities that make the control of the budget-making process important to them. They are aware of the present overall resource position of the institution and know what it is likely to be in the forthcoming fiscal period. In a public university, they have to negotiate with the agencies of state government for basic institutional support. In a private university, they have the obligation to bring to the university's trustees the prime recommendations concerning allocation of endowment income and reserves, tuition income and tuition increases, and other estimates of the institution's income base.

The senior administration and faculty leadership have some general vision of where the institution is and should be going—in other words, a sense of institutional priority. They are aware of what is needed for academic development and for appropriate responses to the important pressures and opportunities facing the institution. Individual academic and administrative units, properly enough, see first and foremost their own domains of concern and not those which may cut across all branches of the institution. In addition, the senior administration has or can obtain significant information for the processes of monitoring, comparison, and control. From the central campus database of enrollment and registration statistics, the workload variations among departments and schools can be calculated. From the space inventory files, the allocations of building space to various academic and administrative uses can be monitored. To the extent that there are judgments of the general vigor and quality of important academic and administrative operations, these are generated by, or flow to, the central administration. Finally, and most important, the senior administration will have to assemble the final budget by reconciling competing claims and fitting them into the foreseeable resource situation.

Individual academic and administrative units also have important contributions to make to the budgeting process. They are familiar with their problems and their aspirations. If they are simply handed the budget as a fait accompli, with no opportunity to speak to their needs, they are likely to take the view that the constraints of the budget are not of their making. They may then feel free to circumvent the budget if they are able to, rather than support it as the document that accurately describes the institution's fiscal position and commitments. We return to this issue in the discussion of resource management and incentives.

Each unit is likely to make expenditure requests that reflect aspirations and hopes much more heavily than considerations of efficiency. As any budgeteer knows, the first round of a purely grassroots budgeting process reflects the sum of hopes: the amount of money that it would take to go as rapidly toward goals as one could imagine, without winnowing out anything unnecessary, questionable, or obsolete. If the first round of budget making simply answers the question, "What would you like to have?" the second round— scaling requests to manageable proportions—is likely to be all the more traumatic on account of the hopes that have been aroused and the necessity to dash those hopes.

There is a persuasive argument for an open, decentralized budget-making process guided by a conception of institutional objectives and supported by an adequate system of financial information.

What is needed, then, is a dialogue between the two valid perspectives: that of the decentralized operating units and that of the central administration. The mechanism needs to include at least one round of responses from each level of decision makers, no matter which does the initiating. One way to start from a semblance of realism is to have the central administration send out budget guidelines for the forthcoming fiscal period that include the preliminary forecasts of revenues and workload changes. These guidelines are used by each unit as a starting point in assembling its request. The president and senior staff of a public university system typically sound out the executive branch of the state government for its views as to the likely budgetary climate in the upcoming fiscal period, and these signals help to shape the guidelines.

Some state governments and higher education coordinating agencies go much beyond providing signals of budget expectations and specify both the format in which the budget is to be prepared and the dollar or percentage targets of major budget categories. Format and target controls can greatly reduce the public university's capacity to manage the budgetary process.

The university's normal internal budget guidelines can also include, if necessary, an allocated amount of economizing adjustment that each operating unit is initially expected to absorb. Then, each unit is free to assemble its expenditure request and its justification for the request, either accepting the guidelines or deviating from them.

Generally speaking, the budget-making mechanism needs to include at this point, or after another iteration, a discussion involving the budget officer, senior administrators responsible for the area in which the unit operates, and the head of the operating unit. The discussion can be well-focused if the issues of concern have been worked on carefully by both sides. The budget director and senior administrators raise questions of program scope and efficiency, and the operating unit head raises questions of program opportunity and unmet needs. Studies of budgeting behavior show that differential power of units and unit heads materially affects the outcome of budget negotiations, for the budget officer and senior administration cannot ignore the centrality and institutional significance of a major unit. (See Pfeffer and Salancik, 1974.) Budget negotiations are by no means a purely technical exercise.

The negotiating process can proceed rapidly if there are no major cuts to be absorbed or serious questions of program goals and efficiency to be hammered out. But the latter questions deserve more attention than they often get. They are often ignored or incompletely addressed, being postponed for more leisurely attention when the unit comes up for a periodic multiyear performance review.

A budgeting process that relies heavily on the current year as the base year—with only infrequent reopening of the questions of program goals, performance, efficiency, and budgeting standards— is bound to reinforce the status quo allocations and more or less proportional expansions of them (for example, when enrollment increases necessitate workload adjustments). Innovation in any institution that emphasizes this budgeting mode is likely to be confined to incremental change within the existing terms of reference of each academic unit. Significant departures from established goals or performance standards cannot usually be accommodated within the narrow limits of workload budget adjustment, and without the necessity to react to more drastic shifts of resources, significant changes are not contemplated.

Zero-Base Budget

The most onerous dialogue between central administration and operating units occurs in *zero-base* budgeting, where each operating unit is put on notice that it should justify, from the ground up, all elements of its current expenditure pattern as well as any upward adjustments that it advocates. If it is not actually a realistic possibility that the forthcoming budget might be reduced to zero (that is, the department's claim to budget would be eliminated), the zero part of zero-base budgeting is simply an agonizing charade and not worth the trauma that raising such questions entails. The more sensible course is to divide the problem. This means that the question of continuation of the activity is raised in a full-scale performance review only occasionally (but more frequently than never); however, the annual budget process uses workload guidelines and also requires that the operating unit show what it would do if it were to receive a cut of some more or less tolerable magnitude, for example, 5, 10, or 15 percent. The responses can be expected to form a continuum, from "burdensome inflexibility" to "cut in service delivery and quality by such and such degree" to "strictly infeasible (in view of contractual employment and other commitments) in one year." The pattern of resource use in operating units is far more flexible upward than downward at the margin in short periods, and the opportunities to accommodate budget cuts by reducing the quantity and quality of work done are often held to be minimal in the very short run.

Budgeting Expertise and Systems Support

As the discussion so far shows, budgeting depends on the availability of extensive data and on the use of systems that enable budget analysts to assemble, analyze, and project budget figures quickly and conveniently. From the technical standpoint, budgeting and planning are intimately linked, and in principle, the annual budget is nested in a longer-term view of the university's future.

For the purposes of budget control, each operating unit also needs systems that help it maintain control of expenditures (including commitments or liens made but not yet processed as transactions) so that budgeted allocations in particular categories are adhered to.

Calendars

Even in ordinary circumstances, the senior administration and budget office of a university may have to keep track, simultaneously, of up to four fiscal year budgets and their interrelations:

1. The most recently completed fiscal year budget, which is a complete and fully known base
2. The current fiscal year budget, which requires control and administration in the present and serves as a base for the following year's budget
3. The following fiscal year budget, which must be prepared and defended
4. The budget for the fiscal year beyond the next, which will provide the earliest indicators of developing issues

In a complex university, with dozens of budgetary standards, hundreds of activity centers of identified functions, and thousands of line items, it has been necessary to develop aids to budget accounting and control, and methods of partially automating the budget accounting and its interyear ties. Given the level of complexity and the demands of reporting and justification, the budgeting process is always in danger of bogging down in detail and mechanics. Thus, it is necessary to apply conscious pressure to save time for substantive issues of policy.

State budgeting calendars and procedures differ, and some work on a biennial rather than a one-year budgeting cycle. In California, the governor releases to the legislature the executive budget for the upcoming fiscal year in late January of the current fiscal year. It is considered in budget hearings during the following months, and legislative action is not normally completed until June. Then there is often a flurry of activity as the governor vetoes various items. (In California, the governor may reduce any line item of the budget by any amount.) Finally, in late July or August, the legislature attempts to override some budget vetoes and restore cuts with which it disagrees. Meanwhile, the fiscal year that was the object of budgetary scrutiny has already begun. For fiscal year 1992–93 a severe revenue shortfall and a consequent budget deadlock prevented passage of the new state budget for many weeks after the beginning of the new fiscal year. The state controller was forced to issue warrants—IOUs—because the state's cash balances were depleted, and all state agencies faced near paralysis because they had no information as to the magnitude of mandated budget reductions. The situation presented the University of California and the California State University with exceptionally difficult budget adjustment problems.

A private university does not have to run the same gauntlet for its basic support budget; because negotiation with the state is not required, certain steps in the process are eliminated. But the private university faces two other exigencies that are more onerous for it than for the state institution. First, it relies proportionately more on extramural research funding and foundation grants than does the state-supported institution, and it is also more sensitive to variations in the income yield from endowments and in the income from tuition. Revenue forecasting must therefore be very meticulous. Second, because support for administration, academic units and faculty, library, and other basic operations is not underwritten from a more or less stable state source, the private university may have to react quickly to cuts in research funds or other extramural funds. It must preserve capability for quick within-year adjustments.

In 1990–91, for example, U.S. public institutions obtained 16 percent of their revenues from tuition and fees, 10 percent from federal sources, and 1 percent from endowments. The corresponding percentages for private institutions were 40, 15, and 5 (National Center for Education Statistics, 1993, pp. 171, 322–323).

Budgetary Standards and Indicators

A budgetary standard can be defined as the amount of resources deemed to be required per unit of workload in a particular activity.

Standards are usually experience based, and in a public university they often embody informal agreements between the university and the state financial and budgeting authorities.

By far the most significant example is the student-faculty ratio. This ratio usually involves much more than a simple count of the number of bodies in each category. Thus, the first level of refinement is to adjust head count (usually downward) to full-time equivalents (FTE) and get the ratio of FTE students to FTE faculty. Some institutions accord separate recognition to the more intensive tasks—and the generally smaller-scale character of instruction—in advanced graduate programs, as compared with undergraduate programs. This led to the development of weighted FTE student-faculty ratios, where higher weights for the graduate components of enrollment reflect the presumably greater staffing requirement.

Whatever the form, the student-faculty ratio can be used to calculate the number of faculty positions that should be added to the budget to meet the presumed demands of additional students. In its easiest and most plausible form, the increment is calculated at the preexisting average ratio.

An enrollment increase of 100 FTE students, at an FTE student-faculty ratio of 20, would mean adding five FTE faculty positions. At this point, a secondary budgetary standard—the average rank level of new positions—might be invoked, to guide control of staffing and to fix the number of dollars added to the faculty salary budget.

A clever budgeteer might object to this way of calculating incremental faculty positions, because the more pertinent issue is: what should the marginal ratio be? Among the considerations that might come into play are: the preexisting size of the faculty; the extent to which the institution's leadership or (in a public institution) the state budgeting agency wants to thin out the staffing pattern; and the composition of enrollment increases, which should be examined to determine whether they are mostly in areas where class sizes could be increased with little need for new staffing.

This example may help to illustrate both the uses and the potential weakness of a simply stated budgetary standard. Such a standard makes for administrative convenience and ready calculation of budgetary needs. It can also be used to assess the approximate internal allocation of a resource increment among academic units. However, the budgetary standard rests on commonsense presumptions about resource needs in relation to workload or activity rates, and these presumptions often prove, on examination, to have incomplete justification.

In some cases, therefore, in-depth studies are made to provide deeper justification. Building maintenance standards, for example, have been studied to determine whether, at the historical rates of expenditure per square foot, buildings of various ages and construction types are receiving enough care to avoid the buildup of a backlog of deferred maintenance. A growing backlog indicates that the operating budgets of previous years have been inadequate.

Budgetary standards may sometimes be adjusted for the size of operations. Statistical studies at various campuses of the University of California showed that, as campus size increased, the percentage of general administration expense in the total budget could be allowed to fall. Such an economy of scale could then be built into a declining-percentage budgetary standard for general administration expense budgeting.

Capital Budgeting and Space Standards

For preparation of capital budgets, space standards are conceptually analogous to the operating budget standards just discussed. Occasionally, external regulatory requirements impose the standard. An example is the set of regulations promulgated by the U.S. Public Health Service for the care of laboratory animals. These specify space and service requirements (such as air-conditioning) for proper care of various animal species, and their effect is to set capital requirements on animal care facilities.

Space standards embody educational policy. For example, the number of assignable square feet (ASF) for a faculty member in the laboratory sciences or engineering is much greater than the number stipulated for a faculty member in the social sciences or humanities. If a field of academic activity has historically justified a large amount of space per person, the implied capital costs are gradually built into the institution's cost structure. Actual costs may, of course, deviate from the standard. During growth periods, there is a tendency for staffing and enrollments to outpace the completion of space to house them. Fields that experience declining enrollment and activity are rarely penalized right away for occupying excess space. Their administrators usually argue that enrollment and staffing declines may soon be reversed. And often, the physical location or functional characteristics of the excess space are inappropriate for other uses unless heavy renovation and relocation investments are made. Thus, space standards may have very real importance in an institution, but deviations from them may be prolonged.

Budget Concepts and Categories

Traditionally, operating budgets in public agencies (and in most educational institutions) were laid out using *line items* or *object classes*, such as the number of personnel in various categories and their budgeted salary costs, minor equipment purchases and maintenance, purchased supplies, travel expenses, and building maintenance. A line item was any separately labeled expenditure. Object classes were the standard categories for each type of budgeted resource. The dollar total in each of these categories could in turn be broken down into the allocation for each unit. Because each new building is a large, one-time investment, the capital outlay budget is typically a line-item budget, with each fiscal year phase of design, construction, and equipping of the building a subitem. Only for deferred maintenance and renovations might there be a pooled capital budget total without prior designation of the amount to be spent on each project.

Traditional operating budgets are focused entirely on object classes—the various categories of input. An early, valuable step in the budgeting process is to compute the required change in inputs from the change in activity or workload. When this can be done via agreed budgetary standards, two further steps are enough to produce a plausible and enforceable expenditure budget. One is to correct for year-to-year changes of the unit prices of inputs. In an era of inflation, it is important to do this carefully, but academic institutions have had difficulty using or constructing the appropriate price indices and still more difficulty predicting price changes.

The income or revenue side of the budget also needs to be constructed. It will show income by category, indicating how carryovers will be treated, and dealing with any intentional gaps between income and outgo. These steps, together with the breakdowns to organizational units, are sufficient to produce an enforceable budget—assuming, of course, that the budgetary pattern plausibly reflects the conditions of operation and that no strong shock to income or expenditure comes from the environment.

Budget administration and enforcement are issues in themselves. When a unit manager sees reasons for shifting funds from one budget category to another, such a "budget transfer" ordinarily requires approval of the budget office. The structure of the unit budget is preset in the requisite categories, and savings in a given category cannot be reallocated unilaterally without loss of control. (Responsibility center budgeting, discussed below, decentralizes category-by-category budget administration to the unit managers, which motivates them toward more efficient local management.)

The trouble with the object-class budget is that it is almost completely devoid of any conceptual representation of what the institution is doing. A better tool is what may be called the *function and performance* budget. This type of budget is cut into significant areas of functional operation, such as the departmental budget that consists of instruction and departmental research, organized research, libraries, organized activities, public and community service, maintenance and operation of plant, student services, and general administration. Activities or performance areas under each of these headings are broken down into finer categories. The library budget, for example, may be divided between two functional areas: acquisitions and acquisitions processing; and circulation and services. Whenever possible, agreed budgetary standards provide a basis for determining the amount of change in budgeted expenditure that is justified—using a pertinent measure of workload—between the current year and the next.

From the point of view of budgetary administration and control, the function and performance budget gives an improved basis for focusing budgetary responsibility on organizational units and for determining whether deviations between the budgeted expenditure rate and the actual rate are justified by unexpected workload changes or changes in other conditions.

Program Budgeting: A Noble Experiment

Object-class budgeting is based purely on inputs. Function and performance budgets are based on areas and rates of activity. Program budgeting is a conceptual schema for allocating resources according to the objectives of the institution. This is a praiseworthy aim. The first step toward it in higher education institutions was to rearrange the format of the operating budget so as to divide the areas of functional activity into major programs and supporting programs and to work out reallocations of some functional budgets among the major and supporting programs thus identified. Even this modest step requires a great deal of exacting effort in any large-scale institution.

An extensive review and critique of "planning, programming, budgeting systems" (PPBS) in higher education were made by G. B.

Weathersby and myself (Weathersby and Balderston, 1972). In the early 1960s, PPBS held out the promise of imparting a new degree of rationality to public sector resource allocation and management.

The experience of the U.S. Department of Defense under the leadership of then-secretary Robert McNamara and his assistant secretary and comptroller, Charles J. Hitch, provided the widely heralded first example of PPBS (Hitch, 1965). Hitch emphasized that the implementation of a planning, programming, budgeting system in the Department of Defense did not mean that object-class budgeting was entirely abandoned. The old and the new had to be carried forward together, partly because congressional committees insisted on continuing to receive the traditional layout of resource commitments. The implementation of PPBS depended on a large accumulation of quantitative and qualitative analysis of defense programs and problems. This analysis was carried out mainly at the RAND Corporation. Other executive agencies attempted to follow the lead of the Department of Defense, in response to President Johnson's 1965 executive order mandating PPBS in federal agencies, and many state governments soon followed. Implementation proved frustrating in many areas of government, and there was eventually a pullback from the mechanics of PPBS in the federal budgeting process. State agencies, including public universities, also experienced difficulties.

One problem that soon developed was the lack of quantitatively definable objectives in many areas of government service, including higher education. There are broadly definable aims for a university and for elements of university mission, but measurement of the quantity and the quality of results achieved is not very highly developed.

Until there is reasonably clear agreement on what the accomplishments (or outputs) of a university are, it is not possible effectively to budget for results. Furthermore, there is still much work to be done in:

1. Identifying the processes of activity
2. Showing what organizational units or combination of units are responsible for the work
3. Demonstrating how the organizational units and processes are affected by a richer or more scant allocation of resources
4. Indicating how the processes contribute to the attainment of objectives

A university abounds in multiple processes, and the analysis of costs and results in the presence of substantial jointness and interdependence is difficult.

But even if adroit compromises are reached on the use of less than ideal ways of measuring results and on rule-of-thumb approaches to jointness, the remaining problem of time horizons has proven to be, politically, the most serious of all. One basic idea in PPBS is to specify what is to be accomplished in each program in each future year; it is then necessary to calculate how many resources will be needed for a program and to specify when these resources have to be acquired, and at what cost, in order to meet the schedule. The system forecasts the costs of the program over a series of years and sets forth the timing of these costs, thereby avoiding the trap of making seemingly innocuous first-year commitments to programs that eventually turn out to be far more expensive than contemplated. It is still quite possible to make a poor choice of program or to underestimate costs. PPBS did not altogether solve the problem of mistaken and misunderstood commitments. But it was certainly a far more sensible conceptual approach than the political jockeying that got programs started on false promises and then built them into large and unstoppable claims later on.

Universities found that although they tried to show the multiyear budgetary implications of programs, their funding sources were unwilling or unable to look beyond very short commitments—typically, the single budget year. Administrators were very much aware that most of what they were trying to sustain in existing programs or initiate in new ones had implications for costs, and horizons for results, that stretched far beyond the upcoming fiscal year. But they have generally not been able to use a multiyear horizon except for very contingent internal planning—or by announcing noble hopes whose realization would be heavily dependent on future decisions by outside funding agencies. A more sophisticated analytic spirit, both within the university and in state and federal agencies, is perhaps the most enduring legacy of the program budgeting experience.

Responsibility Center Budgeting

Universities find two major advantages in decentralization: decisions are made and actions are taken close to the locus of service delivery, where information is immediately available; and the focus of responsibility is centered on the local unit. One method of achieving this focus is, first, to provide for explicit, decentralized authority and initiative, and second, to set agreed budget targets that will gauge the performance of the unit manager. For such an arrangement to be meaningful, the unit manager must be able to control costs; thus, the accounting system must provide prompt (ideally, on-line) information concerning the transaction flow for which the unit is responsible and the status of expenditures relative to budget. (Traditional financial accounting systems often did not provide supporting information promptly, and they often did not include provisions permitting the unit manager to show liens against the available budget components. To overcome these deficiencies, unit managers had to maintain their own informal departmental accounting records—a duplicative, wasteful, and sometimes inaccurate substitute for a well-functioning accounting framework.)

Responsibility center (or cost center) budgeting can serve as a support to a decentralized, performance-focused management system, provided the unit manager has the support of an effective departmental accounting system. The University of Pennsylvania installed a responsibility center budgeting system with good effect.

We discuss in Chapter Fourteen a still more far-reaching approach to the transformation of university administrative management: comprehensive decentralization and team or networked organization, supported by accessible databases and state-of-the-art information systems.

Budget Adjustment Strategies

Universities pass through phases of ebullient growth, managed stability or drift, slow decay, and occasionally, sharp financial crisis. Whatever the phase, budgetary control has to be exerted. Aspirations for new programs and a higher institutional living standard produce a continual gap between desired expenditures and fiscal realities. Besides these pressures for programs, amenities, and experiments (a worthwhile motivating pressure, in principle, and one whose absence would indicate serious institutional illness!), a specific feature of institutional organization gives rise to the need for budgetary control. General institutional resources are always at a premium. Demands for them come from three different sources: induced or required matching of special and restricted funds; the underwriting of direct academic programs that are valid commitments of the institution but do not have any extramural support; and most important, the budgetary support of core activities that are indispensable but unloved. The sum of these demands on general funds of the institution is invariably more than can be comfortably met within available general fund revenues, and so rationing through the budgetary process is unavoidable.

Close observers of higher education have noted that institutions often behave as if they were seeking to maximize expenditures—the larger the budget, the better. Many of the indicators of quality and vitality—high faculty salaries, generous allocations to the library, ease of funding new academic ventures—are associated with a high and rising expenditure rate. But such a pattern of intended expenditures puts an even higher premium on the careful assessment of revenues and the planning of revenue growth. The president of a private university needs to worry about money-raising and tuition policy. The president of a public university must worry about keeping the confidence of the state's governor and legislature, because the state appropriation is the most crucial element of the institution's general funds.

Budget Administration and Incentive Issues

Control and adjustment of the expenditure pattern can have positive or detrimental effects on incentives and efficiency within the institution, depending on the manner in which the signals of control are designed and interpreted.

"Lapsing" of Unspent Balances. End-of-year "lapsing" or recovery of unspent balances is a classic device of governmental budgeting. The perverse incentives it creates are seen also at the university when budget managers require the return of unspent balances to a central, budget-balancing pool. Yet they may have to do so to avoid budget overruns.

At the very least, this policy produces short-term incentives to spend the whole of the budgetary allocation. In order to control against this, still another layer of restraint is sometimes added—a bar against new equipment and supplies commitments after a cut-off date late in the fiscal year.

The disincentive to economical management is compounded if the following year's budget allocation is thought to be based on the *expenditures* made in the current year. Under these circumstances, any savings and resulting unspent balances actually harm the unit's future budget. (The chilling effects of this sort of budgetary control—which may be forced on a public university by state budgetary rules—can be reduced by making it clear that future budgets will not be reduced when unspent balances are reported, and reduced still further if a unit that makes economies is permitted to carry over or apply in a discretionary way some substantial part of the savings.)

Reasons for Year-to-Year Allocative Changes. The budgeted expenditure pattern reflects the priority status of programs and functions. Year-to-year changes in the allocation for a given activity may be made because of shifts in earmarked revenues (control of the volume of an activity by the funding source), efforts to offset price inflation that is eroding the real basis of support (influence of market events), movement of enrollment interest toward some fields and away from others (influence of student demand), or a change in the priority assigned to an activity (control according to institutional objectives). What is at stake, then, is the type and direction of control exerted over the activities of the university.

As we observed in Chapters Five and Six, the many units of a university operate according to their perceptions of what they should be doing individually, and they also acknowledge interdependencies and their obligation to contribute to the larger purposes of the institution. Other administrative units of general administration, such as the accounting office and the personnel office, are necessarily regarded as overhead and budgeted from institutional funds.

All budgeted units, academic and administrative, derive incentive signals from the scheme of controls through which the annual budget is administered and from the budgetary adjustment strategy that is used. Some major consequences of the university's resource allocation policies can be summarized by examining the specific incentives created by these signals and strategies.

The budgetary strategy of proportional adjustments conveys perverse managerial incentives because all units receive the same percentage budget cut regardless of how well they manage or how much they contribute to longer-term institutional aims. No differential reward is given for exceptionally efficient or effective performance. Also, some units can absorb a given percentage cut in budget with relative ease, while to other units it may be devastating.

Self-Funded Units and the Pricing of Their Services. Units are sometimes self-funded parts of the institution, seeking to confine their expenditures to the amount of internal revenue they obtain by billing their customers in the institution for services rendered. However, this does not guarantee that the unit will be operated at the highest possible level of efficiency, because the prices it charges are designed to cover costs even if these costs are higher than they should be. Allowing outsourcing for the services can impose a salutary cost discipline on the self-funded unit.

A price system for services rendered to individuals or organizational units makes the customers consider carefully how much of the service to buy and—if several qualities of service are available at different prices—what quality they find appropriate. Customers may economize on the service to save funds for other needs. The alternative to charging a price for a needed service that costs something to produce is to allocate it among users by means of administrative decisions. Making people wait in queues is one rationing technique. Another is to classify some users as eligible and others as ineligible.

An industrial corporation that has several decentralized operating divisions often uses a system of internal prices (transfer prices) to focus responsibility on each division manager for contributing to the overall profit performance of the corporation. The division receives revenue credits on the books of the corporation for the volume of components, subassemblies, or other items that it produces and sends to other divisions. The division that receives these items has to recognize their cost (the number of units multiplied by the transfer price). If the transfer prices are set correctly, the contribution of each operating division to the overall profits of the corporation can be determined. The manager who contributes most can be rewarded, and the manager who does poorly can be penalized. Such internal pricing is an approximation of the invisible hand of a market system, as opposed to the visible hand of administratively determined allocations.

Links to Accountability

The expenditure pattern and the revenue-drawing capability of the university are linked by demands for accountability. Donors to the private university may be reluctant to give if they perceive gross waste or if they are dissatisfied with the direction the university is taking. State governments are concerned about efficiency issues and also about the university's success or failure in adhering to numerous policy constraints imposed by the state. These are some of the concerns about the focus and style of adjustments of both revenue and expenditures.

Budgetary Adjustment Strategies

The size of the swings to be dealt with, upward or downward, also affects both the type of budgetary adjustment strategy that can be used and the intensity of the response required. Universities are usually far more capable of accommodating growth than of absorbing the pain of retrenchment. For retrenchment, both adjustment time and the absolute or percentage amount of reduction must be considered. With these considerations in mind, we now turn to an examination of several budgetary adjustment strategies.

Enriching or Reducing Budgetary Standards. These budgetary adjustment strategies all focus on programs, activities, or organizational units, and on different ways to arrange related budget adjustments. But a different dimensional approach can be taken: namely, to adjust—upward or downward—a budgetary standard that is important enough to affect most facets of the university's operations and have important effects on the budget, for example, adjustments in the student-faculty ratio or in the standard for building maintenance.

A change in an important budgetary standard can produce substantial dollar impact on total budget because many units of the institution are affected. A question raised about a budgetary standard, such as the student-faculty ratio, is in a different domain of argument from a question about a particular program or activity. The student-faculty ratio, after all, is based on a rough judgment of average academic staffing needs across many departments, with differing compositions of undergraduate and graduate enrollment, different scales and styles of work, and different stages of development.

State budgeteers may propose to increase the ratio so that the upcoming year's enrollment-induced entitlement to more faculty positions will be negated. The institution's president and the academic deans and department chairs may have trouble constructing an opposing argument. They may take the position that other institutions, similar to theirs in character and quality, have a richer academic staffing standard than the one proposed and that therefore raising the student-faculty ratio would undermine the university's quality. But this argument lacks concreteness. Alternatively, they may undertake a detailed analysis to indicate adverse consequences of the proposed change, department by department and program by program. But the use of a generalized standard such as the student-faculty ratio is in the first instance designed to avoid issues of detailed academic judgments. If such judgments are discussed at all, those who raise questions (whether they are private university trustees or state budget officers) will be put in the position of offering counterjudgments about the merits of academic programs and their staffing requirements.

Thus, it is easy to see why budget cutters may choose to attack the existing budgetary standards and why it is difficult for institutional spokespersons to counterattack.

Freezes. A "freeze" singles out a budget component—for example, office supplies or unfilled faculty or administrative positions—and requires that no budgeted academic or administrative unit take any expenditure action concerning that item. Freezing positions enables the senior administration to control against increases in payroll and other expenditures for the duration of the freeze. Freezes often damage efficiency in unexpected ways, because vacated positions, for example, cannot be filled even if they are high-priority, whereas other personnel whose contribution is not so significant are left untouched. Nevertheless, freezes are less unpopular within the institution than are layoffs and phaseouts.

Proportional ("Across the Board") Adjustments. Suppose that a specific budget increase or decrease is determined to be necessary. The university administration may simply apply to every relevant unit the same upward or downward percentage adjustment. Such a rule of simple proportionality seems fair, since all units share equally in the pain or gain. Especially in the early stages of budgetary retrenchment, or in response to what appears to be a temporary or one-time adjustment need, the institution's budget administrators often adopt this tactic. It is politically safe, because it avoids invidious distinctions between the contributions of various units. It is also easy to calculate and enforce.

An alternative to simple dollar proportionality is workload proportionality. For example, projected FTE enrollment for the fiscal period could be used as the basis for distribution of the given dollar change in the aggregate budget. If the budget allocation has customarily been made in accordance with a workload standard, this method has internal plausibility throughout the institution and contains the presumption that resource needs change in accordance with changes of workload. However, it equates the average requirement with the marginal requirement, which may not make much sense. Also, the distribution of resources within the institution is then governed by shifts of student enrollment in programs. Carried far enough, this approach may compel the crippling or even the closure of departments that are valuable to the university from the standpoint of compositional balance and longer-range institutional commitment.

Although a scheme of dollar proportionality or workload proportionality may work for a time, persistent budget adjustment pressure must eventually arouse doubts. The short-term advantage of proportionality adjustments is precisely in avoiding questions about objectives, efficiency, and quality of performance. Nevertheless, in any institution, there are implicit views concerning the most important aspects of its academic operations. There is also an internal distribution of power and influence in the academic leadership. Even during the early stages of application of a proportionality adjustment rule, some affected units may demand partial or full exemption from the cuts. Some of these demands, backed with cogent arguments about consequences at the margin or lack of adjustability of the unit's budget, may indeed be persuasive. But the granting of exemptions then increases the adjustment burden to be borne by other units.

Eventually, some units and their spokespersons may suggest that selective choices (presumably, in their favor) should be made, even if these must be based on the primacy of some objectives at the expense of others or on hard judgments about efficiency and quality. Meanwhile, however, repeated application of proportional adjustments has had two bad effects: the gradual weakening of performance and morale throughout the institution, among strong units as well as weaker ones; and the loss of deliberative time. If the issue of selective priority arises late, it arises as an emergency question. The response under these circumstances is unlikely to be sound and coherent, because substantial lead time is needed for adequate investigation of the merits of one scheme of selective priority over another.

"Every Tub on Its Own Bottom." Proportionality rules need to be administered centrally. "Every tub on its own bottom" is a way to avoid even this degree of central administration responsibility. The concept is an old one, but its modern use and its nickname were popularized by Nathan Pusey, former president of Harvard University. Each decentralized school or major program ("tub") is made responsible for generating its own operating revenue

("bottom") through extramural grants, contracts, and gifts; and sometimes the tuition income generated by enrollment in a program is left with the program to finance its budget. The essence of the system is: let the market rule. If the program attracts funds and students, it can survive and even grow. If not, it may be given a grace period for a dignified passing instead of a sudden one, but the presumption is that it must die.

Fixing the responsibility for program survival on the program's entrepreneurial leadership provides strong motivation. The scheme has a measure of quality control built in, provided that funding sources use expert panels of peers to place contracts and grants where scholarly reputation and the prospect of excellent work are highest. The judgments of funding agencies and donors are not, however, valid indicators of academic quality in programs where applied work is pursued according to terms imposed by the funder for its own programmatic reasons.

If tuition revenue is left with a program, and if it has de facto control over student recruitment and admission, the program may pump enrollment for the sake of income, without adequate concern about the qualifications of students. It may also tolerate class sizes that are too high.

This allocation policy cannot be applied individually to academic areas that are strongly complementary and interdependent, as they are in undergraduate liberal arts. At Harvard, the main reach of the policy is toward the professional schools and some graduate programs. It does not extend to Harvard College. The policy would also defeat most infant programs in an expanding university, as they need seed money for their early years of development.

Even if the hazards of interdependence and of choking off young programs are avoided through judicious application of the policy, two deeper problems remain. The policy assumes that decentralized coupling of revenue and expenditure works to the institutional interest because funding and enrollment market signals are valid, and each program is in this way subject to realistic controls on quality and size. But these signals may not be fully valid as a basis for institutional policy, and they may change much faster than the adjustment capability (particularly, the downward adjustment capability) of the program.

Decentralization poses yet other problems. Most decentralized programs are not totally freestanding. Students often need to circulate among them. Faculty may need to be borrowed back and forth. Services of the central administration in business management, accounting, and other functions are generally characterized by economies of scale. If decentralized units perform these services for themselves, costs are high; if they use centrally provided services, careful cost accounting and recharge billing through an internal pricing scheme are necessary to allocate costs to the revenue-generating locations. Similar observations can be made about computer centers, libraries, and major laboratories. The "every tub" philosophy may only too easily be taken as a mandate for excessive, autarchic decentralization of some functions, and it may weaken the quality of central administration and centrally provided academic support services. The decentralized resource policy may also inhibit the responsiveness of units to institutionwide policies and requirements—for example, affirmative action in hiring—or even to demands for sufficient information to enable the central administration to understand, interpret, and defend the institution.

The positive appeal of the decentralized revenue-and-expenditure control policy—aside from the opportunity that it gives the central administration to escape the onus of adjustments—is the appeal of decentralization in any organization: authority and responsibility are firmly coupled, and the entrepreneurial capability of the leaders and members of the decentralized unit is both stimulated and tested. The question is whether this very great virtue is more than offset by the hazards and defects that have been pointed out.

Budgetary Adjustment According to Selective Priorities. This policy requires assessment of the program commitments of the institution and comparison of the resource costs and apparent efficiency of each one with what it delivers, quantitatively and qualitatively, toward the objectives of the university. On the basis of this assessment, differential treatment is accorded to individual programs and areas of activity. Some may be permitted to remain at stable size and resource commitments; some are given targets of resource reduction while remaining at the same scale; others are permitted workload growth and corresponding resource allocations; and still others may be provided resources to do new things or improve quality of performance. Certain programs may be deemed unnecessary and may be phased out, with more or less time given for this painful process. The selective priority approach may also entail plans for reorganization, use of a different technology or style, or consolidation of activities.

Of all the approaches discussed, this one is by far the most disruptive of the organization and decision-making style of a university. Precisely because it is costly in time and institutional energy, a selective priority scheme can accomplish only a modest number of major changes in each fiscal period. Selective priority usually becomes acceptable to constituencies within the institution only after repeated experience of fiscal and program tightening (as one governor has called it, "cut, squeeze, and trim"). The strongest case for selective priority is that the alternatives are worse. During a period of institutional expansion, selective approaches are needed for otherwise uncontrolled and ad hoc proliferation of programs, some of which will likely weaken rather than strengthen the institution. Selective priority is equally necessary during a period of retrenchment, for the alternative is some form of proportional budget cutting that would produce anemia everywhere, weakening strong and essential programs in order to keep less important programs alive, even though the latter cannot be accorded enough resources to overcome performance difficulties.

A scheme of selective priority should have the following ingredients:

1. A technical capability to analyze costs, interactions, and goal contributions of programs, along with access to comparative data to buttress the findings
2. A way of joining credible and expert academic judgments with fiscal information
3. An institutional process that meets conditions of fairness
4. A quality and range of academic and administrative leadership that can reach and enforce decisions without losing the ability to function in the future

Budgeting People

The preceding discussion has been cast in terms of dollar budgets, which are indeed the usual means of resource planning and control. However, we also need to take note of other important resources—in particular, personnel and building space—that are planned and allocated in parallel with the procedures for dollar budgeting.

Governmental agencies have long practiced *position control* in addition to dollar budgeting. In most governmental activities, the workload of an agency is reflected, through rule-of-thumb conventions, in a manning table: a certain number of workload elements are assigned to each first-level employee; a specific number of first-level employees are assigned to each supervisor; and so on. The table of organization is built on this basis, provision also being made for people who coordinate the interactions between line units, for support staffs sized in some ratio to the operating staffs, and for a top executive structure. Each position level is accorded a rating that denotes salary range. Thus, if all authorized positions are filled, the total wage bill of the agency can be estimated easily from the manning table and the salary rates, and this wage bill constitutes the major part of the dollar operating budget. Fringe benefits are calculated as a percentage of salary in each category. Nonwage budget items are usually tied by other rules of thumb to the number of authorized employees.

Why not budget in terms of dollars and merely ask the agency head to determine how many employees are needed to meet the workload? The University of Minnesota System does exactly this, focusing the attention of administrators on dollars and salary costs. Why not do without position control? Classically, there are several reasons. The most important is that, once hired, a civil service employee acquires job and retirement rights that are totally extinguished only on death, voluntary separation prior to vesting of retirement benefits, or dismissal for cause after elaborate due process. Also, the assessment of the resources needed by the agency proceeds naturally from activity workload to personnel requirements to dollar budgets. Position control provides additional assurance that an agency director will not step outside the prescribed boundaries of operation. It also shows those who are reviewing an agency's budget request for the forthcoming fiscal period how the estimated workload increase translates into staffing requirements, assuming that a standard ratio of units of workload to units of staffing is agreed. Furthermore, position control enables budget reviewers to intervene at a critical point if they want to force a productivity increase or a decline in the apparent quality of the service of the agency. This can be done by applying a new and less generous staffing allocation either to the workload increase or to the total workload of the agency.

Public universities find that position control is most crucially enforced through the student-faculty ratio that is used to determine how many faculty positions the institution will be permitted in the forthcoming fiscal period. The number of new faculty positions allocated (usually on the basis of increased enrollment) together with the number of positions vacated by resignation, death, or retirement provides the total of allocable faculty slots that can be assigned to the academic departments. These slots, or faculty FTEs, are precious coin in the process of resource allocation. The salary budget allocation to each academic department is adjusted to reflect the salary cost of a faculty FTE awarded to it. On the other hand, the mere availability of dollars does not permit a department to recruit a new faculty member if a slot has not been provided. This restriction prevents a department from engaging in short-term trade-offs between one dollar category and another, when the effect would be to increase not only the department's but also the institution's longer-run costs.

Budgeting Space

Building space is another major resource. Most universities keep comprehensive inventory records of the space they own and control. Records usually exist, also, of the current assignments of space. But the extent to which a particular building or room is capable of accommodating different uses is often not evident from the records. Rather, it is part of the judgment and lore of the campus administration. (See Chapter Ten for detailed discussion.)

Space for academic and administrative uses is typically not budgeted; there is no regular cycle of review and determination of need. Initial assignments are made on the basis of administrative judgments about the amount and type of space that is appropriate and available. Once assigned, space is often considered to be all but owned by the unit that occupies it, and any proposed reallocation becomes a major administrative issue.

Academic and administrative space allocations are administrative actions, heavily influenced by the internal power politics of the campus. Once having gained control of a block of space, a unit has little or no incentive to give up any excess, and it typically has incentives to ask for more. In principle, space costs and usage could be included in operating budgets of units, and a unit willing to give up unneeded space could reallocate budgeted funds (at least in part) to other purposes. This approach would increase the rationality of resource allocations, although it would not deal with issues of allocation for "close neighbor" efficiency, nor would it resolve the problem of space for which the capital cost was originally provided by a donor and is therefore restricted to the donor's intended use.

Assuming that—as is almost always the case—the space is allocated by negotiation and administrative decision, the university should require periodic space justifications from all units, management of space allocations should be closely checked, and all space allocations should be coordinated with other allocations of resources. If such steps are not taken, it cannot be said that university space is budgeted.

Chapter Eight

Revenues and Enrollments

A university obtains the revenue to support its operations from numerous sources. Some are *enrollment related* or *enrollment driven*. This is true of student tuition and fee revenues, and it also holds for public budgets that provide an appropriation tied by formula to the amount of enrollment. Tuition and fee income of public institutions formed 16 percent of total revenue in 1990–91; private institutions obtained 40 percent of their revenue from tuition (National Center for Education Statistics, 1993, pp. 322–323).

Other revenue components trace to different sources and are subject to change over time, in response to various influences. *Endowment* is a function of past benefaction, and the income stream from it arises from investments, their yield over time, and the apportioning of total return to spending in the current period as against the future. Public institutions obtained 1 percent of their revenue from endowment in 1990–91, and private institutions 5 percent (National Center for Education Statistics, 1993, pp. 322–323).

The all-important university revenues from research grants and contracts divide into two portions: *faculty-initiated* grants applied for under announced programs, which are generally peer reviewed and awarded on a competitive basis by federal or state agencies; and negotiated *institutional* grants and contracts, under which the institution commits to operating a laboratory or a program that is mandated to achieve programmatic objectives. Research revenues and trends are discussed in Chapter Twelve.

Federal and state funds for *student financial aid*—grants-in-aid and work-study for undergraduates, doctoral fellowships for selected graduate students—are administered through university channels. Details of financial aid programs are discussed in Chapter Nine. The student is the direct beneficiary, but the institution is assisted indirectly, because these programs reduce the call on institutional funds for financial aid.

Still other revenue streams arise from the provision of *specialized services*. (Often, these are referred to as institutional services or auxiliary enterprises.) Almost one-fourth of institutional revenue is derived from sale of services. Patient income of university teaching hospitals is one example. Revenue from intercollegiate athletics is another. Rental income from room and board in university-operated housing is a third. (Each of these has its own peculiar demands: for a justifying policy, to ensure that the activity contributes to the institution; for effective management, to ensure that the activity is conducted so as to achieve revenue objectives net of operating costs; and for market effectiveness, to ensure that those who make payments receive a service that is satisfactory to them.)

Multiple Sources of Funding

U.S. universities, both public and private, cultivate *multiple sources of funding* to a much greater extent than do universities in European countries and elsewhere. Having a variety of sources reduces the risk of subordination to any one funding source—an inherent problem for European universities, which are all but totally dependent on an annual budget allocation from their nation's ministry of education. A deeply felt desire for independence of action heightens the importance of multiple sources in American eyes. Endowment that produces an effectively unrestricted income stream facilitates autonomy in a similar fashion; but no major U.S. university has sufficient endowment to avoid taking an interest in other income sources.

Revenue Forecasting

University trustees and senior administration are guided by multi-year revenue and expenditure projections, because the current-year and forthcoming-year annual budgets must be cast in a frame consistent enough for reasoned expectations. In his well-known *New Depression in Higher Education* (1971), Cheit defined "financial stress" as a continued gap between the growth of revenue and the growth of expenditure. During several periods since then, temporary phases of relief at U.S. universities have been succeeded by deficit trends of shorter or longer duration. The revenue side of such projections is of interest to us in this chapter.

For private universities, the largest single revenue component is tuition and fee income. For public universities, the state appropriation for operating purposes is the largest component (40 percent of revenues); but this in turn is usually arrived at with considerable reliance on enrollment-driven formulas.

Revenue can also be analyzed according to whether it is largely *trend related* or *episodic*. Tuition and fee income, based on enrollment with relatively modest year-to-year changes and on yearly adjustments in tuition—not always at the same percentage rate of increase—follows an upward, though usually nonlinear, trend. A state's college-going population plus its admission standards and enrollment policies produce a similar demographically related trend for total enrollment. College and university enrollments in the 1980s were expected to stabilize and then fall as a result of echoes of the variations in previous birthrates. Particularly in the northeastern region of the United States, these predictions have been more or less borne out; but continuing increases in the percentage of women attending colleges and universities, and increases in enrollment of "returning students" from higher age brackets, have sustained a positive trend of enrollment. In the latter 1990s, another upsurge of enrollments is expected to occur.

Episodic revenues arise from unexpected large gifts and from *campaigns*. Annual giving campaigns are now professionally managed and produce a generally predictable income stream, whereas capital campaigns for major building projects and for major additions to endowment produce results that are erratic. Correspondingly, the prudent institution takes such large infusions into its balance sheet but does not allow them to affect current operating expenditure levels quickly. Their effect is either confined to transfers within the capital base (financial capital plus fixed capital and equipment) or spread over multiple operating periods by means of rules limiting the annual expenditure rate to, say, a rate of investment return.

Predicting Enrollment-Related Revenue

A private university must be good at predicting its tuition revenue and also its own expected costs of institutionally provided financial aid. The resulting net revenue from enrollment becomes a crucial part of the basis for annual budgeting and multiyear projections. The public university must also predict income from tuition and student fees, but in its case the proportion of total revenue is smaller. The university's prediction (and in due course, its negotiated settlement) of the state appropriation is the most significant component of expected revenues.

Student enrollment is meat and drink to the university, though—like other meat and drink—too much of it can produce pain and discomfort. The university seeks to meet both academic and social objectives in its admissions and enrollment policies. The fiscal aspects are two: enrollment produces tuition income (and in the public university is the basis for much of the state appropriation decision); and enrollment induces costs—not only the cost of providing instruction, but also other student-related costs of administration. Tuition and financial aid policies are so important that they are discussed in detail in a separate chapter, Chapter Nine.

Public universities receive an annual state appropriation to cover a major portion of their basic operating budget. Some, like the University of California, are funded under an agreement with the state government whereby nonresident tuition is applied against the approved state-funded budget. In-state residents have traditionally paid a substantial "registration fee," but this covered health services and other student services and was not to be used for academic operations. Thus, historically, the university could not utilize for academic operations the tuition revenue from enrollment and enrollment growth, but as enrollment grew, the university ordinarily expected to win expanded appropriations for operations in the annual state budgeting cycle. Severe fiscal problems from 1991 through 1994 eliminated the state's commitment to a no-tuition policy for California residents.

Other public universities operate under very different agreements with their state governments, whereby tuition revenue is expected to cover a significant portion of academic budgets. The University of Vermont has been, historically, a "high tuition" public university. The University of Michigan has "privatized" to an increasing degree, funding its budgets partly through tuition and attracting more out-of-state students whose tuition is higher.

Where the state does provide a high proportion of the operating budget, the marginal cost of each additional student—to pay for academic operations and student-related administrative services—is typically lower than the *average* (budgeted) cost; thus, the public university ordinarily gains some net fiscal advantage from enrollment growth. But enrollment grows within agreed guidelines. Most public universities have some agreement with the state on certain broad parameters: the fraction of the state's high school graduates expected to enroll; the curricula that should be offered to them; and the eventual destinations for which they should be prepared.

California's Master Plan for Higher Education, enacted in 1960 and periodically reviewed since then, provides one such agreed framework—a division of labor among three segments of public higher education: the University of California, the California State University (CSU), and the California Community Colleges system.

Differentiation of function between these three segments includes:

1. The assignment of scholarly and applied research to the university, with some recognition of research activity in the CSU
2. A mandate to the university to offer the Ph.D., with provision for joint doctorates in which CSU departments may participate
3. Authorization for undergraduate and master's degrees programs, which may be offered by both the university and the CSU campuses

Responsibility for the education of undergraduates is divided among the three public segments according to a principle of selectivity:

1. The university is obligated to provide enrollment opportunity to any high school student in the top one-eighth of the high school graduating class.
2. The CSU must provide such opportunity to anyone in the top one-third of the graduating class.
3. The community colleges must be open to anyone who possesses a high school diploma or who has turned nineteen.

When demographic trends in California result in an upsurge of prospective students, the three segments request additional "workload" budget; but in 1992–93, severe budgetary stresses prevented augmentation and in fact resulted in late budget reductions below the earlier governor's budget. Part of the gap was closed by significant tuition and fee increases. Additional fee increases were enacted for 1993–94 and 1994–95, although the legislature limited the latter increases to 10 percent.

This episode illustrates how public institutions are caught between the general expectations of educational access and the realities of fiscal constraints. These stresses, if they continue in future years, could challenge the viability of the California Master Plan. (See Rothblatt, 1992.)

Private universities confronted, in the early years of the 1990s, a challenge to maintain enrollment in the face of a nationwide decline in the number of high school graduates. Because tuition and other costs of attendance rise inexorably from year to year, adroit marketing and aggressive administration of student financial aid—including loan programs—have become critical to the maintenance of enrollment. In the latter part of the decade, demographic trends point toward greater enrollment demand for both public and private institutions.

Public universities have the general advantage that their student fees are historically lower, but state budget pressures are forcing large percentage increases. Financial aid is critical to the maintenance of enrollment and access. In addition, the public university that does not reach out vigorously to attract applicants from all community segments is not doing its job. "Diversity and excellence" has become a political necessity as well as a catchy, ambiguous slogan. Admission standards become a focus of intense pressure and controversy, as potential applicants from some minority communities have to overcome deficiencies in early education in order to compete successfully as university students.

The best-known public university campuses cannot accept more than a fraction of qualified applicants; if more is done to accommodate members of one group, the members of another are seen to pay a price. The intertwined problems of admissions policies, financial aid policies, and academic assistance to new students are even more of a challenge to the public than to the private university, because of the political pressures that are brought to bear on the public institutions.

Increased financial aid to students is an important element of growth in the cost structure of many institutions. Many private institutions that have increased their incomes by raising tuition have felt obligated to devote significant portions of the new revenue to financial aid for needy students. And many have accepted new financial responsibilities for minority students who were formerly underrepresented in their enrollments. It has been of great importance to American society that our colleges and universities, both public and private, undertake these new responsibilities. But their discretionary resources are clearly not adequate to the job of redressing deep imbalances in the previous distribution of parental income, assets, and educational opportunity.

There is a strong case for federal finance to meet this need. Congressional action in 1992 appeared to signal recognition of the issue, but federal budget problems may well continue to prevent full funding.

That this is not a new dilemma is exemplified by Jenny and Wynn's 1971 analysis of financial trends at a group of private liberal arts colleges over the period 1960–1968. Both their original study and their 1972 follow-up underscore the importance of financial aid as a growing component of institutional expenditure (Jenny and Wynn, 1971, 1972a, 1972b). For the full decade of the 1960s, Jenny and Wynn report that the colleges had compound annual rates of income growth per student of 6.4 percent, while the rate of growth in expense per student was 6.8 percent. Thus, for the decade, the gap was 0.4 percent per year. Jenny and Wynn found that student aid had the most rapid growth rate of all the expense categories. The authors also calculated the year-to-year marginals— the changes in income and expense—and found that for 1960–1961 about eight cents of each dollar of extra tuition and fee income went to student aid, whereas for 1969–1970, thirty-two cents went to student aid.

Marketing the University

If managing the university is a concept repugnant to many in academic life, *marketing* the university may well be beyond the pale.

Yet a university does need to determine what it offers to its various constituencies, and it may need to provide information, signals, and persuasive messages to influence the way each constituency perceives it. The university seeks to attract students in particular categories. Numerous market segments of undergraduates can be identified, including:

- High-ability, high-income students
- High-ability, low-income students, both minority and nonminority
- Children of the university's alumni
- Students from other geographical regions and from foreign countries
- "Returners" (older students who come back to education to finish a degree program or prepare for new careers)
- Other recent high school graduates
- Transfer students

Patterns of college choice and the reasons for choices differ among these groups. Each segment of the market can be studied to ascertain its members' preferences and perceptions regarding formal education and its meaning for them, lifestyle aspects of college or university choice, and the attractiveness and reputation of each university in the potential student's choice set. Then, the university needs to determine what channels of communication can be used to reach the members of each market segment, and what their respective costs are. When the relevant segments are understood and prioritized, the marketing budget must be decided.

The aura of high reputation surrounding a major university is an important marketing feature. Of course, reputation has many dimensions, and members of different segments perceive and evaluate the standing of the university on each reputational dimension in different ways and according to different standards. It is generally believed that undergraduate students react most strongly to the glamour and lifestyle aspects of an institution and to the availability of a wide range of curricular options. Many undergraduate students do seek to evaluate both the quality of the formal education they can obtain and the prospects of future advantage from it: employment opportunities and prospects for successful application for graduate study in a field of their choice.

The prospective graduate student is likely to take a sharper, more instrumental view: will this professional degree program, or this program of doctoral studies, enable me to enter a rewarding professional career? The research reputation of the faculty and the placement successes of the program are likely to be influential. Therefore, the prospective student tends to rely on published reputational ratings and the opinions of trusted advisers in choosing a graduate program.

Students in the United States normally apply to several institutions or specific programs, and they often visit one or more of their highest-rated options. U.S. universities thus live in a milieu of competition—for the highest-quality academic (and sometimes, athletic) talent; for adequate numbers of undergraduate and graduate students in each program area; and for the most promising members of underrepresented minorities, to enhance the diversity of the student body and meet the university's felt obligation to contribute to wider opportunity throughout American society. This element of competition distinguishes the U.S. university system from those in countries such as France and the Netherlands, where students traditionally enroll in the nearest university.

The university must also market itself to faculty and prospective faculty, to administrative staff, to research granting agencies, and to corporate, foundation, and individual donors. Again, these segments differ considerably in the reputational dimensions they consider important. They must be reached through varied channels of communication.

University reputation in faculty circles is partly general to the institution and in greater part associated with the scholarly reputation of the particular academic discipline or specialty in which a faculty member is interested. Institutional reputation is enhanced when a faculty member wins a Nobel Prize or other highly visible honor, and when the university can claim that the scholarly opportunities it offers to faculty and advanced students are superior. Among the major considerations are faculty salaries, library resources, funding of research programs, and the quality of graduate students and postdoctoral fellows.

Revenue from Extramural Research Grants and Contracts

A university's research establishment depends crucially on extramural grants and contracts. Enhancing and predicting this revenue source is significant to the entire budgeting process. We discuss the organization and conduct of university research functions in Chapter Twelve. Here, we concentrate on the revenue-generating aspects.

Research agencies and foundations are not indifferent to general signals of university reputation. They may also be influenced by the university's performance in meeting contract obligations on large grants and contracts and by the relative ease or difficulty of dealing with the institution (as distinct from the individual faculty member). Peer-reviewed grants for basic scientific research have historically been of greatest importance to the research universities. However, alarming tendencies exist toward politically inspired research allocations. Examples of this were the decision (later canceled by Congress) to locate the Superconducting Supercollider project in Texas, despite doubts about the quality of scientific leadership there; the award of a seismological research institute to the State University of Buffalo, although major academic research in the field had for many years been concentrated elsewhere; and the shift of the federally funded Institute for Electro-Magnetic Research from the Massachusetts Institute of Technology (MIT) to the

University of Florida, nudged by the State of Florida's commitment of $58 million in special funds. (See, on the last of these, "Cracks in the Ivory Tower," 1992.) In the 1993–94 federal appropriations bills, more than $700 million in research grants were allocated by congressional earmarking action outside the peer review and panel review system.

Federal funds provided about $11.1 billion for basic research in fiscal year 1991, when total spending on academic research and development was $17.2 billion (National Science Board, 1991, appendix table 5-1, p. 347). State and local government, industry, and institutions' own funds supplied the rest. The growth of very large research establishments between 1950 and the 1980s made U.S. research universities the world leaders in basic and applied science. As this growth abates, however, the adjustments to static or declining federal funding are painful. Big-science projects are taking away part of what otherwise might be allocated to university research. Declines in appropriations for the Department of Energy and the Department of Defense are also likely to reduce their historically substantial support of university research.

The story of a relative decline of U.S. leadership in R&D spending and performance is presented in detail in *Science and Engineering Indicators* from the National Science Board (1991). While the United States remains well ahead of its international competitors in absolute terms (figure O-2, p. 4), the percentage gains of Japan and Germany are impressive, and their R&D spending as a percentage of gross national product has surpassed that of the United States.

A university's success in attracting research support via the competitive, peer-reviewed mechanism depends on the quality, reputation, and initiative of its leading scientists in each field. The very importance of extramural funding accentuates their role and increases the institutional value of the "star" professor as principal investigator and research organizer. In turn, the research leader has high leverage within the university and can demand building space, budget support, and even special powers to control junior faculty appointments. (It is said that the head of MIT's Whitehead Institute exacted the right to control a number of faculty appointments in the biological sciences, which evoked concerns about university governance among some members of that university's faculty.)

A more subtle but potentially more serious problem than the number of federal research dollars is a shift in the perspective of federal research-funding agencies. Hannah Gray, former president of the University of Chicago, is quoted as observing that universities, instead of being research partners with the National Science Foundation and other agencies, have become vendors, thereby having to submit to "the greater centralization and regulation that accompany the federal funding system" ("Cracks in the Ivory Tower," 1992, p. 1199).

The quest for research support has also led to alliances between universities and major U.S. and multinational corporations. MIT entered into a long-term funding agreement with the Du Pont Company. Massachusetts General Hospital, affiliated with Harvard Medical School, accepted from Hoechst AG, the German chemical/pharmaceutical combine, funding of about $18 million for a new building and a support arrangement amounting to $10 million per year over five years. In return, Hoechst gained rights to future patents; it will also have the right to place its resident scientists in the laboratory and will have first-look privileges on research results prior to publication. (See Balderston, 1990.)

Carnegie-Mellon University's former president, Richard M. Cyert, is president of the Carnegie-Bosch Institute, endowed and sponsored by Robert Bosch Industrietreuhand AG, of Germany. The mission is to support research and continuing education in industrial management. High-technology topics are pursued under the guidance of the faculty of the Graduate School of Industrial Administration. Bosch provides a resident financial officer for the institute and has rights to any patents generated via its research support.

Alliances of this kind have the advantage of positive linkage in applied science between university researchers and the executives and research leaders of industrial corporations. Problems and risks are also present. Will these arrangements weaken the independence of the university as an institution or the intellectual freedom of the research investigator? Will the research agenda be modified in inappropriate ways through the influence of industrial funding and relationships? No easy answers have appeared on the horizon so far.

Donors to the University

Each university has a base of individual donors: alumni in particular, but also community leaders who become interested in the institution. Private universities have historically relied heavily on the donor base, both for capital gifts and bequests to endowment and for contributions to an annual fund. Princeton's annual fund, representing unrestricted current support, garnered $21.5 million in 1991–92 (*Princeton Today*, 1992, p. 3).

Public universities, facing constrained state funding, are increasingly active among potential donors. Presidents and trustees, deans and directors of development and of alumni affairs, and some influential faculty members engage in extensive cultivation of alumni and of key individuals in the donor base. The University of California, Berkeley, exceeded an ambitious goal of $400 million, and the University of California, Los Angeles, is engaged in its second major capital campaign of the last ten years, for about the same amount.

Fund-raising has become a highly professional activity. Both annual giving and capital campaigns have required development of extensive databases of alumni and other potential donors. A capital campaign is typically designed after substantial preliminary research on key donors and identification of the most salable projects. Presidents and other key fund-raisers engage in long-term cultivation of major donors, for the following purposes:

- To solidify cordial and loyal ties to the institution
- To ascertain and shape the specific interests of the donor, so that an eventual gift will be of a size and nature that will contribute strongly to a university goal while at the same time satisfying the donor
- To head off, if possible, a decline of interest or a diversion of attention to some other philanthropic activity

Two endowment campaigns launched by private universities in the early 1990s set themselves particularly ambitious goals: both Harvard and Princeton announced campaigns for $2 billion.

Responses of the Public University to Dwindling State Support

A survey conducted by the American Council on Education (ACE) in spring 1992 found that almost 50 percent of U.S. public universities expected no increase, or a decline, in their operating budgets in 1992–93, as compared with the previous year ("Cracks in the Ivory Tower," 1992, p. 1197). By contrast, only 14 percent of the private institutions surveyed faced static or declining budgets. In the ACE survey of 1993, 30 percent of the doctoral universities reported a midyear cut, and 50 percent of them expected budget cuts in 1993–94 (El-Khawas, 1993, p. 28).

State governments all across the United States faced increasingly difficult fiscal circumstances in the early 1990s: increased costs and expanded demands for state-financed social services while state revenues were reduced by recessionary economic forces and by "no tax" political sentiment. Political bargaining over the size and composition of the state operating appropriation has intensified, and long-agreed formulas for budgeting and enrollment targets have eroded in many states.

Public universities have responded to their budget problems by cutting and pruning on the expenditure side, and by raising student tuition and fees. The 1992 ACE survey also disclosed short-term reductions in building and equipment plans and library acquisitions, as well as increases of class size and freezes on faculty hiring. Long-term impacts are expected to be similar, with a buildup in deferred maintenance, equipment obsolescence, and slower growth of enrollment and faculty.

Rising student fees, even though partly offset by increased financial aid, will push public universities closer to a "privatized" status. Public institutions can still, however, offer lower attendance cost than private ones. In addition, public and private universities are seeking to engage more actively in revenue-generating activities and programs.

Creating Revenue: Self-Funded and Income-Producing Activities

Traditional self-funded activities, which are intended to take in enough revenue to cover or more than cover their operating costs (and sometimes debt service as well) are exemplified by the student residence hall system and the parking system. Football and basketball, the major revenue earners in intercollegiate athletics, usually carry the expectation (or the hope) that they will earn enough net revenue to cover operating costs of the other intercollegiate sports. However, a great deal of money is also raised from alumni booster clubs to support such activities. University teaching hospitals take in huge patient revenues, but they also have higher costs than many competing hospitals because of greater reliance on advanced tests and procedures. For this reason, medical schools in public universities sometimes receive patient income subsidies as part of their state-supported budgets.

Potential producers of net income include:

- Continuing education courses and seminars
- Service activities for industry and community organizations

- Library and information services, as a subordinate activity of universities' extensive library collections and databases
- Aggressively administered patent programs and R&D alliances with industry

Universities now increasingly seek opportunities to establish programs that will be self-supporting or even produce net revenues to contribute to other academic purposes. At some business schools and engineering schools, special continuing education seminars and programs are contributing mightily to support budgets.

Industrial liaison programs, which give industrial companies access to university research in progress, in return for a fee, are now offered by many leading institutions. These programs can also draw the member companies and the university into service relationships, applied research contracts, and eventual sharing of the economic value of new technology.

A broader institutional strategy is to establish a business park or a series of joint ventures and "incubator" activities. Rensselaer Polytechnic Institute was one of the first to establish a new-venture incubator. Stanford established an industrial park in the early 1970s, initially motivated by the need to earn a return on land that the Leland Stanford Trust required the university to retain in permanent title. The resulting success of long-term leases by growing high-technology companies increased Stanford's visibility as a leading center of applied science research. It also fostered symbiotic linkages between the university and these companies.

University patent offices have also grown in professionalism and aggressiveness, seeking to capitalize on the potential economic value of the flow of research results. Typically, the royalties are shared between the inventor and the institution.

Chapter Nine

Tuition, Fees, and Financial Aid

The university's tuition is the price it charges students for their academic program. The student (or the student's parents) normally make a net payment that is less than the posted price, because of grants of financial aid, which can be regarded as "discounts." Some universities also impose compulsory student fees, and these add to the net payment. Average costs in four-year public institutions were approximately $8,000 in 1993; costs in private institutions were approximately $17,000. The student's total cost of attendance includes room and board, books, transportation, and various incidentals, as well as tuition, compulsory fees and optional fees. This cost and the financial status of the student (and if the student is financially dependent on parents, *their* financial status) are analyzed to determine the components and total amount of the aid to be offered. Usually, the offer includes loans as well as grants-in-aid, which complicates the interpretation of the "net price" that the student is asked to pay.

Several major issues confront the university in managing its tuition policy and the consequent stream of revenue that tuition and fees generate. Whatever course is followed must adhere to federal law and regulations controlling federal grants-in-aid (Pell grants) and federally guaranteed student loans, and state laws and regulations governing student financial aid programs at the state level.

Federal Student Aid Programs

The federal framework of financial aid policy is a compromise. In part, it is directed toward ensuring access to undergraduate higher education regardless of the income level of the student and the student's parents. But under the 1992 reauthorization of the Higher Education Act, it is also designed to relieve the problems faced by middle-class families in financing their children's higher education ("The Higher Education Amendments of 1992," 1992).

All graduate students are considered financially independent or, as the terminology used to say, "emancipated" (from parents). They are not eligible for the federal Pell grants, but they can obtain substantial subsidized and unsubsidized loans.

Parental income and assets are regarded in public policy as a major source of financing for the undergraduate student, and the 1992 reauthorization retains twenty-four as the minimum age for an undergraduate's financial independence but makes it virtually impossible to prove self-sufficiency after that age unless the student is married, a parent, a veteran, or an orphan. Because of these tightened restrictions, many students who had been able to claim independent status in prior years (and therefore qualify for a larger package of aid) became dependent for 1993–94.

Each student who wishes to establish eligibility for financial aid is required to fill out the Free Application for Federal Student Aid (FAFSA), which under the 1992 reauthorization consolidates all of the standards for need determination and is processed directly by the U.S. Department of Education. The student must be a U.S. national or an eligible noncitizen. The student budget—outlays for tuition and fees, books and incidentals, and living costs—is the starting point of need determination. It should be noted that the full-time student has a major implicit cost of attendance that the student budget does not include: the wage income forgone during the academic year. Economists' studies of the returns to higher education have, quite rightly, included estimates of income forgone along with estimates of the outlays that are in the student budget, and it is this total cost per student year that enters into economists' calculation of the size of the educational investment. (See Hansen and Weisbrod, 1969, p. 15; also, Solmon and Taubman, 1973, pp. 18–22.)

The FAFSA Self-Help Expectation (SHE) includes student earnings, savings, and outside scholarships, plus the amount that is normally to be borrowed in federal loan programs (these are the Perkins loans, at 5 percent interest, and the Stafford subsidized loans, with interest pegged to the U.S. Treasury bill rate). For 1993–94, for example, the Self-Help Expectation at Berkeley as determined by the campus financial aid office began at $5,500. The parents' contribution is computed from the FAFSA as a function of income, age, assets, the number of dependents, and the number of family members in college. Here, the 1992 reauthorization helped middle-income families by excluding the value of home equity and the value of a family-owned farm; this change broadened eligibility for both grant and loan programs.

If the student seeks to borrow an amount that exceeds officially determined "need" but that falls under the annual borrowing limit for Stafford subsidized loans ($2,625 for freshmen and higher amounts after that) he or she may borrow through the Stafford unsubsidized loan program, and parents of dependent children may borrow through Parent Loans for Students (PLUS) at unsubsidized rates to bridge any remaining gap between the student budget and the amount of the student aid award. This option is especially important to parents of students attending private universities and to upper-income parents who do not qualify for grant or loan subsidies.

The Pell grant is computed from the need determination, with an authorized ceiling of $3,700 for 1993–94 but (because the congressional appropriation was limited) a de facto ceiling of $2,300.

Some states, too, provide grants-in-aid, especially to assist with tuition and fee costs. If provided, such grants reduce the amount of residual need that must be borrowed. State financial aid programs supplement the federal system, and they provide a greater amount of assistance to students attending private institutions than to those enrolled in public ones.

This framework provides full access to undergraduate education to any student who is willing to incur substantial debt. It also ensures to institutions the revenues necessary to meet the costs of academic programs and to pay for room and board in college dormitories when students choose to live in them. Significant increases in tuition and in the other costs of attendance do increase the level of concern of students and parents, but this comprehensive financial aid system enables colleges and universities to increase tuition and dormitory charges (and thus the student budget) by some reasonable amount each year without serious resistance.

Furthermore, the system of financial aid to undergraduates is comprehensive enough to substantially reduce the amount of institutional contributions needed, except for the scholarships that are financed from the income of restricted endowments. Nevertheless, universities do use large amounts of institutional funds for undergraduate grant aid and to finance fellowships and grants for graduate students—particularly, doctoral students of exceptional talent.

Issues of Institutional Financial Aid and Tuition Policy

Universities face a number of complicated issues in their administration of financial aid and in setting tuition levels.

Optimizing the Use of Federal Grants and Loans

The federal financial aid system is complicated in its procedures, and the university's first obligation to students is to administer applications, awards, and payments at a high level of efficiency. Annual changes in tuition rates, state budgets, and federal appropriations are often made with little lead time. One university completed the calculation of each eligible applicant's 1993–94 financial aid package in May 1993 only to find that last-minute changes in its budgets and fees, by state action, would require recalculation of many thousands of awards.

From the student's point of view, grants are always better than loans, and subsidized loans are always better than unsubsidized ones. Financial aid administration should therefore be directed toward the goal of maximizing use of the preferred aid components. The greatly broadened opportunity to borrow at unsubsidized rates does raise new issues for financial aid counselors. They need to reassure the reluctant student that necessary borrowing is a valid option, but at the same time, they should coach students to restrain their living expenses rather than incur excessive indebtedness.

The university also helps students, and helps itself, by maximizing its provision of federally subsidized work-study opportunities. The federal share of work-study was 50 percent for 1993–94. On-campus part-time work that is *related to the student's academic goals* reinforces persistence to the degree, according to some research findings, and work-study is a major means of financing such experience.

Tuition and Aid Policies in Relation to Size and Composition of the Student Body

The university has recognized objectives for enrollment size, academic selectivity, quality of the student body, gender ratio, ethnic and geographical diversity, and other characteristics. The institution is located in a particular academic marketplace, with other institutions competing against it to attract enrollment. Tuition and financial aid policies can facilitate or impede attainment of the institution's enrollment objectives.

The university's attracting power for undergraduate students depends on its reputation for general academic strength, perceptions of the quality of its student life, and the prospects either for successful career preparation (as in engineering, science, or business curricula) or for eventual entry into graduate school. The university also attracts students to its graduate professional schools and its academic doctoral programs.

An elite private university attracts undergraduate students from a regional or nationwide pool, whereas many public universities are limited by state policy to a predominantly in-state population. The strong private and public universities attract graduate enrollment from both national and international sources.

Success in marketing the institution is achieved if prospective students know about it, are attracted to it, have a good sense of what they would experience there (so that they will not face disappointments and become dropouts), and feel themselves well-matched to the academic and other demands of the university. Graduate students, with firmer and more specific goals and greater maturity, are likely to know themselves better than do undergraduates; they also have more refined and secure methods of evaluating their choice of institution. Nevertheless, both graduate and undergraduate applicants sometimes react to aspects of a university that faculty members might consider grossly irrelevant—its perceived lifestyle features and ambience, its climate, and (in the case of undergraduates) its reputation in intercollegiate athletics.

A college or university located in a strong and growing enrollment market and with a reputation for academic excellence and high amenity is bound to have a large number of applications for admission relative to the number of available places. It can be highly selective, offering admission to a small fraction of its applicants and expecting a high "show" rate—the rate at which those offered admission will actually enroll. Thus, tuition can be higher than that charged by nearby institutions, and only a small portion of institutional resources may need to be spent to bolster offers of financial aid.

The demand for undergraduate admission to an institution can be represented as a matrix whose columns show the home origins of applicants and whose rows display their academic qualifications. Entering a year's applicants into the cells of the matrix reveals the profile of the applicant pool the university has attracted. With accompanying data on the number and qualifications of graduating high school seniors in each locality, the institution can calculate its percentage "draw"—and therefore its attracting power—in each cell.

An institution facing highly elastic student demand will find that a small increase in its tuition, while competing institutions hold theirs unchanged, causes applicant numbers to shrink drastically. If most of the application demand is within a small local radius, competitive interaction with a very few other institutions may be critical. On the other hand, a university with national visibility and applicant interest faces more diffused competitive pressures from other institutions. It tends to identify as its competitors for enrollment those other elite institutions, wherever located, that offer similar qualities and types of programs and are similarly selective.

Selective colleges and universities seek a share of the highest-quality entering undergraduate students, as measured by high school academic performance and evidence of leadership and by scores on the Scholastic Aptitude Tests (SATs) and American College Tests (ACTs). A few universities and colleges offer some merit-based scholarships to attract these students, but this is an exception to the general commitment of U.S. institutions to administer financial aid exclusively according to need-based criteria. Institutions do, however, compete to attract outstanding minority students as part of their commitment to student diversity. Aggressive diversity policies involve setting goals for minority participation that stretch the ability of the institution to attract sufficient numbers of minority applicants at its usual eligibility standards. Affirmative action guidelines then help to determine what allowances should be made in order to offer admission to the desired numbers of such applicants.

Competition among graduate schools for outstanding doctoral students is unashamedly aggressive and is national and international in scope. Recipients of "portable" fellowships from the National Science Foundation, the Andrew Mellon Foundation, and other major foundations are wooed vigorously. Other potential high-quality candidates are offered university fellowships, tuition reductions or waivers, and other components of an aid package. Some doctoral programs promise continued financial support, including research assistantships and teaching assistantships, for the four or five years that are the likely minimums needed to complete the doctorate. This intensive competition indicates the significance of attracting the most outstanding graduate students to sustain academic excellence and maintain the high reputation of the university.

Tuition in Relation to Average Cost of Instruction

A private university that has little endowment income to spare may perforce have to set its tuition to cover nearly all of the "full cost" per student of instruction and institutional operation. Full cost is calculated by dividing the total operating expenditure budget by total enrollment. Alternatively, the university may set the fee per course or per credit hour instead of per year, to make allowance for significant part-time enrollment.

Elite private universities do have endowed scholarships, and they also allocate endowment funds and other funds to support academic departmental budgets. The average tuition can then be set at a reduced percentage of average full cost; the typical percentage has been 75.

Public universities, on the other hand, have had a historic commitment to zero tuition or very low fees, going back to the land-grant origins of the leading state institutions. More recently, many of them have faced financial pressures from their legislatures that resulted over time in increased student fees. As of 1993, average fees for resident students were about 30–35 percent of the average cost of instruction at these public universities, the rest of the cost being largely defrayed by state operating appropriation. (It should also be noted that the public university has lower average cost of instruction than does the elite private university; the differences are due to the latter's considerably lower student-faculty ratio and to the former's much higher enrollment size, which permits capture of some economies of scale. Furthermore, elite private universities invest in amenities in order to attract full-pay students from upper-income families.)

A public university with a low-tuition or no-tuition policy collects no money from students to contribute to "educational and general" costs—that is, costs of departmental instruction and research, and costs of academic support. However, it has been argued that students could properly be charged mandatory fees for those student services that the public university provides. Over time, as public universities have faced increasing budgetary pressures from their state governments, the definition of "student services" has broadened in order to justify increased fees, while at the same time the claim is maintained that such fees are not "tuition"—that is, not part of the cost of instruction. The broadening sometimes stretches to the breaking point; the University of California reclassified its entire library budget as part of student services for 1992–93, in order to fund library costs from the greatly increased student fees associated with the fiscal crisis of the state government.

While the level of public university tuition is mainly determined by history and by recent financial pressures within the state, there is no well-established method by which a state can rationally compute the level of tuition as a percentage of the cost of instruction. If a state expects to lose a high percentage of its state university graduates to migration, it should presumably set a high tuition. On the other hand, if the state has experienced shortages of labor in key growth industries, it could reasonably set a low tuition, especially to students who could be expected to stay after graduation. A state that loses very few of its university graduates, educates most of its own talented residents for well-paying employment, and has a progressive income tax structure can expect, over time, to recover the cost of the university education it provides. Furthermore, if its public universities are of high quality, their attractiveness improves the climate for recruiting out-of-state scientists, engineers, and other advanced professionals to the high-technology industries that states tend to favor. (See Balderston, 1974a.) But arguments such as these have not been developed in such a way as to provide a full rationale for any particular level of public university tuition.

Relations between public and private universities in the same state or the same market are another issue. The tuition price differential between the private universities and the best of the state universities has become a point of contention as the dollar spread has increased. Private universities have feared loss of enrollment, and especially loss of enrollment of full-pay students who would not be eligible for large financial aid packages. States vary tremendously in the percentage of their students attending public universities. In states in the Northeast and Middle Atlantic regions where the percentage of private university attendance is high—often, 50 percent or more—the public-private differential is lower than in states such as California and other western states that have a much lower private-university enrollment percentage. Furthermore, states with a high percentage of private university enrollment, such as New York, have experimented with large-scale subventions to students attending private institutions, presumably in order to help the private institutions maintain their enrollment levels.

Pegging the amount of tuition at some percentage of the average cost of instruction would of course result in increases in tuition as the cost of instruction rises over time. (If budget cuts in years of financial distress *reduced* the average cost of instruction, tuition based on a fixed percentage of instructional cost would actually fall!) If the initial percentage were 100, then a one-dollar increase in costs would immediately (or with a one-year lag) translate into a one-dollar increase in tuition, *unless the institution found that it had to take into account the sensitivity of the student to the price of attendance—that is, the price elasticity of demand for attending that institution.* (We return to this issue of price sensitivity in the discussion below.) However, a tuition set at 30 percent of the cost of instruction would imply that for each one-dollar increase in instructional cost, the institution would increase tuition by 30 cents, leaving 70 cents to be covered by other sources of revenue. This is hardly a strong "cost-push" impetus to raise tuition. In fact, if the Consumer Price Index (CPI) were increasing 5 percent per year and the average cost of instruction rose by 10 percent per year (a high figure, perhaps), the tuition rate would increase by 30 percent of 10 percent, or 3 percent per year, or *less than the rate of increase of the CPI*.

The political agonies of public universities in many states during the early 1990s arose from the tendency to increase student fees by quite large dollar amounts and very large percentage amounts each year—changes forced by the severe fiscal difficulties in many state governments. Thus, tuition as a percentage of average cost of instruction was increasing rapidly.

Determination of Target Net Revenue from Tuition

The institution's net revenue from tuition can be defined as: gross tuition revenue, minus tuition waivers funded from discretionary sources and unrestricted institutional funds that are utilized for student financial aid. (Most universities have certain restricted endowments, the income from which can be used only for student fellowships, scholarships, and grants-in-aid. Because of these restrictions against use for any other purpose, such funds would not be counted in the calculation of the net revenue from tuition because these restricted funds cannot flow into the institution's general funds.)

Many public universities charge nonresidents a special tuition approximating the average cost of education, but this revenue is often simply subtracted from the amount of the state appropriation for operating budget. This is another of the areas of political bargaining between the state government and the public higher education system over tuition and other revenues.

A private institution having no endowment or financial reserves, no service contract or research income, and no gifts, grants, or subsidies, would perforce have to budget for a target net revenue from tuition equal to its expected operating expenditures, plus perhaps a small cushion for contingencies. If it faced an elastic demand for enrollment, it would have to control its operating expenditures very carefully, or it would risk losses of applications and enrollment.

A strong and visible private research university could anticipate a less elastic demand from applicants, which would imply that it had more latitude to increase tuition. On the other hand, its non-tuition revenues, including endowment income, extramural research grants and overhead, and income from services rendered would all enable it to limit tuition to a lower percentage of total operating expenditures. Private colleges and universities facing relatively inelastic demand did become accustomed to substantial annual rises in tuition and fees, and for many years these were greater than the rate of increase of the Consumer Price Index. Gradually, the fraction of the U.S. college-going population enrolled in private (or "independent") institutions has fallen, as access to public higher education has widened and as costs of attendance have galloped ahead.

Antitrust Implications of Interuniversity Financial Aid Agreements

In 1992, the financial aid practices of universities attracted the attention of federal antitrust monitors, which added a curious fillip to the issues of public policy and student aid. The U.S. Department of Justice brought a civil suit against the Massachusetts Institute of Technology, claiming that MIT had violated federal prohibitions against price-fixing. Federal District Judge Louis C. Bechtle found MIT guilty (DePalma, 1992).

MIT and the eight Ivy League universities had been members of the Overlap Group, which was organized to share information about the financial status of applicants and their parents and to apply a common formula to the determination of the financial aid package that would be offered. This effectively eliminated variations among these institutions in the amount of aid that an applicant could receive. The other eight universities signed a consent decree agreeing to discontinue this practice, but MIT elected to defend its policy in federal court. The school argued that as a charitable institution, it was entitled to spread available aid funds among as many students as possible, but Judge Bechtle rejected this argument, leaving MIT vulnerable to student lawsuits that could possibly seek recovery of triple damages. The suit and the verdict shocked academic administrators. It also served as a warning that the Department of Justice might examine other practices of interuniversity cooperation, treating universities simply as economic entities that might be seen as engaging in collusion.

While the case was on appeal, MIT and the Department of Justice reached a compromise settlement.

Issues in the Design of Tuition

Tuition can be uniform, or it can be set to vary according to the costs of particular majors or academic programs. It may be cost-based or demand-based. It may even incorporate elements of progressive taxation through a sliding-scale formula. These issues are discussed here.

Uniform Versus Variable Tuition

Historically, the posted tuition at most colleges and universities is uniform for most full-time students. However, public universities are often obliged by state governments to charge a higher tuition to "nonresidents"—that is, students whose legal residence is in another state. The plausible rationale for this is that taxpayers in the state where the university is located should not be expected to subsidize the education of someone who is not a resident or (if a dependent) the child of a resident of that state.

Also, a student who is enrolled only for a fraction of a full-time course load may be charged a lower tuition, or the tuition may be set per credit hour or per course, as is often done in the extension division or other part-time programs offered by the institution.

A uniform tuition for full-time students is defended on the plausible grounds that it enables the student to choose curricula and indeed individual courses with concern only for their academic relevance and attractiveness, so that considerations of dollar cost will not enter in. During the freshman and sophomore years of college, when exploration of interests and preferences takes the form of sampling courses in many disciplines, it does seem likely that a uniform tuition supports and encourages such exploration among fields of knowledge. However, it is also true that the upper-division cost per student-year varies widely between one academic program or curriculum and another.

Cost accounting systems in universities are often not set up to trace the direct and induced costs per student in different academic programs. Courses and curricula in the experimental sciences and engineering typically have high costs, however, and such fields as major foreign languages and literatures, English literature, and the major social sciences are lower in cost per student-year. Costs *per student* are of course greatly affected by the number of courses offered in a given major program and the course enrollments in that program. Thus, a low average teaching load, a low program enrollment, or a lack of constraint in the number of required and elective courses in the program results in high cost per student-year, because the total academic salaries are increased by the first and third of these factors and the faculty wage bill must be amortized over few students if the second condition prevails. Given that public resources are being used to support instruction in a public university, it is argued that the student who absorbs large amounts of these resources should pay more than the student who absorbs less. Berg and Hoenack (1987) make this argument and demonstrate some consequences of such a policy, using the University of Minnesota as a case study.

Graduate curricula are typically higher in cost per student-year than undergraduate programs. Advanced instruction in experimental sciences requires laboratories with exotic equipment; in non-experimental fields, research libraries are needed, and often, access to other advanced materials and field study. In addition, average enrollment in graduate courses and seminars is typically much lower than in undergraduate courses. Thus, one might expect that cost-based tuition for graduate curricula would result in a large variety of tuition levels. Berg and Hoenack state, however, that in the academic fields, the laboratory sciences have high average enrollment per course, which more or less offsets their higher cost per course offering. Graduate tuition at Minnesota was therefore made uniform for academic fields. Professional school curricula, however, were separated, and differential tuitions were established for them. An interesting political counterpressure *against* cost-based tuition came from the health professions, which succeeded in getting support for the "capping" of their tuitions (Berg and Hoenack, 1987, table 3, p. 294).

Berg and Hoenack do point out that such fields as law and business management have high enrollment demand and can therefore tolerate levels of tuition at a higher-than-average percentage of instructional costs. This brings us to the issue of tuition pricing that takes demand specifically into account.

Demand-Based Tuition

Our previous discussion of the university's desired profile of student enrollment, and the relation of that profile to tuition and financial aid policies, described the general framework of competitive interaction among institutions. Here, we focus on specific demand-related features of tuition policy. Berg and Hoenack point out that entering freshmen, and lower-division students generally, display a more elastic demand for attendance than do students at more advanced levels. They claim that the University of Minnesota successfully predicted the size of undergraduate enrollment at the main

Twin Cities campus by taking into account various differentials in attendance cost (such as travel expenses) and other factors. Berg and Hoenack argue that it would be unwise to set different tuition levels for lower-division students in different curricula. The first years of study are years of exploration and uncertainty, and tuition policy should not discourage such exploration.

Specific demand-related adjustments become quite plausible for those graduate professions—medicine, law, business management, and some fields in engineering—that have historically provided assurances of high career income. At a private university, these professional degree programs and the faculty involved in them may even become financially autonomous. When applicant demand is strong, a "market-based" tuition policy may be designed to capture an amount of operating revenue that, combined with endowment income, research grants, and miscellaneous revenues, will sustain the professional school.

A market-based tuition policy may need to be adjusted for objectives of enrollment quality, size, and composition. Special financial aid offers to minority and female candidates may be necessary to attain diversity objectives and to offset the aversion of low-income students to heavy reliance on loans. Some programs in engineering (especially graduate programs) do not attract sufficient numbers of highly qualified domestic candidates, and they rely increasingly on foreign applicants. The same problem often occurs in doctoral programs in the sciences, where graduate students from other countries earn the majority of Ph.D. degrees in some fields.

Public universities historically maintained low-tuition policies for graduate professions and the doctorate, but there is now pressure for a larger graduate tuition differential or for specific, large tuition differentials in the most sought-after graduate professions. The university then faces the important issue of determining what allocation of general budgetary resources to make to the program that is earning significant tuition income. A few public universities even seek to "privatize" their law schools and business schools—that is, make them autonomous and more or less self-supporting—

but it is not clear what should be the terms of accounting and academic separation, and what policy adjustments should apply to the privatized program in a public university setting.

One plausible lower limit of the "tax" that the autonomous professional school could be asked to pay to the campus as a whole would be its imputed share of campus overhead services: library services (over and beyond its own specialized library), computing services, accounting, building and grounds (usage and maintenance), personnel management, contract and grant administration, and campus security. Elaborate cost accounting to trace one school's appropriate share of each of these might not be worth the candle, but the principle is clear: the autonomous academic unit could be asked to bear its share of general overhead. On the other hand, the autonomous unit might also be providing some services to students, faculty, and administrative units elsewhere on the campus, and could therefore request recognition of the value of these as offsets against overhead contributions that are asked of it.

In a different category is recognition of the costs and values of student cross-enrollments between the autonomous unit and the rest of the campus. An issue of academic policy is whether to encourage or discourage cross-enrollment, and one would normally suppose that students should not be discouraged from seeking out the sources of teaching capability that serve them best. However, complications do exist: whether, for example, the course credits earned are to be recognized in the student's specific curriculum, and whether overloads of enrollment in particular courses may occur when students from other programs seek to enroll in popular courses in the high-tuition program.

The "balance of payments" between the autonomous unit and the rest of the campus can be reflected in appropriate fund transfers at some level of accuracy. However, the institution faces the broader policy challenge of determining the value contributed to the campus by the autonomous unit (implying that it could qualify for some implicit subsidy) and the value contributed by the campus to the viability of the autonomous unit (implying that some "tax" beyond those already discussed might be justified). In view of these qualitative considerations, it may be expected that the campus administration and the dean of the autonomous unit will negotiate a commonsense bargain over net payments in one direction or the other.

A multicampus public university system also faces an additional dimension of demand: some of its campuses may be much more popular than others. Even though the minimum standards of eligibility for undergraduate admission may be uniform among the campuses, some may receive four or five applications for each available enrollment place while others struggle to meet enrollment targets. Setting higher fees at the campuses that are in greater demand might be criticized as discriminatory against applicants from the local "drawing" radius, who may seek to enroll in the nearest campus in order to save money by living at home with their parents. But such applicants are likely to be a small percentage of the total applicant flow and could be accommodated with some admission preference. There could then be a rational case for charging higher fees at the popular campus, and a market-like reallocation of application demand would help to keep the system as a whole in better equilibrium. However, significant campus-by-campus variations in student fees might prove difficult to defend politically, especially if the fees are ostensibly based on costs of student services. The campuses with high enrollment demand are also likely to want to keep any differential fee income to finance their own unmet budgetary needs, rather than sharing it among other campuses of the system. Again, the eventual disposition of such fee income would be a subject of negotiation between campus and systemwide administrators, within a fairly wide zone of indeterminacy.

Sliding-Scale Tuition Based on Parents' Income

During the California fiscal crisis of the early 1990s, when large increases in fees for public higher education provoked great controversy, State Senator Tom Hayden and others proposed a "sliding scale" fee structure that would exempt students from the lowest-income families and require fee payments at increasing percentages of higher incomes. Such a fee structure would be similar in effect to a progressive income tax, except that it would be paid only by parents of currently attending students. It would also give students of high-income parents a stronger incentive to choose private higher education.

The irony of this proposal, seemingly a populist "winner," is that it would double the effects of a financial aid system that already awards the most dollars and ascribes the highest percentage of "need" to low-income students and requires high-income students to pay the full cost of attendance or borrow a portion of that cost at market rates. When the low-income student now enrolls in a public institution of higher education, the federal grant-in-aid pays a portion of the cost, including tuition, and other aid and loan programs pay most of the rest. Thus, the real effect of the "sliding scale" proposal would be to reduce federal aid payments and shrink the budgetary support that public institutions receive from student fee revenues. Administering a sliding-scale tuition would also require that every student (including many who do not now apply for financial aid) submit data of family income and circumstances sufficient for a determination of the applicable amount of tuition.

The Role of Loan Programs

A student might, in principle, pay the costs of attendance by borrowing at market rates, accruing the interest due during the years of attendance, and then repaying interest and principal from his or her (presumably higher) earnings stream after entering the workforce as a college graduate. If the individual is held to capture the entire eventual benefit of the higher education investment, incurring loans for the full cost of the education and then repaying interest and principal later could be justified as a "human capital" investment.

For a portion of their costs of education, millions of U.S. students do exactly this, but government guarantees assist them in gaining access to the capital market from which they would otherwise be excluded, for lack of collateral and a credit rating. An *unsubsidized loan* is at a market rate of interest, adjusted for risk of default, and entails full accrual of interest due. Elements of subsidy can enter as:

1. Below-market rates of interest
2. Forgiveness of interest during the years of attendance in higher education
3. Government guarantees of repayment, which are activated if the student defaults on loan payments

Subsidized Loan Programs and Their Rationale

Explicitly *subsidized loans* are a major component of present-day financial aid packages. Much of the subsidy takes the form of forgiveness of interest due during the years of college attendance. This is a clearly bounded and temporary commitment of government subsidy. More significant is the potential cost to the federal government of loan guarantees. The former student may escape from repayment obligations by declaring personal bankruptcy, which is easy to do in some states. Numerous scandals have occurred in the past when students were recruited into aggressively marketed vocational programs, some of them sham; resulting default rates of 50 percent or more caused the federal authorities to modify the conditions under which guaranteed loans would be granted.

Proposals for Income-Contingent Loan Programs

Students may be deterred from entering into substantial loan programs by worries that the alleged gain in earning power may not be substantial enough to provide an income margin for loan interest and amortization. To remedy this, economists have proposed an *income-contingent loan program*. The 1992 federal financial aid reauthorization bill contained provisions for this type of program, but it had not been implemented as of 1993.

The income-contingent loan is designed to provide a kind of insurance policy, in that annual payments during the years of income earning are set as a percentage of income, not a flat dollar amount of interest and amortization. Thus, if income is above expectation, more dollars are paid; if below, fewer. If the income-contingent loan program contains a large population of future income earners of varying abilities and prospects, the issuer of the loan funds (a federal agency or its surrogate) can obtain total revenues that will keep the program solvent in the long term. In the first few years, the student earns modest income and pays less than the amount that would be due on a flat-rate loan; but in later, higher-income years, the former student pays more. Borrower and lending agency share the risks on any one loan (risks of income interruption or career-long low earning power), but the program as a whole rests on the average borrower's experience. The lending agency has to find ways to finance the cash-flow deficit of the program's early years—a larger deficit than in a flat-rate program. The agency also faces the classic insurance problem: will it be subject to adverse selection, attracting a high proportion of borrowers with below-average earnings profiles over their income-earning careers? (See, for an extended earlier analysis of income-contingent loan programs, Johnstone, 1972.)

Krueger and Bowen (1993) discuss important policy features of income-contingent loans and provide illustrative calculations of the earnings percentages that would be required under plausible assumptions (constant purchasing power dollars; a 3 percent real interest rate; a zero rate of real income increase over time). Absent any systematic adverse selection, they calculate the percentage of wage and salary income that would have to be paid to service a $10,000 loan. Men and women with some post–high school education who faced a payback period of ten years would have to pay 7.1 percent of average earnings; this would be reduced to 2.8 percent for a twenty-five year payback. But average career-long earnings of women have been shown to be much lower than those of men; if separate percentages were established, women would have to pay more than double the rate for men. Krueger and Bowen also explore the implications of a predominantly low-earnings career profile: men and women earning only at the 25th percentile would have to pay 17.7 percent of income on a ten-year payback, or 8.4 percent over twenty-five years.

These numbers show that income-contingent programs designed to fully amortize loan interest and principal, with no defaults, would impose significant extra burdens on the average career incomes of many college graduates.

While an income-contingent loan program has conceptual appeal, it does not fully resolve the issue of encouraging access to higher education. Outright grants-in-aid and scholarships are a more powerful inducement to enroll in higher education, and students from low-income families who fear indebtedness may be attracted into higher education only if they do receive such outright support.

The Politics of Public Tuition

Target net revenue from tuition and mandatory fees at a public university can be set merely to finance the budget for necessary student services; even a "no tuition" policy permits this. (In addition, nonresident students may be charged a genuine tuition that is set to recapture for the state's taxpayers the approximate average cost of instruction.) But if revenue is sought beyond the demands of student services, there is no obvious end in sight. The entire range of other costs that are enrollment-related may come into play in the setting of the target net revenue. As mentioned earlier, at the University of California, the entire library budget (acquisitions, circulation, and administration) was shifted into the category of items to be paid for from increased student fees when a serious budgetary shortfall threatened. In view of the extensive usage of library services for faculty research, such a shift could be a conceptual embarrassment and could also complicate the cost-accounting efforts that are required in establishing the rates for indirect cost recovery on federally funded research.

Individual Benefits and Social Benefits of Higher Education

An alternative approach would be to attempt to establish what benefits of higher education flow to the individual student and what benefits are received by the state's general public. Howard Bowen argued persuasively in *Investment in Learning* (1977), that the individual would grow, change, and benefit from successful exposure to higher education and would start on the way to a satisfying and productive life. Systematic research has shown convincingly that higher education has a positive impact on both cognitive and affective development, and also broadens and deepens the values of the student (Astin, 1993). But at least as important as these benefits to the individual are the benefits to society of the broader contributions of the educated person (Bowen, 1977).

The exercise of financially quantifying these social impacts of higher education is conceptually difficult, and it does not solve immediate fiscal problems of the state or of its public university. Nevertheless, it is of interest to list some of the elements of public benefit from a larger cadre of the highly educated:

- A larger number of highly prepared entrants to the work force, reducing upward pressure on salaries in high-technology and other growing sectors of the state's economy.
- A more productive and more flexible workforce for public sector as well as private sector activities.

- Increased sensitivity to the need for social change and increased tolerance of racial and other differences.
- A wider interest in matters of culture.
- Assurance to parents that children with high potential will have extensive educational opportunity, without serious financial barriers to attendance—this last makes the state more attractive as a place of employment.)

Provided the state retains most of those whose higher education it has financed and loses very few to migration, the higher education investment can claim greater justification. If the state has a progressive personal income tax, the incrementally higher income earned by the public university graduate can be successfully taxed for delayed "repayment" of the state's investment.

Those who do not share in the personal benefits of a state's higher education investment may oppose being taxed for advantages they do not obtain. This group includes:

- Parents of those who attend independent colleges or universities or who go out of state for higher education
- Adults who do not themselves enroll in the state's higher education system
- Adults who completed all the education they want prior to becoming residents of the state
- Adults who do not have children who can benefit from the state's higher education system

The Politics of Access and the Demand for Excellence

If the state provides higher education through its public system to the great majority of its eligible young people, this reduces the political antagonism toward state budgeting of higher education. Political support for adequate budgets for the various sectors of public higher education is then founded in great part on the *politics of access*—the effort to assure citizens of the state that their children, and they, can obtain what they want and need from the public system. Quite naturally, local community colleges, as the first line of access, have the easiest task of demonstrating the merits of their claims for budgetary support. Proponents of the politics of access generally favor policies of zero tuition or very low tuition, and they also advocate grants-in-aid and easy loans for students from families of low and modest income.

' One interesting variation on the theme of access was an attack in the early 1990s on efforts to tie the student fees in the California State University system to the cost of instruction. Patrick Callan, former executive director of the California Postsecondary Education Commission and, as of 1993, head of the foundation-financed California Higher Education Policy Center, castigated the state's elected political leadership and its institutional leaders for failing to adhere to policies requiring student fees to rise by no more than 10 percent per year. He also called for stricter observance of the requirement that students and their parents be given at least ten months' notice of any change in fees (Callan, 1993a, 1993b).

Callan refused to acknowledge that the rapid decline of state revenues and a mounting budgetary crisis were an adequate cause for what he regarded as a retrograde series of fee increases. He was silent on the issue of alternatives to the actions he criticized, but his message of alarm regarding the potential decline of access to higher education was clearly in keeping with the politics of access.

Balancing the demand for access and the demand for excellence is the root issue of public policy in higher education. The state's public research university usually has selective rules of eligibility for undergraduate admission, and it must certainly limit admissions in graduate professional-degree and doctoral programs. If, therefore, it wishes to claim to be a contributor to the accessibility of higher education, it must base its case on its ability to meet the educational objectives of high-talent students and of students who have already progressed toward graduate and professional education.

The public university also finds it necessary to appeal to the *politics of excellence* to justify public budgetary support. It will maintain that its obligation is to educate scientists, doctors, lawyers, and engineers to a high standard, not merely to provide advanced education to everyone who seeks it. The university justifies the commitment to academic research partly on the grounds that quality advanced education requires a research milieu, but it also makes an independent, pragmatic claim for the research role: that it pays off in eventual benefits to the state's population, through scientific discovery, which spawns new technology, which leads eventually to new and vital industries. As for the university's scholars in the languages, literatures, and cultures of the world, their presence is justified by the necessity to cultivate wide understanding of an increasingly interdependent planet.

Because the interests supporting, respectively, the politics of access and the politics of excellence are often in danger of diverging, advocacy on behalf of a state's public higher education system is a difficult exercise in coalition building.

Chapter Ten

Academic Resources and Facilities

A university's faculty is its crucial and most powerful resource—difficult to build up at a high-quality level, sustainable only with constant effort and leadership, and subject to deterioration and defections if the university fails to meet faculty needs.

The Institutional Pyramid

The research universities of the United States—88 Research Universities I and 37 Research Universities II—are seen by most career academic people as being at the apex of the higher education system in terms of both reputation and working conditions. (The categories and figures in this section are from the 1994 Carnegie classification.) These universities have national and international visibility. They contain professional schools as well as strong and comprehensive arrays of departments in the scholarly disciplines. Some have extremely large enrollments, while others are relatively small. They have larger total budgets and higher budgets per faculty member than other types of institution. They attract the lion's share of federal research funds. Their faculty salaries are systematically higher than salaries in other sectors of higher education.

Following these are 111 Doctoral Universities. Most are regional in character. Some are large in enrollment size. Many have pockets of scholarly excellence; nearly all aspire to become classified in due course as Research Universities I.

The liberal arts colleges—now called Baccalaureate Colleges I and II—differ from both of the above categories, as they do not offer the doctorate and do not have professional schools. The best-known and wealthiest of them, however, have faculty cadres with high percentages of Ph.D.'s and pay salaries that are closely competitive with the research universities.

Master's (Comprehensive) Universities and Colleges I and II offer a variety of master's degree programs. Some have the name "university" and may aspire to the offering of the doctorate and to provision of research support, major libraries and laboratories, and other facilities characteristic of the doctoral institutions and the research universities. Because the conduct of research and original scholarship is less emphasized in these institutions than in the doctorate-granting institutions, their faculty members have higher teaching loads and, in general, lower salaries than at the research universities.

Finally, two-year institutions—Community Colleges and Technical-Vocational institutions—have faculty cadres with a still lower percentage of Ph.D.'s and a still higher average teaching load. They typically shape the academic curriculum to permit transfer of student credits to four-year institutions; at their best, they design courses and instructional methods so as to help students overcome previous deficiencies in preparation.

Supply and Demand for University Faculty in the 1990s and Beyond

National projections of demand for arts and science faculty, which are compared with projections of supply, provide the university with a framework for understanding the hiring and retention conditions it can expect to face in the future. Major early studies (Cartter, 1971; Radner and Miller, 1975) sharpened analytical perspectives. These studies showed, first, that the individual university's attrition rate must not be taken as the faculty replacement rate for the entire university sector, for a faculty member departing from university X is very likely to fill a position at university Y. Second, Radner and Miller showed the sensitivity of projected demand for faculty to the student-faculty ratio (actually, they used its reciprocal, the faculty-student ratio, for technical reasons).

William Bowen undertook a major study of letters and science faculty (Bowen and Sosa, 1989) and showed that, on the basis of enrollment demographics and the available age distribution information, an exceptionally high demand for faculty will characterize the latter 1990s. Two policy conclusions follow, assuming this projection to be correct: (1) universities should plan for rising faculty salaries, as their competitors bid strongly in the markets for faculty; (2) expanding the number of graduate students recruited into doctoral training in the early 1990s would have made sense, as it takes at least five to seven years to complete the doctorate.

The first of these is a lesson for the individual university. The second is a national policy issue. If Bowen's assumptions are correct, the higher education associations should have been pressing for additional doctoral fellowship funds, and the National Science Foundation, the National Academies of Science and Engineering, and the American Council of Learned Societies should be campaigning for such additional fellowship support. However, financial stringency in the early and mid 1990s may counteract the growth trend, for it has resulted in efforts to reduce the number of faculty. Twenty-five percent of institutions overall, and 40 percent of doctorate-granting institutions, reported such downsizing efforts in the American Council on Education survey, 1992–93 (El-Khawas, 1993, table A7, p. 33). From 1991–92 to 1992–93, 40 percent of doctorate-granting universities reported a net gain in number of faculty, and 35 percent reported a net reduction. Many institutions made generous early retirement offers in order to trim faculty numbers. (See also a major article covering this issue by Magner, 1994.)

The Flow of New Doctorates

Ehrenburg (1992) reports important findings on the flow of new doctorates—the almost exclusive source of future new faculty appointments. The number of new doctorates awarded annually was approximately constant from 1970 to 1988 at thirty-four thousand, in contrast to the doubling of the number of first professional degrees. Of the doctoral total, nonresident aliens earned an increasing proportion of degrees (table 1.4, p. 836). From 1960 to 1988, the share of doctorates in social sciences and life sciences remained constant, gains in engineering doctorates approximately offset loss of share in physical science, and humanities doctorates declined by one-third (table 2.1, p. 840). The share of doctorates in education increased to almost 20 percent of the total.

The pool of young scholars available for academic appointment thus dwindled appreciably. In the physical sciences and engineering, the trend was reinforced by the attractions of industrial research posts and by the significant numbers of nonresident aliens earning advanced degrees. Ehrenburg reports specifically on the employment destinations of new doctorates: between 1968 and 1988, the academic placement share fell from two-thirds to one-half; the shares fell most for physical sciences, engineering, and social sciences—fields offering strong opportunities for professional employment (table 2.4, p. 844).

Discussing the incentives and impediments to doctoral study, Ehrenburg also reports that the average length of time in the pipeline has increased substantially (a disincentive) and that starting salaries of new Ph.D.'s in economics, mathematics, and physics are well below those of new M.B.A.'s and new lawyers (table 3.3, p. 854). Financial support for doctoral study is also in question, even in science and engineering where such support is historically more generous than it is in social sciences and humanities; more than one-fourth of full-time science and engineering students were self-supporting in the 1970s and 1980s (table 3.4, p. 855). National policies and university efforts have not succeeded in augmenting the academic "seed corn" of doctoral supply, and Ehrenburg expresses skepticism about whether the numbers opting for doctoral study and subsequent academic careers would be much affected by increases in doctoral support funds.

As to the demographics of new doctorates, the big news is that women are now earning more than one-third of all new doctorates, with almost one-half of the degrees in social sciences and humanities and sharp relative increases (but still a low percentage) in physical sciences and engineering (table 4.1, p. 862). Still, women have prepared even more aggressively for the active professions than for academic life (table 4.2, p. 863). University departments will need to recruit women faculty candidates actively, as women form an increasing part of availability pools. Universities may also, as Ehrenburg points out (p. 863) need to pay more attention both to disincentive aspects of doctoral study and to what many women consider inflexibilities in the pattern and timing of academic advancement.

By gender and race, the numbers of 1990–91 new doctorates, including doctorates in education, are as follows (National Center for Education Statistics, 1993, table 235, p. 243; table 261, p. 281):

Total	39,294
White male	14,564
White female	10,764
Asian American	1,458
African American	1,212
Hispanic	732
American Indian	102
Nonresident	9,715
Race unknown	747

Universities generally seek to expand the participation of minority members, both in doctoral study and in eventual faculty appointment, but Ehrenburg (1992) reports data showing a discouraging lack of progress in the number of doctoral degrees earned by minorities (table 4.4, p. 866). In fact, the numbers have receded somewhat from an earlier peak. This means that the available pool of minority doctorates from which to recruit candidates for appointment is very small in some key fields. For example, only ten African

Americans received the Ph.D. in mathematics in 1991. The achievement of greater faculty diversity remains a challenging task.

Faculty Recruitment: Nontenure and Tenure Levels

Universities are now accustomed to formalized listing and advertising of faculty positions. Affirmative action requirements and guidelines gave impetus to more highly elaborated and systematic recruiting procedures. Advertisements inviting applications are typically directed to the national and international professional societies in each discipline or specialization. The most promising candidates (even for some nontenure positions) are invited to visit the university, conduct a seminar discussion, and meet with faculty members and students.

Hiring nontenure faculty from within the ranks of graduate students at the same institution, once practiced widely in U.S. universities and still a frequent approach in other countries, has been increasingly avoided because of the dangers of inbreeding and cronyism. Many U.S. universities, particularly the public ones, are now sensitive to the need to encourage recruitment, appointment, and retention of female and minority faculty. Short of quotas or targets for hiring, which are resisted by both university administrators and faculty groups, appointment rates of women and minorities can be increased by the use of devices such as:

1. The broadest possible advertising and search, including the canvassing of graduate programs with substantial numbers of women and minority members

2. Appointments or research fellowships for a year or two, maximizing the prospects of research attainment by the new recruit

3. The identification of teaching and research areas that are attractive to female and minority candidates and the channeling of recruitment efforts toward them (Academic Senate, 1991)

The university may authorize the filling of an open position at nontenure level only, at tenure level only, or at either level, depending on the relative quality of candidates. Some major private universities such as Yale and Harvard are said to have a strategy of hiring at the level of assistant professor, with no significant expectation of eventual promotion to tenure, and of engaging in exhaustive search for a distinguished scholar when a permanent faculty position is authorized. (Often, indeed, a ceiling is set by policy on the number of tenure positions at major private universities.)

Public universities often do not have such a stratified approach, and they are therefore able to recruit women and minority faculty more aggressively, for the nontenure availability pools contain much larger percentages of women and minorities than are present in the tenure pools. Nevertheless, a public university department that is highly sensitive to its reputation may try to appoint a visible senior scholar to replace a retiring luminary if the academic administrators will authorize it. The administration is likely to prefer substantial emphasis on junior-level appointments, however, both for budgetary reasons and to balance the faculty age distribution.

The Criteria of Faculty Appointment and Advancement

The mantra of faculty criteria is "teaching, research, and public service." No research university can promote to tenure unless the candidate has demonstrated research achievement. The question is: how outstanding must the achievement be? Research achievement is gauged from the judgments of the departmental faculty where the appointment or promotion would be located, and from letters of evaluation solicited from outside the institution. The relevant citation index shows how much use other scholars have made of the journal articles published by the candidate. In addition, the quality of reputation and of peer review in the journals where articles have been published is taken into account, "mainstream" journals being accorded more weight than peripheral or secondary journals.

Papers in the proceedings volumes of scholarly organizations have less weight than peer-reviewed articles. Notably, the emphasis is on evaluations made by the scholarly apparatus of a field rather than on independent evaluation of the work by particular individuals of trustworthy reputation.

Quality of teaching is weighed in the tenure decision but is generally a less binding criterion than research achievement. Many faculty members argue that teaching effectiveness is less capable of evaluation than is research attainment.

Public service is weighed not at all in nontenure appointment, and not much at promotion to tenure. The university may, however, attach importance to outstanding and highly visible public service, such as advice to the nation's president, membership of a presidential or congressional commission, or other roles evidencing extraordinary reliance on the professor's expert knowledge.

In research universities, not much weight is given to other kinds of contribution. One potentially undervalued contribution is the "synthesis of knowledge," as distinct from original discovery, in the words of the University of California's Task Force on Faculty Rewards (1991a). Another is the faculty member's contributions as a role model to students. This contribution is valued especially by female and minority graduate students and undergraduates. Traditional academic evaluators tend to resist the role model argument, which is often made in the promotion cases of women and minority faculty, but there is little question that this function takes a great deal of time, energy, and conscientious commitment in many instances. (See Academic Senate, 1991.)

Nontenure faculty members are typically up for promotion to tenure after four to seven years of service; the decision is typically "up or out." (See Metzger, 1993, especially pp. 66–77, for a discussion of the evolving position of the American Association of University Professors on limitation of the number of pretenure years.) Eligibility for advancement to tenure is typically limited to those holding "tenure-track" or "ladder-rank" appointments. Temporary lecturers are not considered for tenure except in very rare cases.

Faculty Compensation Strategies

Universities are of course sensitive not only to the numbers of available candidates and to their academic quality and potential but to the salaries of new as well as experienced faculty. Academic career earnings are characteristically "flatter" than in the professions, with full professors' salaries of generally less than double the salaries of new assistant professors. This "compaction" operates as a disincentive for doctoral study, and it also illustrates the consequences of reduced mobility at the senior faculty level. Average faculty salaries at both the full professor and assistant professor levels are much lower in the social sciences and the humanities fields than in the physical sciences, engineering, and business schools (Ehrenburg, 1992, table 1.3, p. 835).

Each discipline or professional specialization constitutes a distinct submarket, to which universities have to be sensitive in their recruitment and retention policies. Some universities set each faculty member's salary through individual bargaining and adjustment, within general guidelines stating the amount of increase permitted in the total annual wage bill. Other universities—particularly public universities—use salary ranges or scales for each academic rank and attempt to administer these more or less uniformly across disciplines. The appeal of the salary scale is that it conveys a tone of equity across departments or disciplines. A uniform scale, however, gives rise to difficulties when the university must compete in markets where talent is scarce relative to the demand for faculty.

Many institutions provide annual cost-of-living salary increases to each category of faculty (to the extent they can); these are separate from individual increases of salary within rank ("merit" increases) and increases that accompany promotion in rank. Combining cost-of-living and merit funds would permit the most efficient use of salary monies, as professors who contribute most strongly to the institution could be more heavily rewarded on a merit basis and those who are merely marching in place could be accorded much smaller raises. Whether a pooling of compensation elements is feasible depends both on the amenability of the university's funding sources (the state government, in the case of public universities) and on the attitude of faculty organizations. The latter may fear excessive concentration of discretionary authority in department chairs, deans, and the university provost.

Particularly in research universities, there is a consistent drift toward preoccupation with the rewards obtainable outside the institution. Reputation is enhanced by research publication, and in many fields consultancy beckons with offers of money to bolster the professorial living standard. Professors may then become resistant to requests that they take on more teaching or undertake special institutional duties (the department chairmanship or a demanding committee assignment). The department chair is in a weak negotiating position with these faculty colleagues if the chair has only modest influence on decisions concerning faculty compensation. (See Kerr, 1994a, chaps. 9, 10.)

Department chairs in some medical school faculties, on the other hand, acquire significant personal leverage and often serve for periods much longer than the three-year rotation typical of letters and science departments. With control of the patient-income pool—the money generated from clinical work performed by faculty members—the chair has a major influence on a significant portion of compensation.

Similar powers could be invested in the chair in other departments of the university. A base salary would first be established for each individual; then, the department chair would negotiate optional payments for special duties or for a reconfiguration of the faculty member's role. An older faculty member who is no longer productive in research could be nudged in this way to take on additional teaching. Time-consuming assignments in the department or in the broader institution could be rewarded tangibly—with money.

Total compensation includes retirement, health, and other nonsalary benefits. For universities as for other employers, these have become an increasingly expensive part of the package, accounting now for more than 25 percent of salary at some major research universities. These benefit systems ordinarily operate on percentage formulas that are uniform across faculty, although the employee may be able to exercise options—such as added life insurance or payments into tax-deferred annuity programs—for which deductions are made from salary.

Age Distribution of Faculty: Retirement and Induced Retirement

Most universities are "top-heavy," in the sense that full professors often account for 80 percent or more of the regular faculty. Universities have become increasingly aware of the need to control longer-term aspects of staffing: age and rank distributions, and the extent of the institution's ability to hire new blood each year. This concern is shared by all hierarchies that have relatively strong patterns of career-long employment.

To manage retrenchment, the most demanding resource management problem of the early 1990s, some universities with exceptionally well-funded pension plans have enacted early retirement schemes, with incentives for long-service, high-salaried faculty and staff to depart from the institution. The specific age structure of an academic unit and the attitudes of its employees toward retirement are the key determinants of the effectiveness of such a program. At the University of California, Berkeley, fully 9 percent of the faculty took induced retirement simultaneously in fall 1991 (as compared with that institution's normal annual departure rate of senior faculty of about 2 percent); furthermore, the professional schools experienced much higher retirement rates than did the rest of the institution, presumably because their faculty members had more alternative income-earning options available to them.

Beginning in 1993, federal legislation has prohibited the use of any mandatory age of retirement. In the past, tenure systems were bounded by such a retirement age, whether sixty-five, sixty-seven, or seventy. Facing the prospect that some faculty members will seek to remain on active service indefinitely, universities and other employers affected by the new federal law will have to think through the basis of advancement, continuation, and termination of employment. Periodic review of the performance of each tenured faculty member will become a necessity, so that the institution can counsel with individuals whose productivity has fallen appreciably below the institution's standards. This issue is almost certain to arouse greater interest in replacing tenure with new systems of "rolling contracts" whereby the faculty member's employment is guaranteed for, say, eight or ten years, and is subject to a new negotiation for continuance after that. Once such a system is in place, it can serve also as a basis for periodic readjustment of the faculty member's composition of duties—for example, toward a mix favoring teaching over research in later years. But as of early 1993, the problem had hardly been faced. Every tenured professor should be subject to some evaluative review at intervals (say, every fifth year), and there should be available, with the consent of the faculty organization, a mechanism for engaging a review panel in any instance where a faculty member appears to lack the energy, ability, or interest to continue in regular faculty duties.

Retrenchment and the Faculty Resource

Universities seek to manage the faculty resource in new ways, coping with financial stringency by increasing the proportion of teaching done by visiting faculty, temporary and part-time lecturers, and "retreaded" early retirees. There is a danger that greater stratification of appointments will occur, with women faculty, especially, pressed into numerous "non-ladder" positions.

The interests of individual faculty in the research universities are known to run strongly toward research attainment, often with no more than routine attention given to teaching. This emphasis serves the cause of reputation-building among peers in the discipline and improves prospects for advancement in rank. University presidents and university critics periodically call for increased teaching commitment, but universities will have to modify the real and perceived incentives in faculty careers if this is to happen.

The Cornell University faculty made a most interesting proposal to the president: they suggested that he commit to a 4 percent reduction in faculty numbers over a period of several years, in order to generate funds to meet the faculty's increased salary needs. In the characteristic mode of university operation, a reduction in faculty while student enrollment remains constant must entail an increase either in average class size or in the number of courses each faculty member offers per year.

Other universities that face severe budgetary and retrenchment pressures will no doubt consider similar trade-offs. The challenge then will be to adopt and implement changes without causing faculty resistance and a lowering of morale. Gaps in course offerings may also be filled within available budgets, by hiring part-time lecturers at lower salaries.

We discuss in Chapters Fourteen and Fifteen a variety of long-term and short-term policy options. Many of these bear on the utilization of the faculty resource.

University Library Systems

A university's library is, externally, a badge of its eminence as a center of scholarship and, internally, a prized resource and an arena of contest among numerous priorities. Today, libraries are not merely repositories of books and scholarly journals; they are the great gateways to information of all kinds. On-line cataloguing systems permit quick mobilization of sources both within and among campuses. Interlibrary loan systems that enable an individual campus library to call on collections other than its own are utilized to the point of overload.

The university library's acquisition policy for adding to its collections represents its attempt to keep up with at least a significant portion of new materials in each field of scholarship. The increasing worldwide output of books and serial publications makes it more and more necessary to be selective. Accelerating upward trends in the subscription prices of serial publications are a particular source of pressure on library acquisition budgets (Economic Consulting Services, Inc., 1989). Consortia of research libraries are engaging in negotiations to arrive at a division of labor among them.

Library-stack space is also subject to rationing. Despite the qualms and criticisms of faculty researchers, some major libraries have established off-campus regional repositories for seldom-requested titles in order to economize on space costs.

The thrust into electronics—cataloguing, databases, and interlibrary links—is a critical policy issue for major libraries. Librarians are retraining themselves to design and manage these informational resources. On-line catalogues now permit remote bibliographical search via modem from the scholar's own office. Several hundred professional journals are published entirely by electronic means and are available to scholars via the Internet.

Electronic substitutes for books and journals, especially on CD-ROM, are already cost-effective in some applications, but publishers' policies on pricing and reproduction fees have not yet stabilized. Ideally, a scholar would like to be able to search electronically, first for titles, then for specific material within a publication that could be downloaded and prepared for quotation. But copyright protections stand in the way of fully realizing this ideal.

Even though budgets are tight, major libraries have captured numerous benefits of computer technologies, and their progressive efforts are likely to continue.

There are also significant questions of support for special collections. An individual donor, whether bibliophile or scholar, may have a consuming interest in a special collection. But the head librarian must ensure that sufficient private funds are given to provide for both acquisitions and collection management.

Because command of information has become a crucial competitive tool for enterprises and governments, the specialized services that a university library can supply have significant value in the external market. Libraries are therefore beginning to examine how to offer such customer services on a fee or royalty basis.

Building Space

Three issues need to be considered: space and utilization standards; administration of existing space; and maintenance of existing space.

Space Standards and Utilization Standards

State governments, ever since the end of World War II, have faced the difficult fiscal challenge of financing enrollment-driven expansion of public colleges and universities. They have been concerned to provide adequate, but not excessive, amounts of classroom, class laboratory, and other space. Standards for space, like many operating budget components, are computed by formula and reflect the different missions of community colleges, comprehensive colleges, and research universities.

The starting point in the derivation of a standard for a given type of institution is student enrollment. Needs for classroom and class laboratory space are dependent on the enrollment distribution among the lower division, upper division, and graduate levels, and among disciplines. Once estimates of student load are arrived at, two important steps remain. The first is to determine how many square feet each workstation (classroom seat or laboratory bench) requires. The second is to specify a rule for the estimated "load factor," or occupancy rate, of that workstation. This rate, in its turn, is a function of the number of hours per week of scheduled classroom or laboratory use and the proportion of total work spaces expected (by demand estimate or by policy) to be filled in each scheduled hour.

It goes without saying that a class laboratory in upper-division chemistry needs different space and equipment provisions from those required by a class laboratory in mathematical statistics. Therefore, different sizes of workstation (in assignable square feet, or ASF) were designated for different disciplines. Over time, public agencies insisted on more and more detailed elaboration of the standards for each type and use of space, to the point that in a 1990 study by the California Postsecondary Education Commission (CPEC), an effort was made to reduce the number of specialized categories and simplify the system.

The CPEC study includes results of a national survey of public higher education systems. It demonstrates that generally, the states have needed systematic standards, but it also contains extensive discussion of differences in definitions and measurement methods, which complicated the task of comparison.

As the CPEC report states, space standards for faculty offices, faculty laboratories, and academic support space were derived from analysis of the particular needs of faculty in each of California's subsystems of public higher education. The University of California's complex mission resulted in a larger number of square feet per office for faculty members than in the California State University system, with those in engineering and the natural sciences accorded more space than those in the social sciences and humanities. Research space was recognized as a category separate from teaching laboratories and separate also from faculty office space. The report, incidentally, recognized for the first time that postdoctoral fellows, previously invisible in the California system, should be taken account of in computing the total amount of space needed in each scientific field.

Space standards and their companion utilization standards were needed originally to help plan the capital budgeting requirements for expanding systems of public higher education. As the report comments, however, the standards gradually evolved into a scheme of regulation and a restrictive framework within which to design academic facilities. Regulation, for example, was implicit in the

State of California's shift, in 1970, to a schedule mandating an average 75 percent utilization of available classroom seats between 8 A.M. and 10 P.M, Monday through Friday. This state action increased the apparent enrollment-accommodating capacity of existing classrooms; but it also spurred the planners in California public higher education to push for more space in other categories.

The complexity of the University of California's research mission has increased, and the report recognized that laboratory teams have become more common, equipment is larger and more complex, and (as indicated above) postdoctoral fellows as well as regular faculty and graduate students need to be accommodated. Consequently, the state's funding obligation for university research space is computed according to new standards in each major scientific discipline.

The report also emphasized that the changing academic needs of various disciplines and the idiosyncrasies of individual departments should be taken into account in building design, with space standards regarded as general guidelines and not as design standards.

Policies for Administration of Existing Space

Some types of building space are designed for specific purposes, and buildings that are constructed through the generosity of donors or with capital grants from foundations or research agencies have restrictions on their use. Both functional characteristics and assigned uses place constraints on the allocation of space.

The mechanism of allocation and occasional reallocation of existing space is almost always administrative and judgmental, as opposed to market driven, in universities. Only rarely—when the institution must go out and rent offices for a research project and pay the rental with funds provided by an extramural grant—is the attribution of space costs to a particular program activity explicit and price therefore a determinant of space allocation. Otherwise, administrative assignment and rationing is the rule, sometimes based on general space standards.

Once space is assigned, the user has no incentive to economize on its use or to give up space that is not really needed. The unit receives no compensation for the surrender of space, and it loses flexibility for the future. The basic rule, therefore, is: "What's mine is mine and what's yours we can negotiate."

Internal pricing, designed to encourage more rational allocation and more trade-offs, could be an alternative to the customary mechanisms of purely administrative judgment. To the knowledge of this author, no American university is relying substantially on a price mechanism to deal with facilities administration.

Typically, expanding departments are pinched for faculty offices and other space, and their needs are accommodated grudgingly and with considerable time lag. By contrast, departments undergoing gradual decline in graduate enrollment and in the size of their regular faculty are able to provide individual offices for visiting professors and good accommodations for graduate students. Such disparities, and lags in adjustment, are indicative of the essentially political character of space allocations.

Planning, Budgeting/Financing, and Project Management for New Facilities

A major university campus benefits from careful planning for building sites, circulation of people and vehicles, and preservation of open space and amenities. Many U.S. universities are in superbly attractive locations, with opportunities for land planning to preserve aesthetic qualities of the campus. Urban universities such as Columbia, Chicago, and the University of Pennsylvania have had to develop active relationships with their city governments in order to participate in urban renewal programs that will help to solve their problems of land use.

As was discussed in Chapter Seven, universities have methods of capital budgeting, based on fund accounting, that differ sharply from industrial practice. Depreciation is not ordinarily computed as part of operating costs, and institutions do not routinely accumulate reserves for major maintenance and replacement. For example, after many years of accumulated deferred maintenance, Yale University had to utilize endowments and raise substantial new money to undertake an extremely large renovation and rebuilding program. More generally, universities have experienced growing backlogs of deferred major maintenance and equipment replacement; one estimate for the major universities, prepared for congressional testimony, was $4 billion (Baker, 1985).

Universities also face large capital costs for upgrading and modernization of laboratories and other specialized scientific facilities, so that state-of-the-art research and teaching can be pursued.

Budgeting for capital facilities increasingly resorts to debt financing as a component of the financial equation. Universities have long used debt financing for residence halls, parking structures, and other facilities whose identifiable revenue stream can be pledged for interest and amortization. A more recent innovation is partial debt financing of university research laboratories, in the anticipation that indirect cost ("overhead") recovery on extramural research grants and contracts will provide the requisite revenue stream. With stagnant or declining volumes of academic research funding in prospect through the 1990s, this strategy now appears risky.

Project management for major university buildings is a complicated process. The author's own experience as chair of the planning committee for a major new building of the Haas School of Business at the University of California, Berkeley, provides a vignette of the tortuous progress of a major building project. In 1977, the dean of the business school undertook a study of the needed size and configuration of a new building that would replace facilities considered inadequate in comparison with those of the competition. The campus administration was not able to allocate funds for the project, however, and it was postponed indefinitely.

Interest in a new building revived in the 1980s, partly because a survey of prominent alumni and other donors showed stronger support for a new business school building than for many other projects on the campus "wish list." The new dean of the Haas School of Business accepted the challenge to raise privately all of the funds for the building, and a planning consultant calculated the approvable size and characteristics for the building. It came to 204,000 gross square feet, translated after subtracting corridors and public spaces as approximately 120,000 assignable square feet—a big building.

The planning study included a review of several alternative sites, the preferred one being within the precinct of the campus's professional schools. The campus provisionally awarded this site to the project, although two fifty-year-old buildings housing the student health service and some research facilities would have to be demolished and replacement facilities built elsewhere before the Haas School's building could be started.

By 1987, the project was on the university's officially approved list of capital projects for donor solicitation. The target amount for design and construction was $36 million, which eventually grew to $48 million. The business school's planning committee—representing faculty, staff, students, alumni, and campus planning experts—defined functional needs and participated actively in selection of the project architect. In parallel, the dean organized a major fund-raising campaign which was part of a campuswide capital campaign for a variety of priority needs.

The project architect expressed strong interest in obtaining ideas and indications of preference from the entire community at the business school and held informational workshops for this purpose. A team of students from the school conducted interviews with twenty-two focus groups and submitted a major report on needs and preferences. The planning committee and the architect's representatives met weekly throughout the first intensive year of design. The architects presented a plan for a minicampus with a central plaza surrounded by three interconnected buildings; the rationale for this design was that it promoted a sense of community.

Financing and construction of replacement buildings for the student health service and the affected research facilities took many months, delaying the clearing of the site. Several local community groups opposed the new long-range development plan of the campus, of which the business school project was a part, and filed suit to set it aside on the grounds that the Environmental Impact Report was defective. The court rejected the lawsuit in 1992, and construction began in 1993, two-and-a-half years later than originally hoped. The building was to be ready for occupancy in 1995—approximately eight years after the planning study and eighteen years after the first preliminary study of needs.

Perhaps this is an object lesson in the complexities of project management in the contentious atmosphere of the 1990s.

Chapter Eleven

Graduate Education

Education leading to degrees beyond the Bachelor of Arts or Bachelor of Science is part of the distinctive role of the university, and education for the doctorate, coupled with a systematic commitment to research, defines the research university. Of about 3,600 postsecondary institutions, a total of 236 are classified as conferring significant numbers of doctorates. Of these, 88 are Research Universities I, 37 are Research Universities II, and 111 are Doctoral Universities. (The Association of American Universities, the "club" of the best-known research universities, has 59 members.) Specialized professional institutions in such fields as clinical psychology, as well as certain institutions not classified as doctoral but granting a few doctoral degrees, add somewhat to the list of doctorate-awarding schools.

In other graduate education, doctorate-granting institutions overlap with a much larger number of institutions that have master's and professional degree programs. Furthermore, nearly all of the research universities provide undergraduate education as well as education for professional degrees and for the doctorate. There is inevitable tension between these different roles, for few U.S. universities have established a graduate faculty separate from the faculty that teaches their undergraduates.

Entrance to Graduate Education

The student entering a Ph.D. program ordinarily regards it as preparation for a career of teaching and research, although some fields provide the alternative destination of advanced professional practice. However, in many fields, eventual placement in academic career positions is problematical at times, and recipients of the Ph.D. sometimes have to shift to other destinations. Doctoral degrees other than the Ph.D. are identified with practicing professions—for example, the Ed.D. in education, the Dr.P.H. in public health, and the Doctor of Engineering. Recipients of these degrees may opt to teach in the professional curricula of their fields, but they often find themselves, instead, in significant administrative or professional positions.

A Ph.D. program in a major university engages in rigorous screening of its applicants: it scrutinizes grade records and other indications of performance in previous education; it normally requires high marks on the Graduate Record Examination (GRE) or an equivalent standardized test for advanced students; and to the extent that evidence is available, it looks also for creative intellectual promise. Often, the initial phases of graduate admission are controlled by a dean of graduate studies for the entire campus, who sets reasonably high minimum standards for consideration of an applicant by the departmental admissions committee. The graduate dean also controls the selection of recipients of university fellowships. The department does its own further screening and selection, awards special fellowships that fall under its own control, and makes research assistant and teaching assistant appointments.

Two distinct groups of young people consider applying for a Ph.D. program. Top students emerging from undergraduate programs constitute the main applicant flow. Some of these have also enrolled in a master's degree program and have excelled. This applicant pool contains students from foreign as well as domestic universities; in some fields of science and engineering, in fact, fifty percent or more of total enrollees and degree recipients are not U.S. citizens. In 1990, 102,000 out of 402,000 graduate students in science and engineering were foreign citizens. Of 22,673 doctorates awarded in science and engineering that year, 6,286 went to foreign students who were temporary residents, and an additional 1,158 went to permanent residents (National Science Board, 1991, appendix tables 2-23 and 2-24).

The second applicant flow consists of older people returning for advanced education after a substantial interval of employment or childrearing. Doctoral programs in education, social welfare, and public health, in particular, are geared to serve a mixed population: returning students, career changers, and practitioners already in midcareer who need the doctorate for the most prestigious jobs in their professions.

Candidates for the doctorate have to be seriously committed if they are to succeed. Both intellectual gifts and a well-organized passion for advanced learning are important. Minimum elapsed time to degree in the most streamlined Ph.D. programs is about four years. In fields that do not support students with research stipends or in other ways, and in which the curriculum is not punctuated by well-defined benchmarks of progress, the elapsed time often stretches out to ten years or more. (Additional aspects of doctoral program persistence and productivity are discussed in a later section of this chapter.)

Departmental Objectives and Patterns for Graduate Education

A department's faculty members value the doctoral program as an arena for training the oncoming generation of scholars in the field. They vie for opportunities to teach graduate-level courses and seminars, and they want to serve as chairs or members of dissertation committees. Course structure for doctoral students is much more formalized in some universities and some disciplines than in others. At the extreme of informality are systems of one-on-one tutoring and protégé status. These can be highly successful, but they may fail to expose the candidate in a sufficiently systematic way to the topics and methods of the field. At the dissertation stage, however, a mentor/protégé relationship is vital. A significant contributor to the high failure rate at the dissertation stage is lack of sponsoring and motivating attention.

Breneman (1970, 1971a, 1971b) analyzes academic departments as "prestige-maximizing firms," in which the production of well-regarded and well-placed Ph.D.'s is an important contributor to prestige. (The other major contributor to reputation is of course the published research of individuals and small teams in the department.) Faculty research projects, especially those in the sciences and engineering that are extramurally funded, serve as domicile for the doctoral student's dissertation research. The equipment that is needed is supplied through the project; the student is supported during at least part of his or her degree work by research assistantships; and research problems identified by the faculty adviser or the research team are often assigned to doctoral students and the holders of postdoctoral fellowships.

This picture of a tightly connected enterprise of graduate instruction, support, and research is characteristic of the physical and biological sciences and engineering, but the situation in the humanities and in many social science disciplines is very different. Faculty research is mostly conducted without extramural support, and individual faculty members often work in relative isolation from one another. The doctoral candidate, in turn, may have a part-time teaching assistantship but is unlikely to have consistent support for the time and expense of thesis research. These are the fields in which the elapsed time to complete the Ph.D. is longest and the designation ABD ("all but dissertation"), signaling failure to complete, is most common. A major study focused on six arts and science fields and found that both completion rates and time to degree varied systematically between them, with humanities and most social sciences low in completion rates and longest in time to degree (Bowen and Rudenstine, 1992, chap. 7, pp. 123–141). Smaller-scale programs in a given discipline achieved higher completion rates and lower time to degree than did larger programs in the same discipline (chap. 9, pp. 163–176). The program design and the "culture" of the program also strongly influence the completion rate and time to degree (chap. 13, pp. 250–267).

In all university disciplines, doctoral students are important participants in the university's undergraduate education: as teaching and laboratory assistants; as "readers" who grade papers and examinations; and as tutors in remedial courses and sessions. The economy of the research university is designed so that the graduate and undergraduate populations are to a considerable extent symbiotic. If graduate students were not involved in it, undergraduate education would be more costly and more impersonal than it now is; if undergraduates were not present, graduate students could not be supported as teaching assistants. (Though all this is true, graduate education is costly, both in absorbing the university's institutional resources, especially faculty time, and in claiming a portion of the available extramural research funds.)

In 1990, there were 60,315 graduate students in physical sciences, mathematics, and computer science. Of these, 5,365 had fellowships and traineeships, 16,895 were research assistants, 23,277 were teaching assistants, and 14,778 had other sources of support (including their own savings and outside work). In psychology, the social sciences, and the humanities, the proportion of self-support was much greater (data computed from National Science Board, 1991, appendix table 2-21).

Institutional Objectives for Graduate Education

The university's general reputation rests largely on achievements in graduate education and research. A comprehensive university with an array of master's degree programs but no doctoral programs is normally ambitious to offer the doctorate. A doctorate-granting university with a small number of approved doctoral programs seeks to establish more of them. An academic department lacking authorization for a doctoral program regards itself as deprived and is considered to be of low status within the university. The 1982 Survey of Research Doctorate Programs, performed by an association of four major scholarly organizations, reported the results of its peer surveys of faculty quality and of the quality of graduate teaching. High ranking of a department as compared with its competitors was prized as a reflection of its academic strength (Jones, Lindzey, and Coggeshall, 1982). A new survey was in progress in 1993–94, to cover the original thirty-two fields plus some others.

A major university is likely to have a graduate enrollment approximating 15 to 30 percent of its total enrollment; the percentage is greater if the university has a broad array of professional schools, and it is also greater to the extent that the university can successfully fund the high costs of doctoral education.

Doctoral Education and the Academic Labor Market

Over 35,000 doctoral degrees are awarded by U.S. universities each year—35,720 in 1988–89 and 39,294 in 1990–91 (National Center for Education Statistics, 1993, table 235). Of these, 6,800 in 1988–89 and 6,697 in 1990–91 were conferred in the field of education, which awards the Ph.D. or the Ed.D. degree, depending on the program and the character of the candidate's work (table 244). Recipients of many of these doctorates in education expected continued professional employment in the nation's school systems.

Of the remaining 30,000 or so new doctorates, absorption into academic posts depended on hiring conditions in colleges and universities. Total doctorate employment in science and engineering increased at a rate of 2.9 percent per year between 1977 and 1989, but the proportion of such doctorates employed by academic institutions fell from 57 percent in 1977 to 51 percent in 1989, the decline being due to heavier demand from industry, especially for engineers (National Science Board, 1991, p. 77).

Bowen and Sosa (1989) studied the demographics of faculty labor markets in the arts and sciences and concluded that beginning in the mid-1990s, the number of positions that would become available through expansion of faculty numbers and through replacement needs (retirements, deaths, and departures for other employment) would exceed the annual number of projected degree winners. During much of the 1980s, however, new doctorates faced difficulties in gaining academic placement because college and university enrollments of full-time students were not growing. The number of full-time undergraduates in all types of institutions hovered around 6.5 million through most of the decade (National Center for Education Statistics, 1993, table 182, p. 187). In the early years of the 1990s, when some pick-up of enrollments occurred, both public and private institutions faced increasing budgetary stringency.

In his 1971 study, Breneman found that doctoral candidates accelerated completion of the degree when placement opportunities were plentiful and delayed completion in slack market periods. During a slump, they could remain in the safe haven of graduate study a little longer and hope for a better opportunity later. Also, by spending more time on the dissertation, they would strengthen their placement chances and be in a better position to publish articles based on the dissertation.

Postdoctoral education is an important form of advanced research apprenticeship in the sciences. In some cases, it also affords an opportunity for a shift of research fields. The sciences use substantial amounts of their research funding for postdoctoral education, and postdoctural fellows are important contributors in the laboratory. Postdoctoral employment in universities, in its turn, tends to stretch out in slack periods and be shorter when the placement market is strong (National Research Council, 1981; Zumeta, 1985).

Graduate Professions: Master's and First Professional Degrees

Universities award some master's degrees in the academic disciplines as a way station toward the Ph.D. or as a consolation prize for candidates who are discouraged from continuing to the doctorate. Most master's degrees are awarded, however, to students who expect enhanced prospects of professional employment. In 1990–91, U.S. institutions awarded more than 337,000 master's degrees. Of these, over 78,000 were in business and management; almost 89,000 in education; 24,000 in engineering; 21,000 in health sciences; and over 18,000 in "public affairs and social work," presumably social welfare, public administration, and related subjects (National Center for Education Statistics, 1993, table 246, p. 267). Comprehensive colleges and doctorate-granting institutions are larger producers of these master's degrees than are the research universities.

Research universities are dominant, however, in awarding first professional degrees, which are mainly in the health professions and in law. Nearly 72,000 of these degrees were awarded in 1990–91 (National Center for Education Statistics, 1993, table 235, p. 243).

A fully comprehensive university campus has a Ph.D. program in every recognized scholarly discipline, plus representation in many if not all of the recognized fields of professional education. Professional schools are typically incorporated within U.S. universities, whereas they were traditionally freestanding in the European higher education systems.

What does a university gain by including professional schools in its menu of offerings and commitments? First, the graduate professions are themselves a series of influential clienteles. Because these professions often bring high professional incomes to their practitioners, devoted alumni of the professional schools can be a powerful asset. Furthermore, a university can garner prestige if its schools in well-established professions are recognized to be of high quality. The traditional vocations of medicine and law are at the top of the list of such professions. Engineering has also gained a position of prominence; four fields of engineering were included in the 1982 assessment of doctoral programs (Jones, Lindzey and Coggeshall, 1982).

Scholars in the academic disciplines and faculty members in professional schools frequently find common cause in policy research and even in fundamental research. Graduate students cross-enroll in both directions as well. At its best, a professional school enriches the intellectual enterprise; to make this happen, it is important to overcome the tendency of professional schools to isolate themselves from the university mainstream.

Private universities are able to earn a profit, to some extent, from their professional schools. Some use the "every tub on its own bottom" principle to isolate the costs of a professional school and mandate its self-sufficiency. If its dean and faculty cannot raise enough money through the sum of tuition revenue, grants, and gifts to break even, they will face the prospect of closure. Beyond meeting the criterion of immediate self-sufficiency, the professional school may be required by the central administration of the campus to make a net contribution to the general overhead of the institution. After all, even a decentralized professional school relies on centrally provided accounting and other business services, uses university-owned land (and perhaps buildings), and depends in other ways on the resources of the institution as a whole. One major private university, for example, exacted an annual contribution of approximately $7 million from its business school in the early 1980s.

The main motivation for establishing and operating an array of professional schools is not to make money, however, but to enhance the breadth, reputation, and influence of the university. A professional school with high visibility and a reputation for quality is a precious institutional asset. It is no accident, therefore, that so many of the best-known schools of law, medicine, engineering, and business are at private universities, which can thrive only by offering the highest quality of professional education in return for their very high tuition rates—rates much higher than the fees at good-quality public universities.

A professional school depends for its existence on its connection to a major clientele or market. Several types of professional schools have experienced a depression in their specialized labor markets. Dentistry has lost much of its market because routine dentistry practice, concentrating on the filling of cavities, has been all but wiped out in the United States by fluoridation of the potable water supply. Schools of librarianship are in trouble because the profession is subject to shrinkage, even though there are exciting new frontiers in applications of information technology. In both fields, universities have moved to close schools which were not felt to be viable in the current market. The Pew Charitable Trust awarded large planning grants to several major schools of dentistry so that they could plan their transition to new curricula and specialties.

Diversity in Graduate Education: Participation of Women and Minorities

Undergraduate enrollment of women exceeds that of men (National Center for Education Statistics, 1993, table 167, p. 173). Beginning in 1981–82, more women than men earned bachelor's degrees, and more women earned master's degrees in 1985–86. The government projects that this trend will continue into the next century (table 235, p. 243).

Men do continue to lead in numbers of doctor's degrees and first professional degrees, but women gained rapidly during the 1980s. However, participation rates of women vary greatly by field.

Historically, women were a small percentage of enrollment in many doctoral programs in the natural sciences and engineering and in such professional fields as law and business. But as a result of new goals that became real for women in the 1970s and 1980s, impressive gains had been made in enrollment and degrees by the end of the last decade.

University administrators and faculty leaders, facing the needs of a student body with growing percentages of previously underrepresented minorities, have sought to emphasize faculty appointment of women and minority Ph.D.s. However, minority graduate enrollment and eventual award of the Ph.D. vary tremendously by field. In mathematics only ten African Americans earned the Ph.D.

in 1991, and in that year, African Americans earned 1,212 doctorates in all fields combined (National Center for Education Statistics, 1993, table 262, p. 282).

The message of a *Science* special section in 1992, "Minorities in Science: The Pipeline Problem," was that women, African Americans, and Hispanics—the underrepresented minorities in science and engineering—must have high-quality early exposure to mathematics and to basic science instruction, and subsequent counseling and reinforcement in junior high school and high school. White high school students and students of Asian descent took more math courses than did African-American or Hispanic students (National Science Board, 1991, p. 26).

Only when there is better preparation will historic filtering-out effects be overcome. Many students avoid selecting the intermediate-level courses that would qualify them for science or engineering college admission; evidence suggests that they are often counseled not to take these preparatory courses. Colleges and universities have a significant role to play in encouraging women and minority students to major in undergraduate science and engineering curricula; only then will the numbers of qualified entrants to doctoral programs increase substantially.

In addition, doctoral programs that provide consistent and focused support to their doctoral students—minority students in particular—are able to increase persistence to the doctorate and reduce attrition rates of the minority doctoral students they do enroll.

Persistence to the Doctorate

A university's effectiveness can be assessed in part on the basis of its success in maintaining "throughput" of high-quality students. Both private tuition and state funding, however, are typically based on enrollment, without regard to the rates of persistence and attrition. In gauging the success of doctoral programs, both the elapsed time taken to complete the degree and the rate of persistence to it need to be considered, as these programs are the most expensive of the university's academic offerings. (Medical education is probably more expensive than most education for the Ph.D., because of the high costs of clinical training.)

A very broad statistic is the number of years from receipt of the bachelor's degree to the award of the Ph.D. (This may include one or more years of activity elsewhere than in higher education.) Chemistry took a little less than seven years in 1989. Psychology and the social sciences ranged upward from ten years to more than fourteen (National Science Board, 1991, fig. 2–10, p. 56). Recipients of doctoral degrees in 1992 had the following median numbers of years registered as graduate students (*Chronicle of Higher Education, Almanac Issue*, 1994, p. 18):

All fields	7.1
Arts and humanities	8.3
Business and management	7.1
Education	8.2
Engineering	6.2
Life sciences	6.7
Physical sciences	6.5
Social sciences	7.5
Professional fields	8.1

These long periods of enrollment challenge the university to provide adequate support through research stipends, teaching assistantships, and other institutional opportunities.

Cohort analysis is necessary to estimate persistence and attrition. A study of the University of California, Berkeley, reported by Graduate Dean Joseph Cerny and his associate Maresi Nerad, showed that 58 percent of the 1978 and 1979 entering cohorts completed the doctorate by 1991. Twenty percent earned a master's degree, then changed plans and left school. Variations in persistence by discipline were quite marked, as exemplified by completion rates over this long time interval of 72 percent in the biological sciences, 69 percent in the physical sciences, 39 percent in the arts, and 37 percent in the languages and literatures. Engineering is close to the pattern of the sciences, at 65 percent; the other professions are at 48 percent (Nerad and Cerny, 1991, p. 2).

The most wasteful pattern is for the degree candidate to languish for a long time, then drop out just before he or she finishes the degree. According to the Berkeley case study, however, 24 percent of those who did not persist left during the first three years of graduate study (83 percent of these with master's degrees). Ten percent left after advancement to candidacy for the Ph.D., and 8 percent were still pending at the time of the study in 1990–91. Some comparison with the University of California, Los Angeles, and with the University of Michigan indicated that these percentages were not atypical (p. 2).

Nerad and Cerny then investigated through intensive interviews what accounted for dropout and for long-delayed completion of the doctorate. Dominant personal reasons were change of perspective and goals and, for those already holding master's degrees in high-employment fields, a decision to return to professional employment.

The authors then developed a table of the institutional reasons for attrition or delay (fig. 3). Academic fields, of course, vary greatly in style of research. The team atmosphere of the laboratory sciences has promoted timely completion and low attrition. The structural design of the program also mattered a great deal: a required master's degree slowed things down, as did a lack of clear-cut curricular structure, the absence of a requirement for a dissertation prospectus at the time of the qualifying oral, and lack of regular evaluation and feedback to the candidate.

Doctoral completion rates of women candidates followed the same general pattern of variation by field as for men, but women had somewhat lower percentages of completion (fig. 2, p. 3). From

National Research Council data, the same authors determined that both male and female doctorate recipients with one or more dependents required substantially longer to complete the degree (fig. 9).

The extent of financial support for graduate study was an important determinant. Nerad and Cerny undertook a separate study of candidates in five humanities and social science departments, collecting detailed financial support data for each doctorate recipient from 1986 to 1989. For the entire sample, the mean time to degree was 9.1 years. Those receiving support for four or five years took 7.9 years to complete, while those receiving no support or just one year of support took 13.0 years (fig. 7).

This study implies that a university can improve degree persistence and shorten time to degree by insisting that the department set a well-defined program structure, offer strong advice and a positive scholarly environment for the candidate, and provide financial support for four or five years. Availability of housing and child care also materially affects time to completion for those with dependents.

Bowen and Rudenstine (1992) reach similar conclusions in their study of the Ph.D. (chap. 14).

Chapter Twelve

University Research and Scholarship

Research and creative activity infuse the work of university scholars. Faculty members who are active in research at the frontier of a field are best able to teach the most advanced graduate students and shepherd them through their dissertation research. Most university faculty members are devoted to their fields and drive themselves to contribute to them, although the most intensive research activity and attainment generally occurs during the early part of a lifelong academic career. Individual motivations—the joys of discovery, the tasks of integrating and preserving a field of knowledge, the engagement in critical scholarship—are joined with the practical recognition that career advancement depends heavily on achievements in research.

The University as a Domicile of Research and Creative Work

Each research university seeks to be a locus of originality in as many scholarly and professional fields as it can. It gains a great deal when it receives recognition for outstanding quality of research:

- It can attract still more high-quality faculty members with relative ease.

Portions of this chapter are adapted from F. E. Balderston, "Organization, Funding, Incentives and Initiatives for University Research: A University Management Perspective," chapter 2 in Stephen A. Hoenack and Eileen L. Collins (eds.), *The Economics of American Universities*. Albany: State University of New York Press, 1990.

- Graduate students of exceptional promise apply to its doctoral programs and professional schools.

- Undergraduate students are attracted by its fame (although they may also react against rumors that the professors are remote from undergraduate teaching).

- Research funding agencies respond positively to faculty research proposals, call on key faculty members to serve on research evaluation panels, and favor the research university as an important node in the network of active and influential scholarship.

- Donors and industrial sponsors of research are more readily attracted to a university that is already well known for excellent work.

Mechanics of Reputation Building and Their Effects

Each academic field has its professional societies and organizations, with their professional journals, annual meetings, and innumerable conferences. Regular involvement in these scholarly forums—giving papers, serving as discussant or organizer of sessions—builds the scholar's visibility among members of the field. Publication in peer-reviewed journals is the most important medium of recognition for research achievements, though in some fields of the humanities, the scholar's significant contributions are made in books.

The faculty member advances in reputation, rank, and salary in recognition of the amount and quality of research produced. In many fields, citation indexes are now used as signals of imputed quality: the greater the number of citations, the more positive the imputation. An academic department depends for its reputation, in turn, on the visible strength it derives from its faculty cadre. If the department is regarded as strong, it can press successfully for additional operating budget and for improvements in facilities and equipment. Departments also compete for extramural grants, which in turn support both the research process and, through the stipends that are funded, the living costs of graduate students and postdoctoral fellows.

Individual, Departmentally Based Research Versus "Organized Research"

The traditional image of the lone scholar, working patiently in dusty isolation, remains a partially correct characterization of research efforts for the great majority of humanists and for many social scientists. Even in the domains of mostly individual scholarship, however, affiliation with members of the discipline and interaction with them—through seminars and colloquia, informal discussion, and associative connection across specialties—helps to shape research agendas and stimulates creative effort. At its best, the university setting enhances everyone's quality of work; and competitive rivalry, while it can become destructive, serves as a spur to greater effort. Peers in the discipline at other universities and throughout the world are the crucial audience for every individual scholar.

Beyond the academic department, however, universities establish organized research units (ORUs), which can serve as a domicile for scholarly work that cannot easily fit within the administrative frame of a single department. Work that is cross-disciplinary or multidisciplinary may justify establishing an ORU if there is enough of it and if funding is in prospect. The ORU, then, has as its mandate the stimulation and support of mutually engaged faculty members and graduate students who share a common interest. The names are revealing: Institute of International Studies, Center for the Study of Higher Education, Center for African Studies, Center for the Humanities. These ORUs are primarily intended to support basic research and scholarship, although they often develop special library collections and databases and are suited to applied as well as basic research. Affiliated faculty members often seek extramural grants, but the ORU as such does not have a single external sponsor or client.

Programmatic Research:
Specialized Programs and Centers

Programmatic research activity differs from cross-disciplinary basic research. Typically, it is pursued on behalf of an identified sponsor or client and is directed toward a domain of application or policy rather than an agenda of intellectual issues within an academic discipline or across disciplines. For example, when labor-management conflict loomed as a significant problem at the end of World War II, Governor Earl Warren of California called on the University of California to establish an Institute of Industrial Relations. Its studies, public conferences, and training programs advanced understanding of the underlying problems of industrial relations and contributed to the eventual easing of tensions in a number of industries. The presumption was that the State of California benefited and that special state funding for the institute was justified.

Other institutes and laboratories were formed at various universities to accomplish missions in applied science and technology during World War II and the Cold War. Examples are:

The Cornell University Aeronautical Laboratory

The electronics laboratory at the Massachusetts Institute of Technology

The Radiation Laboratory (now renamed the Lawrence Berkeley Laboratory) at the University of California, Berkeley

The Operations Research Office at Johns Hopkins University

Some of these were eventually spun off as independent research organizations, while others reoriented their focus toward nondefense topics.

A programmatic center or institute prospers if its sponsoring client is satisfied with what is being accomplished and if the sponsor has financial resources to continue underwriting the work. The Stanford University Linear Accelerator (SLAC) has substantial federal funding and is a major facility for particle physics research in the United States. SLAC continues to garner significant support, but some other major facilities have lost support when their equipment was superseded by newer and larger machines.

The University of Michigan's Survey Research Center has accumulated infrastructure and expertise in conducting social science surveys of many kinds. As a center of state-of-the-art methodology, it attracts funding from a wide variety of sources, including the Federal Reserve System.

A university has an institutional interest in programmatic research activities, but this interest differs from its concern for the quality and visibility of research in each scholarly discipline. A center or institute with a programmatic mission can become a uniquely visible institutional asset, and its director and senior investigators become experts in cultivating the sponsoring client and obtaining extramural funds. These funds can be used in part for faculty and graduate student support, specialized equipment, and other expenditures that contribute to the university's academic strengths. The hazard of programmatic commitments is diversion of talent, energy, and even some funding from the university's academic purposes and subordination of the programmatic research organization to the client's requirements and needs.

Funding for Academic Research

Much individual scholarly work in a research university is a normal part of the faculty member's duties. For this reason, public universities often design their budgets to reflect the fact that they allocate institutional funds to their *departments of instruction and research*. The departmental teaching load (number of courses per year, plus oversight of student thesis research) is lower than in a dominantly instructional institution such as a liberal arts college or a master's (comprehensive) university or college, but each faculty member is expected to maintain some balance of effort between teaching and research.

In addition to the significant investment of professorial time in creative activity, the academic department may provide funding (to the extent that its institutional budget and discretionary funds permit) for such items as: clerical assistance in manuscript preparation; an assigned research assistant; travel to scholarly meetings and conferences to present a research paper; and (if the department is especially well-off) summer research stipends. A faculty member may affiliate with an ORU and obtain some of these kinds of special support, thus relieving his or her department of some of the budgetary burden. In the medical schools, the laboratory sciences, and engineering, individual faculty members and faculty teams seek substantial extramural grants and contracts. If secured, these provide the principal investigators (PIs) and the affiliated faculty investigators with significant resources that may be used for a variety of discretionary purposes, including purchase of special equipment, creation of graduate research assistantships, and provision of other types of support to graduate students. The well-funded faculty member gains autonomy and leverage as well as the opportunity to undertake intensive research.

In the humanities and most social science fields, institutionally provided funding predominates. Although universities seek private donor support for chair professorships and research programs, most of the creative scholarship in these fields is funded from general university coffers. Some private foundations have specific interests in humanities research, and the federally funded National Endowment for the Humanities is a major source of support. (In the fine arts and performing arts, university scholars can also tap the National Endowment for the Arts.) The total amount of extramurally provided humanities funding is difficult to estimate, but it is very small in comparison with the external funding of research in the social sciences, the "hard" sciences, and engineering.

Federal funding of academic science and engineering research is very extensive, as is reported and analyzed in *Science and Engineering Indicators*, a periodic publication of the National Science Board. Estimated academic research funding for science and engineering in fiscal year 1991 was $17.2 billion, which came from the following sources (National Science Board, 1991, appendix table 4-2, p. 306):

Federal government	$9.65 billion
State and local governments	$1.55 billion
Industry	$1.25 billion
Academic institutions	$3.4 billion
Other sources	$1.35 billion

In constant 1982 dollars, total funding for science and engineering more than doubled between 1969 and 1991, but federal funding increased by only about 70 percent, reducing its proportion of the total from 72 percent to 56 percent. Funding supplied by industry almost tripled but was still a small fraction of the total. The universities themselves doubled their proportion of research funding to almost 20 percent.

It should be kept in mind that the "state and local government" funding of research that is reported by the National Science Board does not include an allocated fraction of the faculty salaries that are paid by state universities, nor does the reported amount of research funding by the universities themselves divide departmental budgets between teaching costs and research costs. Finally, most university facilities and equipment are not subject to annual depreciation allowances. Thus, the university commitment of resources to research is significantly understated in the above data.

Much of the flow of federal scientific research dollars is allocated to projects that are recommended by "peer review" panels. Academic scientists almost universally concur with the wisdom and the general fairness of this system—especially as compared with the alternatives, purely bureaucratic allocations or political earmarking. The hold of the peer review system has weakened somewhat, however. In 1993–94, more than $700 million of academic research was allocated via the political route—by direct congressional earmarking to individual projects and universities, in amendments to appropriation bills. Individual institutions, including some illustrious ones, apparently decided to capture immediate funds rather than observe self-restraint in defense of the peer review system.

Basic Research, Applied Research, and Programmatic Research

Research activity is customarily divided into basic research, applied research, and development (or commercialization). Of the estimated $17.2 billion in academic research spending in fiscal year 1991, $11.1 billion was for basic research and $5.2 billion for applied research. Only a small fraction of the total ($0.9 billion) was for development, as would be expected. The rank-ordering of these three sectors of R&D in the universities was the exact reverse of the expenditure pattern in industry, where development accounted for almost 75 percent of total spending, and basic research for just 4.7 percent, in fiscal year 1991 (National Science Board, 1991, computed from appendix table 4-3, p. 308).

These differences of emphasis imply complementarity, with the universities concentrating on basic research and industry putting most resources into development, some into applied research, and least into basic science. Emerging in the late 1980s and early 1990s were new patterns of joint venture; these are discussed in a later section of this chapter.

Future Growth of Federal Funding for University Research

The number of university research scientists and the costs of their research work have continued to grow, but for fiscal year 1993–94, budgets for the National Science Foundation (NSF) and the National Institutes of Health were not expected to keep pace with inflation. (See "Cracks in the Ivory Tower," 1992.) Federal budgets are tightening as the urgency of reducing the federal budget deficit increases. Furthermore, "big-ticket" projects that have intense political backing tend to outweigh "normal" science in attractiveness to Congress. NASA's manned space-flight program survives as a public relations triumph, despite questionable scientific justification. The Superconducting Supercollider (SSC), under construction in Texas, was endorsed by both major presidential candidates during the 1992 campaign, but in November 1993, Congress killed the SSC in order to save future capital and operating costs. The NSF's own "big science" project is the Laser Interferometer Gravitational-Wave Observatory (LIGO), whose peak period of construction funding was approaching in the fiscal year 1993–94 budget, just as the science foundation's overall funding flattened out. (See Broad, 1992.)

Congressional influence in directing federally funded research toward specific national goals is evident in NSF's operating plan for 1993, under which approximately $100 million will be spent on four strategic areas while NSF's overall budget remains approximately constant. The four areas are manufacturing research and education, advanced materials and processing, high-performance computing and communications, and small-business innovation (Anderson, 1993).

Paradigms of Research and Development

The dominant paradigm for the development of new knowledge and its translation into things of value begins with basic research and proceeds through applied research to development and commercial market introduction. But in recombinant DNA (genetic engineering) research and in semiconductors, to cite two examples, this more or less leisurely progression has been compressed in time and the sequence of development becomes blurred. Newer university-industry relationships are emerging, as will be discussed below.

"Problem First" Research

An alternative paradigm for the development of new knowledge is exemplified by the pattern that developed in agricultural research, beginning with the Hatch Act of 1887 and continuing with subsequent state and federal enactments. Because agriculture was highly dispersed and typically conducted in small-scale enterprises, government stepped in to provide the applied research and problem solving that no single farmer could afford. With this support, American agriculture became extraordinarily strong and scientifically progressive.

In the agricultural experiment station of each U.S. land-grant university, certain funds are devoted to basic scientific research, even though applied research and field assistance are the stations' primary missions. When a new problem or an unmet need arises on the farm or in the marketplace, the agricultural extension specialist in the field reports it back to the station scientists. They assign the problem to a team of applied research scientists. This team has access to basic researchers who conduct long-term studies in plant genetics, entomology, and other disciplines. When a promising solution has been developed in the laboratory, it is field-tested and then disseminated to any who are interested in using it. Sometimes, commercial adaptations are undertaken by for-profit companies, which pay royalties if patents have been granted to the university on new materials or devices. Basic science itself may be enlivened when those in the laboratory are confronted with unresolved field problems.

This "problem first" paradigm prevails in many mission-oriented research organizations. Research at many frontiers between science and technology may follow the paradigm. University researchers normally concentrate, however, on the applied science problems that are beyond the immediate horizon of technological possibilities. By relying on long-term support and by avoiding—as industrial firms cannot—preoccupation with the very next generation of a product or service, university researchers further the more distant goals of technology.

Examples of University-Industry Cooperation

The Microelectronics Laboratory at the University of California, Berkeley, receives part of its funding from NSF and part from the Defense Advanced Research Projects Agency (DARPA), a branch of the federal government. A major component of the laboratory's support comes, however, from twenty companies, each of which contributes $120,000 per year, and more than one hundred companies whose contributions are in the $10,000 to $50,000 range. The laboratory also receives matching funds from the State of California, which have been specially allocated.

The laboratory seeks the involvement of corporate scientists in the definition and formulation of research problems, and there is provision for periods of visitation by these scientists if they can be spared from their company work. The laboratory operates as an open facility, on the principle that the stimulus of free circulation of ideas is highly productive, whereas restrictions on the discussion of work in process or the dissemination of research results would be stultifying. The faculty and students of the laboratory also seek wide contacts with academic scientists across the campus, as new problems that appear on the agenda require fresh insights and leads from basic science.

The Center for Integrated Systems at Stanford University, in a similar pattern, received capital grants of $750,000 each from a number of companies for its laboratory building. The building was designed with the expectation that the infrastructure and equipment requirements for research may change rapidly. Large spaces between floors permit installation of ducts, wiring, and other service systems whenever the multidisciplinary teams that work in the laboratory change the focus of their experimental methods. Sponsoring companies contribute substantial annual grants for operations, and these funds are joined with federal and university support funds.

Single-Sponsor Arrangements for Specialized University Research

The Massachusetts Institute of Technology established a long-term research relationship in biological science with Du Pont. Hoeschst AG, the German chemical and pharmaceutical company, financed a laboratory for recombinant DNA research at Massachusetts General Hospital and pledged $10 million per year for five years to attract an outstanding director and provide facilities.

Carnegie-Mellon University and Bosch AG of Germany established a joint venture corporation, the Carnegie-Bosch Robotics Institute, in 1989–90. Former Carnegie-Mellon president Richard M. Cyert served as founding president of the institute. Bosch has provided a senior staff member to serve as accounting officer of the new entity. The company also has the right to apply for patents on new processes or devices. The new institute augmented the strengths of Carnegie-Mellon in computer science, manufacturing engineering, and related fields.

Ties to a single industrial sponsor, like those created when an applied research program at a university receives support from a single-mission agency of the federal government, entail certain risks of intrusion and control. (See Day, 1976, for a study of contrasts between the client-focused ORU and other research organizations.) The sponsor may demand prepublication clearance of research papers and other reports, or may seek other proprietary advantages from the relationship. In one instance, the industrial sponsor had the right to maintain two of its own staff scientists in residence at the university laboratory to observe methodologies, instrumentation, and results.

In principle, the fruits of basic research are expected to be released into the public domain, and the academic researcher has not only the right but the duty to publish and discuss results freely with other scientists. This "public goods" view of fundamental knowledge stands in contrast to the corporate perspective. The latter justifies research and development as an investment in new products or processes whose uniqueness is to be protected where possible—by patenting or by maintaining proprietary secrecy—because that uniqueness engenders market value.

In the semiconductor industry and some other industries, patents and copyrights are circumvented with relative ease. The race for competitive advantage is to the swift, and lead time with the best new ideas is coveted. The two laboratories at Berkeley and Stanford help their numerous industrial sponsors to maintain state-of-the-art currency through research done on basic problems that must be solved before development of commercial products can begin.

The open-laboratory approach promotes free scientific communication—between scientists in the same and different universities and between the university scientist and the industrial scientist. But this conflicts with the instinct for control that lies behind industrial secrecy and the secrecy cloaking national security. If universities accept industrial support with restraining conditions on publication and free discussion, they not only create internal philosophical tensions but they may also prevent their own scientists from making the fullest possible contributions.

Nelson and Winter (1982) find that patent controls and other restraints on the spread and use of knowledge augment private profitability in some industries much more than in others.

Universities themselves are becoming more aggressive in seeking patent control (and potential royalty income) on inventions by university scientists and engineers. These efforts may precipitate two kinds of conflict: between the university and its inventor-researcher, who may claim rights to personal patent filing outside university control; and between one university and another, where a fight for primacy and first filing may erupt.

Technology transfer has become an important and controversial topic in the major universities. Federal funding agencies often seek to encourage it as a valid means of disseminating research results, and universities themselves are increasingly seeking to capture royalties and other income by exploiting discoveries made by their researchers. Matkin (1990) has a comprehensive treatment of universities' policies and practices on technology transfer.

Megaprojects, Research Consortia, and University Management of Federal Laboratories

Facilities and equipment of great size and cost have become necessary in high-energy physics and in astronomy, with related disciplines also involved in their creation and political support. In fiscal year 1983, total federal obligations to the major university-affiliated Federally Funded Research and Development Centers (FFRDCs) amounted to $2.75 billion (National Science Board, 1986a, appendix table 5.24). A significant portion of this total went to classified weapons research and development at Lawrence Livermore National Laboratory and Los Alamos Scientific Laboratory, whose combined budgets were a little over $1 billion.

When a very large-scale facility is created, it requires expert operating management to minimize downtime and to schedule experiments by scientists from a variety of institutions. The funding agencies want to ensure maximum usage of these one-of-a-kind facilities. However, periodic budget crunches at the federal level impair utilization, because operating support must be reduced and major improvements postponed.

Each university's scientists stand in an uneasy relation to these major facilities, knowing that shared use is necessary yet concerned that the funding of the facilities may cut into the normal flow of project grants. Proposals for new major facilities—the most recent having been the SSC and LIGO—threaten both peer-review research grants and federal budgets. The debate over the SSC included suggestions that the United States should have tried to interest European countries and Japan in a cooperative multinational venture to share the enormous capital cost (originally estimated at $4 billion and, by 1992, revised to $8 billion), so as not to jeopardize other federal funding of physical and biological science research. The politics of big-science grants involves intensive congressional lobbying and direct congressional earmarking of funds for megaprojects. Coherence and scientific priority are often defeated by this process.

New regional research institutes such as the Institute of Physics at Santa Barbara and the Mathematical Sciences Research Institute (MSRI) at Berkeley are NSF-financed consortia. They bring together senior experts and junior researchers on one-year appointments to work on specific themes at the frontiers of the disciplines. Such institutes enrich research opportunities for the individuals concerned, and MSRI seeks to provide stimulus to institutions in the region by arranging for its fellows to lecture at numerous locations each year. One-year rotation minimizes the danger that such institutes could go stale or could drift into the European model of the research institute with permanent career staff, separated from the universities.

As the national research enterprise becomes more complex, consortia and special institutes will probably grow in number. Universities will no doubt compete to become host institutions for these, in the expectation of positive benefits to faculty productivity and scientific communication. They will have to be alert to possible diversion of faculty energies or creation of competing extra-university research organizations.

The largest sponsored relationship of all is the contract between the U.S. Department of Energy (DOE) and the University of California for management of three DOE-owned laboratories: Lawrence Berkeley Laboratory (LBL), Lawrence Livermore

National Laboratory (LLNL), and Los Alamos Scientific Laboratory (LASL). The latter two laboratories conduct classified weapons work as well as nonclassified research in applied science. These relationships began with the World War II research effort on the atomic bomb and the subsequent establishment of LLNL for research on the hydrogen bomb under the leadership of Edward Teller.

At each negotiation for periodic contract renewals, representatives of the University of California and of DOE have struggled with issues of mission, control, and compatibility of the classified work with the commitment of university scientists and scholars to intellectual freedom. The Academic Senate of the University has criticized the relationship on numerous occasions, and in response, the university's president has sought increased academic oversight of the work of all three laboratories. Nevertheless, the classified work at LLNL and LASL defies efforts at normal academic review. The Academic Senate voted in 1990 to have the university phase out its management of these two laboratories. The regents and the Office of the President negotiated continuation contracts in 1992, which were apparently intended to blunt the Academic Senate's criticism by providing new standards protecting intellectual freedom at the laboratories. The university receives a management fee of $14 million per year, which the President's Office can spend for research support unless "unallowable costs" have to be covered. While the annual fee is precious to the Office of the President, from an academic standpoint the support of faculty and graduate student research at LBL—and to some extent the support of unclassified research at LLNL—is far more important.

The relationship remains inherently troubling. The U.S. Department of Energy periodically asserts a need for more specific control of activities at the laboratories. From university faculty groups and some individuals in the administration, on the other hand, come expressions of concern about the adequacy of the university's scientific and academic oversight.

Pressures and Frauds in the Conduct of Academic Research

Pressure to announce results in large-scale research projects exists in all countries where big science is practiced, but "first discovery" probably has greater sway in American science than elsewhere. On occasion, this pressure leads to falsification of data and publication of phony results. One such instance involved David Baltimore, a winner of the Nobel Prize in biological science. After becoming president of Rockefeller University, one of his former faculty research associates at MIT was accused of falsifying laboratory data in a project that Baltimore had headed. A postdoctoral researcher who tried to expose the allegedly unethical behavior was black-balled from research employment for several years. She was eventually vindicated; Baltimore resigned his presidency.

Other egregious lapses from the code of scientific research conduct occurred at Yale University's medical school and at the National Institutes of Health (NIH). In 1992, Robert Gallo, a renowned cell biologist, was found to have misappropriated cultures from a French laboratory and to have falsely announced that he had discovered the HIV virus. In November 1993, Gallo was exonerated by a scientific appeals panel. The dispute continued, however, until the French were accorded recognition for their work.

One of the most curious recent episodes of apparent scientific error was the announced discovery of "cold fusion" in 1989 at the University of Utah. B. Stanley Pons, a professor at that university, and Martin Fleischmann, a professor at Southampton University in England, said that they had succeeded in bringing about hydrogen fusion in a test tube at room temperature—a claim that was startling to the physics profession. They did not fully disclose the method they had used, ostensibly so that they could safeguard their potential rights as patent holders.

Meanwhile, the president of the University of Utah capitalized on the broad promise of the discovery: he asked for and obtained

$4 million from the State of Utah for a new National Cold Fusion Institute. But doubts about the validity of the discovery accumulated, and the institute faced a clouded future. Pons and Fleischmann came under sharp criticism from Oak Ridge physicist Frank Close in his 1991 book, *Too Hot to Handle*.

It is all-important that the scientific community uphold and enforce its standards of appropriate scientific conduct. These episodes also highlight how an institution's reputation can be affected by the misconduct of an individual. There is no easy way to exercise institutional oversight of scientific work; in some circumstances, indeed, attempts at oversight may be interpreted as interference with academic freedom.

Recovery of Indirect Cost or "Overhead"

When federal agencies began to underwrite large-scale university research during and after World War II, the agencies and the universities borrowed from the defense procurement process some techniques for the accounting of a contractor's indirect costs—that is, costs of space, equipment, and services that are essential to the contractor's general operations but cannot be specifically identified with the project in question. Each university now negotiates annually an approved Indirect Cost Recovery (ICR) rate, or "overhead rate," as faculty researchers often refer to it.

Incentive questions arise at several levels in connection with this problem of indirect cost recovery. First, Federal Circular A-21 (Office of Management and Budget, 1993) lays down the procedures for accumulating a series of cost pools (for example, a pool for the totality of library costs, another for maintenance and operation of physical plant). The circular then specifies procedures for estimating the proportion of total usage in each cost category that is traceable to federally funded research activity. Accounting and management problems are sufficiently complicated, however, to leave considerable room for argument. The two federal agencies responsible for determination and oversight of indirect cost recovery are at the Department of Defense and the Department of Health and Human Services. Individual universities have very different negotiated rates, varying from less than 50 percent of total direct costs to 80 percent or more.

Faculty principal investigators on federally funded projects often complain about high ICR rates, arguing that the net amount they can actually spend for their research activity is reduced because ICR payments may come from a fixed total amount of granted funds. One proposal for reform called for an agreed and uniform rate on certain parts of the total federally funded research budget.

Some contributors to *Science,* the magazine of the American Association for the Advancement of Science, have suggested that a set of uniform ICR rates and procedures be established for all universities, to minimize negotiation problems with the federal agencies. ICR rates are said to be much higher for industrial contractors employed by the federal government than for universities. Also, public universities face a situation that is fundamentally different from the one facing private universities. The latter regard indirect cost recovery as a means of financing the basic fabric and infrastructure services of the institution—library, accounting system, departmental administration, and so on—and claim that their base budgets would be severely impaired if rates were reduced or capped.

Public universities, on the other hand, receive state appropriations for most of their basic infrastructure support. Indirect cost recovery, as viewed by many state authorities, is simply federal reimbursement for the portion of these state-supported services that is used in federally funded research activity. By this reckoning, the state government would be entitled to capture all or nearly all of the monies paid in indirect cost recovery. In fact, most states share them to some extent with their public universities, so that part of the recovered funds can be used for university purposes. Even so, the public universities as a group have negotiated rates that are considerably lower than those of the major private institutions. One analysis showed that, of thirty campuses earning a high volume of research dollars, the average ICR rate of the private universities was 63.6 percent in 1986, as against an average of 42.8 percent for the public university campuses. If state governments allowed their public universities to keep more of the funds recovered, or more above some base dollar figure, the universities would probably work harder to obtain larger cost recovery.

In both private and public universities, however, indirect cost recovery is universally unpopular among faculty research investigators. Partly, this is due to the practice of some funding agencies, including NSF, of making total-cost awards, in which overhead costs are subtracted from the amount available for use by the principal investigator. But another reason, much closer to home, is that the faculty investigator usually has a sense that funds received by the university have simply vanished into the administrative maw, with no discernible benefit to the project, the department, or any tangible activity of interest to the academic process.

In fact, some of the ammunition for federal attacks on the universities' practices regarding indirect cost recovery has come from faculty members antagonized by what they feel is unfair allocative treatment. This aspect of the incentive (or disincentive) system is troubling, because it makes antagonists of energetic and devoted leaders in the universities. Some universities now apply balm to these wounds by passing on a portion of the recovered indirect costs to the department and principal investigator, to fund equipment purchases and other needs.

University Research and the Issue of Selective Priorities

Federal funding having flattened out, some research leaders argue that universities should be more selective in their priorities. D. Allan Bromley, White House science adviser during the Bush administration, issued a report of the President's Council of Advisors on Science and Technology (PCAST) in December 1992, which said: "[It] is unreasonable to expect that the system of research-intensive universities will continue to grow" and that it is "ill-advised" for such universities "to aspire to excel in all or most areas of scholarship" (Bromley, 1992). Bromley's report recommends that universities be more selective, cutting away low-quality programs and concentrating resources on those of the highest quality. The report also recommends greater emphasis on teaching, even if this means less research.

Bromley and PCAST also deplored federal agencies' failure to reimburse the full amount of indirect cost. They condemned political logrolling on large-scale grants in Congress, and they criticized self-protective efforts of federal laboratories to hold on to their funds by recasting their missions in the post–Cold War world, even if they could not do so effectively.

One can read into these policy recommendations the question whether the United States can support as many research universities as it now has, much less add to the list from among the several hundred doctorate-granting institutions that seek higher status. (This book has previously cited the increase of sixteen Research Universities I from 1986 to 1993, and similar upward shifts of doctoral institutions to Research Universities II.) Further, Bromley's report predicts, as well as deplores, the continuing politicization of research grant mechanisms. The remainder of the 1990s will be a tangled web for university research.

Nichols (1993) points out that the increasingly political nature of federal research funding has changed the basis of the national research effort. Whereas previously this effort was driven by the scientific goals of each field of inquiry, it now serves specific policy goals: U.S. competitiveness and other utilitarian objectives (pp. 210–211). Also, the federal government has rejected the notion that every qualified scientist has an entitlement to federal support of his or her project research (pp. 202–205).

As Nichols puts it, universities developed myopic expectations that the generous funding of the 1960s and 1970s could be projected into the indefinite future (p. 212–213). He states that universities have not yet faced up to the realities of a changed funding environment—one in which science faculties can no longer expect to gain blanket extramural funding for their desired research activity but must instead develop differentiated research specializations and greater willingness for cross-institutional cooperation.

Chapter Thirteen

Quality Standards
and Assessment

The "quality" of a university must be considered in several dimensions, and it contains a number of paradoxical elements. First, various groups hold strong (and differing) views about the general quality of institutions they have heard about, without necessarily having concrete information on which to base those views. Second, the notion of the "quality" of a university may refer to the reputed knowledge and achievements of its graduates, or to the fame of its faculty and the size of its library and research establishment, or to the sheer notoriety of the institution if it is continually in the news. Or it may refer instead to the processes for learning that characterize the university, quite apart from whether these processes are powerfully effective in imparting knowledge. Finally, contemporary interest in Total Quality Management focuses for the most part on features of performance in administrative services; the academic core of the institution has not received systematic attention from this new and perhaps faddish discipline.

The various dimensions of quality are difficult to define and measure. Furthermore, any particular dimension may be of great interest to one constituency while having no relevance to another. Among the issues of interest are: "global" quality impressions that create a pecking order of institutions; areas of university operation for which quality concerns and measures are relevant; analysis of the markets for reputation; and short- and long-term strategies for quality enhancement.

"Global" Views of the Quality of an Institution

There is a vague consensus about the "best university" (or two, or three) and the "best college" (or two, or three). Such global views derive from institutions' general visibility and their auras of distinction. The views are usually based on general hearsay rather than on direct observation.

Somewhat more specific are the descriptive characterizations of institutions in directories of colleges and universities. An example is the College Entrance Examination Board's *College Handbook* (1992). These directories report, for each institution:

- The degrees offered and the number awarded annually in broadly defined fields
- The undergraduate majors offered
- Admissions policies (SAT scores and the percentage of applicants accepted—indicating the degree of selectivity—and the profile of the student body in terms of academic background, geographical origins, and gender)
- Persistence and completion rates
- Indicia of student life (housing, athletics, student services; and tuition, financial aid, and costs of attendance)

The elements of differentiation among institutions can be summarized as:

- Selectivity in the student inflow
- Extent of localization or wider "draw" of students
- Persistence and achievement of students
- Program variety and number of degree levels represented
- Stated fees and expected cost of attendance

These descriptive features are often reported within categories of institutional taxonomy. The Carnegie Commission on Higher Education formulated its classification in the 1970s as a framework for the analysis of various types of institution in a series of reports and monographs. The main categories are (Evangelauf, 1994):

- Research University I and II (about 3 percent of institutions)
- Doctoral University I and II (3 percent)
- Master's (Comprehensive) Universities and Colleges I and II (15 percent)
- Baccalaureate (Liberal Arts) Colleges I and II (18 percent)
- Associate of Arts Institutions (41 percent)
- Specialized Institutions (20 percent)

The Research University I draws students, especially graduate students, from national and international origins and produces numerous visible contributions to research and scholarship. In the pecking order as perceived by current or aspiring full-time academics, the Research University I has the highest prestige, arising from its emphasis on graduate education and research. The Association of American Universities (AAU) is the representative organization of these universities, with fifty-nine members as of 1990.

A different basis of prestige exists for the predominantly undergraduate institutions, headed by the most selective private colleges that draw students from regional and national origins. In most cases, research universities offer high-quality undergraduate programs, but they organize undergraduate curricula and instruction in ways that are different from those used by the liberal arts colleges, as they employ a cadre of graduate students as teaching assistants for discussion sections or laboratory sections of large undergraduate lecture courses.

Kerr (1991) has written of the intense competition for reputational quality among the Research Universities I, with other institutions also seeking to become highly visible research universities. Kerr attributes the competitiveness among universities to the drive for professional reputation in the research-minded professoriate, the vital competition for extramural (particularly federal) research funds, and the efforts of exceptional institutional leaders to advance the cause of their universities.

While numerous institutions seek greater recognition, some are not favored by history, location, or resources. It may nevertheless be feasible for a university in the Research II category to raise its visibility over time by attracting a critical mass of resources and talent, finding a specialized academic niche, and publicizing its achievements adroitly. Emory University and George Mason University are perhaps good recent examples of such improved fortunes, as was Carnegie-Mellon in the 1960s and 1970s. (Between 1987 and 1994, sixteen Research Universities II became Research Universities I; one Doctoral University I made it to Research University I and sixteen to Research University II; and one Doctoral University II jumped to Research University I while three moved to Research University II; Evangelauf, 1994, p. A20.)

The Doctoral Universities (which offer some doctoral programs but do not have a deep base of research) and the Master's Universities and Colleges often suffer from the disappointed expectations of their faculty members and from lack of achievement drive among their students. Some have developed a distinctive educational mission that helps them to attain cohesion and strength of purpose.

Evaluations by Academic Discipline and Professional Field

There are several sets of published institutional ratings as well as ratings by individual discipline; most major professions have ratings as well. A private rating system by Jack Gourman is published periodically. (See Gourman, 1989a, 1989b, 1993a, 1993b.) It covers fifty-five disciplines and also provides sets of ratings for law, dentistry, and allied health professions. Gourman lists fourteen criteria according to which faculty or administrative respondents at institutions are requested to rate their own institutions. Ratings on the individual criteria are not published; rather, Gourman reduces the information to a single number on the scale 0.0 to 5.0. An institution's program rating in a given discipline, or its "overall rating" for graduate programs, is then rank-ordered against other institutions. Although *The Gourman Report* is widely cited, lack of information about the identity of the rating respondents and about the method of reducing responses to a single number leaves many academic critics uneasy and mistrustful.

In the field of business management, both *Business Week* and *U.S. News and World Report* publish annual ratings, and the latter publication does so for schools of law. The business school respondents include current students, some faculty, and corporate representatives who visit business schools to interview students who are job applicants. Geographical concentration of the raters is one issue; the method of combining evaluations from several sources is another.

Far more carefully conducted and reported are the research doctorate evaluations. Allan Cartter undertook the first comprehensive evaluation effort in 1966, under the auspices of the American Council on Education (ACE), in connection with his studies of the dynamics of supply and demand for faculty in higher education. ACE continued this with the "Roose-Andersen" ratings in 1970. These were important contributions to general understanding of the quality of graduate education in the United States. They were also, inevitably, controversial, and the debate about them included a strong "envy quotient."

More than a decade later, the National Research Council, acting for a consortium of learned societies, published the most comprehensive and objective ratings for academic disciplines. A committee headed by Lyle V. Jones and Gardner Lindzey developed a set of indicators (sixteen of them for most fields), several of which required sampling surveys of expert academic opinion. Twenty-eight academic disciplines and four engineering fields are included in the five-volume final report (Jones, Lindzey, and Coggeshall, 1982). A doctoral program was included in the ratings if it had awarded a minimum of two degrees within the two years prior to the surveys.

Careful statistical methods are described and applied in each case, including normalized scores for quantitative variates. The designers of the assessment system did not attempt to combine all sixteen indicators into a single rating or rank ordering; in fact, they warn the reader against doing so. However, academic administrators quickly turned to the reputational indicators—the peer evaluation of faculty quality, the educational effectiveness of the program, and improvement of program—in each field and used these as the prime markers of program quality.

A new survey was conducted in the spring of 1993, which included the same list of disciplines as in 1982 plus several others. When published, the ratings will provide a new "scorecard" of quality indicators, comparing all the U.S. university doctoral programs in a given field. This will make possible a review of the changes in status of each university's departmental programs between 1982 and 1993. The report is sure to be required reading in every university president's office.

From this discussion of rating systems, two inferences may be drawn. First, if rating comparisons are made on just one dimension of institutional offerings, consumers of the ratings should be informed of the sources of the data, the methods of scoring, and the way in which the comparative index has been constructed. Second, if two or more dimensions are involved, the data sources and measure for each should be disclosed; and if an overall index is constructed to facilitate comparisons, the method of combining dimensional measures and of constructing the overall index should be explained. The Gourman ratings fail to meet these criteria. The National Research Council's *Assessment of Research-Doctorate Programs in the United States* (Jones, Lindzey, and Coggeshall, 1982) discloses its sources of data and displays results responsibly; and it intentionally avoids the philosophical and political dilemmas of constructing an overall index.

Whether institutional and discipline ratings are analytically valid or not, they are paid much attention by prospective students and by many others in the academic community. Therefore, a university administration cannot afford to ignore the signals that ratings convey.

Assessments of Student Achievement

What does the student learn? How can achieved learning be assessed? Universities such as Oxford and Cambridge have traditionally awarded the B.A. degree, and honors, on the basis of performance in comprehensive written examinations at the end of the undergraduate years. Every year's degree candidates in a given field sit for the same examination. Assuming that the examiners are conscientious and that there is consensus about the content of knowledge in each field and the standards for judging proficiency, the comprehensive examination permits enforcement of a minimum passing standard and also makes possible the rank ordering of degree candidates. A relatively small number of U.S. collegiate institutions use comprehensive examinations; Swarthmore College and the undergraduate programs of the University of Chicago are among them.

Undergraduate curricula are designed by faculty in each U.S. university for each major or field of concentration. They consist of required courses, advanced and elective courses, and "breadth" courses, but institutions vary in each major's curriculum and passing standards. The student earns a certain number of credits by passing each course. The bachelor's degree is awarded when the student has completed the required courses in the major and assembled both the credits for the major and some minimum total number of credits. Usually, a required period of residence in the institution is also specified, to prevent excessive use of transfer credits. The course grades in the major and in the totality of all courses taken are recorded on the student's transcript of academic record, and the Grade Point Average (GPA) is often printed on the transcript. The GPA is important as a general measure of the student's achievement, and it is typically used as part of the basis for later admission to graduate study.

Although completion of requirements for a major and success in accumulating a record of high course grades and high GPA provide evidence of industrious application, they fall short as a basis for answering important questions about the student's achievement and for producing a rank ordering of students in a given major. No two students completing a given major are likely to have taken exactly the same list of courses, nor is it likely that instructors in different courses will award course grades according to the same expected standards of attainment. Beyond these differences in the de facto content of knowledge exposure and in the standards for measuring performance in each course, the system avoids imposing a single broad criterion of academic achievement, analogous to the comprehensive examination systems discussed earlier.

"Absolute" Levels of Achievement

The GPA and the comprehensive examination system are alike in attempting to assess the student's general level of absolute achievement at the time he or she is awarded the bachelor's degree. Neither method addresses two other issues of assessment: the student's promise of creative performance in a chosen occupation or in advanced academic or professional studies; and the "value added" that the educational program has provided.

Both methods reward systematic and orderly application of effort to conventionally defined topics. Evidence of original and creative achievement would have to be secured by different means: assessment of a thesis project, a creative work, or a performance of some kind. This sort of evidence is provided and assessed in connection with academic prizes and some types of honors awards that can be pursued by outstanding students at their individual option, but it is not typically built into regular undergraduate curricula.

"Value Added" in Education

A student's level of competence or mastery of a subject at the beginning of an interval of study can be compared with the competence achieved by the end of the interval. "Value added" is the difference between the two, or the gain in mastery. The question of value added addresses the contribution of the institution itself to the student's achievement. A university or liberal arts college that prides itself on accepting the highest cut of entering students can impose strict standards of grading and yet expect the great majority of its students to persist, earn the bachelor's degree, and be eligible to go on to graduate study. The institution has imparted intellectual and cultural sophistication and a sense of high achievement standards to these students and has helped them to prepare themselves for graduate school. While this represents added value, it is a very different educational contribution from the one made by some other institutions, and the achievement by the individual student is also different.

Many students face college or university education from an inauspicious starting point: elementary and secondary education may have been inadequate or uneven; the family setting may have been such that academic achievement goals were not strongly reinforced; or the student may have been uncertain of his or her educational goals—or preoccupied with the pains of maturation—and hence dropped out, to come back to formal education later. A college or university that makes a place for such a student and helps that student achieve at a reasonable level, with persistence to the bachelor's degree, has performed a role quite different from the elite role of the highly selective institution. It has assisted the student in completing a transformative experience, and it has accordingly produced enormous added value to that student's life. Society, in turn, benefits by receiving a graduate whose life prospects are brighter and whose contributions are more valuable than they otherwise might have been.

The famous names in U.S. undergraduate education are, naturally enough, the names associated with high selectivity in admissions, strenuous curricula, demanding grading standards, and a high percentage of students continuing toward graduate study. Yet the American system as a whole does provide opportunities for value added. Many private liberal arts colleges draw from a limited geographical radius and accept high school graduates with average records. Community colleges in some states, including California, allow state residents to enroll even without a high school diploma; then, if the student does well in an academic-transfer curriculum, a four-year institution or the state university will accept the student for transfer at the upper-division level. The student may receive counseling and other assistance in choosing what steps to take, but the process is voluntary and self-managed in many respects.

This opportunity to start late or to try again for a second chance is different from the traditional systems in, for example, the United Kingdom and the Netherlands, where very early separation of secondary school students into academic and vocational streams has been the rule. The "ordinary level" (distinguished from the later "advanced level") examinations in Britain, at approximately age fifteen, often have had an all but irreversible impact on life consequences for young people. Britain's Open University now operates as a new kind of gateway toward a university degree, often for students at a later age.

From the public policy standpoint, high selectivity in admissions, high persistence to the degree, and completion within a compressed time period offer prospects of reducing the overall cost of a college degree, regardless of how it is financed. The approaches that facilitate value added include differentiated or remedial early courses, tutoring and other support systems during the college years, opportunities to start again or start late, and flexibility to stretch out the time taken to complete the degree. All of these tend to add to the overall cost of a college degree. The political appeal of widened access and greater diversity of students is significant, but it competes with the cost-increasing tendencies that accompany efforts to provide broad access with a reasonable success rate.

Assessing the Quality of Instruction

Three steps in an evaluative process—quality control, quality assessment, and quality assurance—can be seen as a sequence of efforts to deal with the quality problem from different vantage points. Tony Becher (1992) of the Institute of Continuing and Professional Education at the University of Sussex, England, has identified these distinct elements of the quality management process. He also points out that pressures toward quality assurance mounted in the United Kingdom when universities experienced a loss of public trust and confidence in the late 1960s and the 1970s.

Although the academic department has jurisdiction over the conduct of a course, it has become less customary for other professors to visit a course, observe the quality of lecture and discussion, and engage in other forms of quality assessment. Departments do occasionally redesign curricula and individual courses, often with the subsequent approval of a broader faculty oversight body. However, the course instructor is expected to initiate incremental improvements, bring topics and content up to date, and make the course attractive and challenging to students.

Quality assessment often focuses on the process of instruction and not on the results. Size of classes is a gross measure; conventional opinion holds that small is good and large is bad. The lecturer's organization of material and appeal to students may be observed and evaluated, and the conduct of discussion or laboratory sessions, as well as the lectures and examinations, are often rated by students at the end of the term. In 1986, Richard Light of Harvard organized the Harvard Assessment Seminars, which brought faculty members together to discuss questions they had posed concerning the quality of teaching and learning. These discussions focused on teaching processes, not on outcomes ("Harvard University," 1990).

Assessment according to results would entail some form of external or standardized test, but this could cause academic instructors to avoid any element of course design or course material that was not to be dealt with in that test. The features of a course of instruction include:

- The design of the course, that is, the topics and coverage chosen
- The presentation of materials, in readings, lectures, and demonstrations
- The course performance expected of the student—papers, reports, and projects; laboratory experiments; quizzes and examinations; participation and interaction with other students and with the instructor

The enrollment size of the course is also an important feature. A lecture course with an enrollment of five hundred students necessarily functions differently in all of the above dimensions from a small seminar of ten students:

- Tests and examinations are likely to be designed as multiple choice, in order to facilitate machine grading.
- The lecturer is a performer and not a discussion leader.
- The course must be administered in a highly structured, orderly manner because of the necessary division of labor between the course lecturer and the teaching assistants.
- Opportunities for individualistic variations by students are at a minimum.

Quality control is exercised by a department chairman, who sees to it that course meetings are regularly held and not canceled at whim; that examinations and papers are graded fairly (or at least with minimal complaints to higher authority); and that teaching assistants are properly supervised. The department may also engage in quality assessment—that is, by observing the clarity and challenge of lectures and by reviewing the examinations to ensure that they provide adequate coverage of subject matter. (*How* these observations are made, and how they are summed up for the course instructor and for the administration, becomes a very delicate issue of departmental politics.) A system of quality assurance then seeks to impose standards of expected performance with respect to each element of course design and course presentation.

The highest quality of instruction is often associated with *enrichment* and with *individualization*. An enriched course or entire curriculum is enlivened by student field trips and experiences, by special guest lectures, by experiments with computer-based exercises and materials, and by other imaginative departures from normal instructional routine. Variation of course content, required performance, or mode of presentation to fit the individual student can produce exceptional learning impact; the ultimate form of individualized instruction is the one-on-one tutorial.

Both enrichment and individualization drive up the expense of instruction, and academic administrators are therefore resistant to them except where academic priorities are high (as in doctoral student supervision) or where the institution obtains a clear benefit.

Quality of Instruction from the Professor's Viewpoint

The professor in charge of a course usually feels an obligation to emphasize content that is as close as possible to the state of the field. As knowledge in a field grows and changes, new scholarship and findings are incorporated first in graduate courses, then in advanced undergraduate courses, and finally in introductory undergraduate courses. Research universities often take leadership in imparting this new knowledge through incremental improvements in existing courses, initiation of new and experimental courses, and occasionally through restructuring of an entire curriculum.

The faculty member's own rewards for high-quality instruction are normally greatest when course content and student readiness permit a dominant focus on the frontier of the subject and on the faculty member's current research interests. Graduate courses and seminars are attractive teaching assignments for this reason. The faculty member may, however, find enduring satisfaction in teaching the introductory course in a subject. Some academic departments have a tradition of assigning outstanding faculty members to this duty. Furthermore, lectures to a large student enrollment are performances, and some faculty members relish audience response and attention, pouring enormous energy into lecture preparation.

Faculty members are conventionally judged for advancement on the three general criteria of teaching, research, and public service. Peers both within and outside the university participate in evaluations of research achievements, the main ground for advancement. Achievements in teaching are usually felt to be more difficult to evaluate. In some universities, students fill out rating forms at the conclusion of each course. Less frequent now than formerly is class visitation by faculty colleagues. When a case for advancement is being prepared by a departmental committee, members are obliged to undertake a review of teaching, including the faculty member's work in design and conduct of courses. Occasionally, a department arranges for student interviews at the time of graduation, and it also may interview former students several years subsequent to graduation to obtain views of course teaching that had enduring impact.

If faculty advancement and salary actions were more clearly dependent on a convincing demonstration of good teaching, there would be more consistent interest in the development and use of good methods of teaching evaluation.

Quality of Instruction from the Student's Viewpoint

What is a student's primary goal? To gain the certification of course completion and a diploma? To learn the basics of the subject matter he or she is studying? Or to excel in the subject and even use it later on? The answer to this question shapes the student's views of what constitutes high quality of instruction. If the purpose is to excel, then the faculty member's mastery of the subject and his or her encouragement of originality are prized. If the purpose is certification, then getting by with minimum effort is likely to be the paramount criterion.

Students do vary greatly in their perspectives, in general and course by course. Thus, interpretation of student ratings is ambiguous, especially when computer-processable forms are used without provision for narrative comments. Students do like to be entertained and challenged, and they flock to the popular lecturer. They also face many time pressures; therefore, they have a preference for efficient learning—that is, organization and presentation of a course that economizes their time and effort for achieving success in relation to their own objectives.

The supporting environment for students has significant effects. Many institutions have established learning centers and have provided coaching on effective methods of study. Places for quiet individual study are essential. Evidence that students can help each other to learn has prompted Uri Treisman of the University of Texas at Austin to organize mathematics courses in which students are assigned to study in teams.

Assessment as an Instrument of Public Policy

Assessment has an important public constituency: governments that vote appropriations for public universities and for much student financial aid. In England, governmental budget allocations, even down to the individual discipline at a university, are already based in part on assessments, and a controlling bureaucracy uses them to assert policy priorities (Trow, 1993).

In the United States, reliance on assessment in the making of public policy is also on the rise. "While at mid-decade just three or four states took an active role in promoting assessment, some 40 states are now taking steps to require or promote assessment" (Hutchings and Marchese, 1990, p. 16). State governors and legislators first evinced anxiety about the failings of K–12 education, and they turned to assessment for a "base" from which to evaluate incremental improvements. Complaints from college students and their parents about poor teaching, unavailable courses, and other deficiencies prompted moves toward state-level assessment of higher education as well.

Hutchings and Marchese describe a long struggle beginning in 1985 between the University of Virginia (UVa) and the State Council on Higher Education for Virginia (SCHEV), as the latter organization pressured the state's postsecondary institutions to establish assessment mechanisms. SCHEV wanted to see that each institution put in place a credible, explicit, and comprehensive assessment program. UVa first launched a trial program with five academic departments; SCHEV criticized this as inadequate both in substance and in coverage. Then UVa, led by a new university provost, moved toward the articulation of a more complete assessment scheme (1990, pp. 17–21). As of fall 1994, the process of interaction between UVa and SCHEV on issues of assessment was still ongoing.

In part, the states' moves toward assessment trace to underlying dissatisfaction with, and suspicion of, education and educators; but Hutchings and Marchese also cite the view of education historian Daniel Resnick that there are long swings in public sentiment—for a while, to preoccupation with access and expansion, and then to consolidation and budgeting pressure. U.S. public higher education moved into the latter phase in the late 1980s and shows no signs of emerging from it. The sanctions of budget cutting are not far from the consciousness of university administrators as they confront issues of how to conduct and report assessments. When approval of an institution's funding hinges on successful assessment, it may of course go through the motions, deliver voluminous reports, and propitiate the authorities—all without necessarily reaching deeply into the merits of the quality of instruction.

Accreditation bodies also promote assessment, in their role of oversight and certification of colleges and universities. The accreditation body, through its executive, first requires extensive documentation to be submitted by an institution undergoing certification or recertification, including statistics of academic programs and some evidence of teaching quality.

The implicit sanction is the threat of decertification, which would render the institution's students ineligible for federal and state financial aid programs. When an institution receives its accreditation report, it is sometimes able to use it to obtain funds and repair deficiencies in its library resources, its proportion of full-time faculty, and other academic resources.

Assessing the Quality of Academic Programs: Shaping University Priorities

Every university contains some weak academic programs. When resources are plentiful, these may slide along for many years without systematic diagnosis of the weaknesses. Budgetary stringency directs urgent attention to these weaknesses. (It would be sensible to review programs during periods when resources are expanding, for program consolidations and phaseouts are far easier to manage when the rest of the institution is well-off. But this is not the usual way of such things.)

When the university is preparing budgets for operating and capital resources, it may ask a department to submit intermediate-range plans and to attach a report on the strengths and weaknesses of its own academic program. Such self-reporting is partly discounted because it is, necessarily, a means of advocacy. Campus administrators may therefore convene a "visiting committee" or external panel, charged to review the academic program and make recommendations about its future. Sometimes the charge is very broad.

In other cases, the panel is asked to focus specifically on a few issues: the department's balance (or lack of it) among subfields; questions of faculty renewal; or questions about the future of the academic field.

When the national assessment of research-doctorate programs is newly available, its reputational rankings serve as a good starting point for judging the status of the program among its competitors. But it is easier to arrive at a judgmental assessment of strengths and weaknesses than to address the action questions. If a program is woefully weak, should it be phased out, or should the university devote substantial investment over a period of several years to remedying the deficiencies?

The department's faculty leadership is normally asked to respond to the external findings and recommendations. Academic advisory bodies at the college and campus level also are entitled to review them. Their deliberations usually extend over a number of months, and they may or may not be clear-cut. The process is cumbersome, and expensive of the time both of external panel-members and of campus faculty and administrators. Many compromises are likely to emerge from the review process. Without prompt and incisive final recommendations, implementing actions are difficult to bring off.

Quality and Consolidation Pressures in Europe

Ministries of education in several European countries have undertaken to restructure the universities whose budgets they control. Acherman (1984) describes in detail such an episode of consolidations and program closures in the Dutch universities. The Thatcher government in Britain gained direct control over budget allocations to the British universities, eliminating the University Grants Committee structure and pressing the universities to do more with less. (See Trow, 1993.)

Intercampus Academic Program Review in the Multicampus University System

Multicampus university systems can approach issues of program review in a manner that is dimensionally different from that of the single-campus institution. One crucial issue of long-range planning for academic quality is to determine what range of academic programs should be expected to develop on each campus. A second issue is to compare across campuses the strengths and weaknesses of programs in a given field, so that the key programs for the future of the system can be identified. Balderston (1985) contains a detailed review from which the following condensed discussion is taken.

The Academic Senate of the University of California appointed a select committee in 1975 to analyze the university's long-term expectations for enrollment and to make proposals on how to sustain high academic quality with growth. The university consists of nine campuses: the San Francisco medical campus and eight "general campuses," of which the largest are Berkeley and UCLA. Three campuses had been established in the 1950s and early 1960s to meet the university's enrollment obligations under the California Master Plan for Higher Education. Berkeley and UCLA were already close to their agreed enrollment ceilings of 27,500 students.

Anticipating that the newer campuses would expand undergraduate enrollment and instruction rapidly, the Senate committee proposed that the universitywide administration and Academic Senate oversee an expansion plan that would create one or more centers of excellence at these campuses. The campus would be asked to define a cluster of related disciplines, and within these, concentrated capital and operating budgets would facilitate a relatively rapid buildup to first-rank research and to graduate as well as undergraduate teaching. The cluster would offer the Ph.D. in each of the related disciplines. Other fields would also be represented in the faculty, but these would offer mainly undergraduate instruction. Their development toward the research facilities and faculty necessary to mount Ph.D. programs would be deferred.

The Universitywide Academic Senate received and debated the committee's report. (The present author served on the committee and participated in the debate.) Meanwhile, however, the new president of the university, David Saxon, was deeply committed to campus autonomy and campus-level initiative. (This was an old struggle within the university, beginning with UCLA's battle in the 1920s and 1930s to establish itself as a full-scale university campus.) The chief officers (chancellors) of the new campuses opposed the concept of specialization, as it would have meant the foreclosing of broader program opportunities in return for intensive resources on fewer academic areas.

Just five years later, Saxon faced severe budgetary pressures from the California state government and set in motion a planning process that permitted faculty layoffs and program reductions, if these were found necessary. The Academic Senate and the president cosponsored the formation of a Program Review Steering Committee. (Once again, the present author served as a member.) Its mandate was to oversee cross-campus program review in a number of selected fields. The committee made its selections for the initial wave of reviews, set the charge for each review, requested nominations for a review panel, and reviewed the draft report before it was circulated to Senate committees and campus chancellors.

In a number of instances, the review panel faced resistance to its requests for campus-level evaluation documents from a particular field, and information therefore had to be developed independently. Campus administrators and faculty alike were opposed, with varying degrees of intensity, to the notion of cross-campus reviews. They wanted to undertake their own internal program reviews and make their own hard choices of program reductions if those became necessary. But the smaller campuses, especially, feared that cross-campus reviews would all too often show their fledgling academic programs to be relatively weak and thus candidates for consolidation or closure.

In two years, the Program Review Steering Committee initiated a total of five major cross-campus reviews: in engineering, law, foreign languages, humanities, and education. At that point, the Universitywide Senate committees called for a "stocktaking." Around the same time, the university's new president, David Gardner, and the newly elected governor, George Deukmejian, reached a meeting of minds on the university's support budget. One week after this news was announced, the chair of the Universitywide Academic Senate called on the president to abandon plans for final adoption of retrenchment and faculty layoff policies on the grounds that they were no longer needed. Cross-campus program reviews, being a part of the process, were stopped, thus ending an experiment in rationalization of academic programs.

The *academic department and the campus*, not the university as a whole, turned out to be the natural units of affiliation and loyalty for serious discourse on quality. The university president could have enforced a retrenchment policy via the budget-setting mechanism, but this would have been dangerous and difficult. Thus, even though a multicampus university system should, in principle, be able to advance the cause of academic quality by setting priorities across the system, it was difficult to bring this off.

The University of Wisconsin system and the University of Minnesota system do manage to maintain sharp and effective program control. The Madison campus and the Twin Cities campus are "flagships." The other campuses have a consciously limited and restricted role, and their ambitions are correspondingly controlled.

Issues of Quality in University Services and the University's Climate for Learning

In the early 1990s, the concept of Total Quality Management (TQM) caught hold in many universities, drawing new attention to the quality and effectiveness of administrative services. The hope was that university administrative systems could be reformed and redesigned, making better use of information technology. At its best, a system could improve performance and save resources at the same time, as American industry had done. The goals typically called for improved accuracy, clarity, and timeliness of response. Both student services and business services were on the reform agenda.

Some quality improvements, however, could come only at increased cost. Improved student counseling and academic support are examples. More generally, the atmospherics of student life are important to the student's maturation, sense of community, and motivation for learning. These aspects of quality tend to receive comprehensive and costly attention in the great private universities and the elite liberal arts colleges. Public university campuses are in most cases much larger and more impersonal. Facilities and opportunities may be present, but the student's quality of life depends more on his or her own mature initiative.

Application of TQM to the instructional process has so far lagged behind its application to administrative services. Faculty resistance may be partly responsible for this lag, but also at issue are the inherent conceptual difficulties of diagnosing quality and addressing the issue of how to achieve improvements while economizing.

Strategies for Quality in the Short and Long Terms

A university can and should utilize several short-term strategies to influence quality perceptions. By recruiting outstanding students, making highly visible faculty appointments, and publicizing its successes, it can impress its publics favorably and reinforce quality aspirations within the institution. In its announced plans, it can set challenging goals for strengthening existing academic programs and adding new departments and professional schools. As the presidents of Harvard, Princeton, and Stanford individually did in 1991–92, it can initiate bold new programs for the improvement of under-graduate education.

Long-term efforts count most, however, toward ensuring the quality of academic programs and the more general quality of the institution. As the faculty resource is crucial, the university admin-istration needs to commit itself to the most intensive searches for the strongest possible faculty appointments and to high standards of teaching and research activity as criteria for advancement.

Over time, the sense of striving for high attainment should be built into institutional and individual expectations. The best uni-versities have a palpably demanding atmosphere. They exude vital-ity, and they have an excitement about them that attracts scholarly visitors, promotes greater alumnus and public support, and enlivens the work of students, faculty and staff. Such a supportive atmos-phere is built only with continued effort over a long period of time. It is in itself an important resource, and it must be guarded vigor-ously by those who are devoted to the institution.

Chapter Fourteen

Efficiency
and Productivity

Suppose the following goal for a university's operation: to function so that its costs will increase no faster than the general rate of inflation. The rate of increase of the Consumer Price Index (CPI) is a good enough yardstick. What would be the implications of this sort of management goal? What sacrifices would be required, and from whom? Would adoption of the goal inevitably mean that the university must turn its back on innovation, slowly degrade academic quality, and lose institutional momentum and morale?

Before tackling these important questions, we should point out that some organizations and institutions do, in fact, perform so that their products or services do not rise in real cost over time; and a few sectors, blessed with rapid advances in technology, such as the semiconductor and computer manufacturing industries, experience significant and continued *reductions* in real costs.

Furthermore, there would be enormous benefit to society and to the clienteles of universities if their cost performance could be improved. Such improvements would eliminate or moderate the present battles for relative growth of state appropriations in the state universities, the inexorable and alarming increases of tuition in private universities, and the intensifying efforts of both private and public universities to raise capital and operating funds from individuals and corporations.

William G. Bowen, provost and later president of Princeton University, suggested a fundamental relationship that may pertain to all of higher education. He noted that higher education may be a constant-productivity industry surrounded by other sectors of society whose productivity is rising several percent per year (Bowen, 1969). He presents long-term comparisons (1905–1966) of direct costs per student in higher education with an economywide cost index, as well as detailed cost data from a sample group of major universities. The figures show a continued rise in relative costs for higher education. To get out of this trap, academic institutions can try to obtain whatever economies of scale are available and can also use more capital and technology per staff member where this might cut costs per student. But Bowen has exposed a problem of rising costs that—in the absence of significant productivity gains—could be dealt with only by cutting the quality of educational operations, reducing the real wages of those who earn their living in higher education, or continuing to raise tuition costs and the public subsidy of higher education.

Universities are organizations whose technology of production, or basic ways of doing things, does not change appreciably over time, while in most other sectors, overall efficiency does improve through advances in technology and the opportunities to use more capital relative to labor.

The performing arts must be reckoned to have *rising real costs* over time, as their use of resources cannot improve while that of other sectors does improve. Universities operate according to an approximation of the "live audience" principle, so that unless they reorganize fundamentally, they may face the grim long-term prospects associated with rising real costs. (This comparison does depend on a narrow definition of the "performing arts," emphasizing performance before a live audience only, and not the modern audience extensions via film, television, radio, and recordings of all types.)

We now turn to specifics of university costs and the challenge of bringing about gains in efficiency. Lack of systematic progress in measuring the output of higher education prevents a full analysis of the productivity questions, although trends in cost per student per year can be estimated. What is needed, and not now available, is an estimate of trends in the cost of achieving a given amount and quality of educational results. It may be possible, when more is known, to moderate the cost push by reorganizing some aspects of the educational pattern and by using new technologies. These strategies will take time, development money, and—above all—courage. The necessary development efforts are beyond the purse of the individual institution and will require help from foundations and from such special sources as the Fund for Improvement of Postsecondary Education at the U.S. Department of Education.

The cost structure of public two-year colleges will probably be least vulnerable to further rapid increases in operating cost per student. The community colleges rely most heavily on academic personnel whose salaries are not pushed up strongly by specialty wages in the general labor markets, and they face fewer urgent needs in other areas of rapid cost increase, such as library expansion and high-tech research laboratories. However, to the extent that two-year colleges need to expand their technical-vocational programs—which have higher costs per student—more rapidly than their academic programs, they too will experience new cost pressures. And those community colleges that play a vital role as gateways to new educational opportunity face intense demands for counseling and other educational services.

Note also that a university's costs of operation are traditionally open-ended: it will always spend as many dollars as it can capture. Howard R. Bowen (1980) enunciated this principle in his well-known study of higher education costs. The mandate of the university is to be as comprehensive as possible and to be outstanding in quality. These two factors are sufficient in themselves to increase costs.

A profound issue of dynamics is also at work. The frontiers of knowledge are ever-expanding, so that research proliferates and becomes more expensive (the "easy" and cheap discoveries have already been made in most fields, it is said). With the advent of new knowledge and the changing agendas of society, new topics, courses, and fields of study are candidates for addition to curricula. Not many fields and topics can be discarded to make way for the new ones.

Reputation, Quality, and Efficiency

A university seeks to maintain and enhance its reputation for outstanding scholarship and quality of learning. "Efficiency" in the sense of instructional service and throughput is usually not emphasized as a positive goal, though it is usually a felt constraint: the budget has to be balanced, and enrollment in a public university has to be large enough to capture budget under existing formulas, or large enough in a private university to yield the institution's target revenue from tuition. Nevertheless, we can first examine "efficiency" as if the university were engaged in quantitative production.

Universities are organized to "produce" educated people and to contribute new knowledge to society, as well as to preserve the heritage of the past. Because the impact of education on the life prospects of the person receiving it is so difficult to assess, universities (and their funders) often fall back on more mundane measures of instructional output: degrees granted and student credit hours earned. While we must pursue the issue of efficiency using these mundane measures, the possibilities for achieving great results in education, in the broadest sense, should not be ignored.

Efficiency Within an Academic
Department and Program

In principle, an academic department should operate at or above the minimum efficient scale for its field. Assuming that it offers both undergraduate majors and the Ph.D., it needs:

- Enough faculty to cover the main specialties or subdivisions of the field

- Offices and facilities to support both teaching and research
- An enrollment and enrollment composition ratios of beginning, intermediate, and advanced students that are compatible with its faculty size and budget, so that the instructional output of student credit hours will approximately accord with expectations

When a university initiates a new department, the nucleus of faculty and other resources is large relative to enrollment, and unit costs of instruction are therefore higher than at steady-state. Even at steady-state faculty size and student enrollment, the department may offer some courses that are low in unit cost, others that are intermediate, and some that are very costly per student because enrollment is low. (See Bowen and Douglass, 1971, for methods of comparing instructional costs under different forms of organization.)

Efficiency improves if a minimum enrollment size per course is enforced, together with the authority to cancel courses having below-minimum enrollment and to reassign faculty to other needed courses.

How Much Teaching Load for University Faculty?

State legislators have often criticized university faculty members for their excessive interest in their research and scholarship and their alleged neglect of obligations toward students—particularly, undergraduate teaching. Critics of the university's intellectual establishment have supplied colorful ammunition (Huber, 1992; Anderson, 1992). But populist liberals sometimes join in the chorus with political conservatives on this issue.

As budgetary stringency increased in the early 1990s, the perennial critics were joined by presidents of highly respected universities—Rudenstine of Harvard, Casper of Stanford, Shapiro of Princeton, among others—who call for relative increases of teaching load and relatively less emphasis on free time for research. The trouble, of course, is that universities compete for outstanding faculty, and a university that expects a teaching load higher than the perceived average among peer institutions will have difficulty recruiting and retaining high-quality faculty. Teaching loads in regular courses also vary greatly by discipline, the humanities fields having the highest and the laboratory sciences and some professional fields the lowest. Analysis of the amount and quality of teaching is an important topic, discussed in Chapter Thirteen. Suffice it to say here that the necessity for trade-off must be kept in view: faculty members who seek low teaching loads because of their research obligations should be expected to be highly productive in creative scholarship; if they are not doing research, they should be required to accept increased teaching assignments.

Summary: Efficiency-Improving Steps When Future Conditions Are Known

1. No course should be offered below a critical minimum enrollment (set in many universities at fifteen for undergraduate courses and ten for graduate courses).

2. Every program and department should operate at or above minimum efficient scale.

3. Teaching load within a program or department should be differentiated so that faculty members not engaged in significant research and scholarship are assigned to additional course teaching.

4. To economize on salary costs, initial ladder-rank or "regular rank" appointments should be made mostly at the junior, nontenure level in order to provide a counterbalance to the high salaries of long-service, tenured faculty.

Efficient Departmental Composition of a University

Some academic fields are inherently costly, others are relatively inexpensive. As a generality, the laboratory sciences and engineering require much more budgeted cost per faculty member and much more space, facilities, and equipment than do the social sciences and humanities, though the latter sectors do have significant demands for library resources. A university can have lower than average overall costs if it concentrates on programs that are cheap to operate. However, in doing so, it falls short of the ideal of comprehensive coverage of the disciplines and professions.

Bocconi University in Italy, a recently founded private institution, concentrates on economics and management. In Indonesia, Korea, and elsewhere, a huge demand for undergraduate enrollment exceeding the capacity of state-supported universities has spawned many private institutions that concentrate on management, computer science, and social sciences—high-demand fields with little need for high-cost facilities. Among the professions, the fields of law, management, and education are low-cost, whereas engineering and medicine (human and veterinary) are high-cost.

The Efficient Frontier

Assuming a given mix of departments and programs, a university that seeks efficiency when prices and wage rates are known and technology is unchanging should minimize the resource inputs required for a given enrollment. By operating every program at a scale no smaller than the efficient minimum, and by eliminating "slack," the university can operate on the efficient frontier of resource usage. (See Radner and Miller, 1975; Carlson, 1972.) As for technology, the efficient frontier is the locus of points consisting of minimum resource combinations to produce a given output. If one key resource (say, faculty) becomes more expensive relative to another (say, computers), the manager of the system will change the input mix to use less of the increasingly expensive resource.

Uncertainty and the Search for Efficiency

A university can successfully choose its most desired mix of departments and programs *under conditions of certainty*. It is more difficult to make a successful choice when the future is uncertain. An institution faces statistical uncertainties, first of all, in the number of new students who enroll each year, the number of continuing students, and the number who pass out of the university through degree completion or through permanent withdrawal. The number of new students is a function of demographics and the university's attractiveness to applicants in the geographical region of "draw," and of the admission standard. The statistical variations in persistence and degree completion are generally within a manageable band, but there are occasional unpleasant surprises.

More variable than total new enrollment is composition by student major. Students may have intense enrollment interest in a given field for a while, causing the university to approve more faculty positions and build up that department. Then, as fashions change or as future employment prospects in the field are perceived to decline, students may veer off to some other field. The institution must then live with a long period of overinvestment in the field that has fallen out of favor. One way to reduce this risk is to appoint higher proportions of non-ladder and temporary faculty in the programs with great uncertainty of continued enrollment interest.

Uncertainty also attends questions of curriculum change. The entry-level course in a given field may be compulsory, and intermediate courses may be eligible to satisfy "breadth" requirements; but then the university faculty may legislate changes that increase or reduce these enrollment demands, in ways that cannot be fully anticipated and that may result in an imbalance in faculty allocations.

Reputation-Maximizing Strategies

We now amend the preceding picture of the efficient institution to include allocations that maximize academic reputation. Let us assume that the university has achieved a mix of programs and enrollments that places it on the efficient frontier. How can it then take steps to improve its reputation?

A university's reputation derives in large part from having highly productive faculty members who are well regarded in their fields. The reputation-maximizing university is therefore willing to pay the sometimes large difference between the salary of a journeyman full professor and that of a "star," in the fields it considers important. Academic reputation among peers is largely a function of the research and scholarly attainments of individual faculty members and faculty groups. (See Rosovsky, 1990.)

The university also selects fields in which it can stimulate entire departments toward exceptional reputation. Tufts University, for example, under the leadership of President Jean Mayer, a nutritional scientist, developed a distinctive reputation for its program in nutritional science and policy. Though a university may attempt to be outstanding in virtually all of the basic scholarly disciplines and all of the major professions, this is an enormously expensive strategy to implement, and it is risky if the buildup is meant to be rapid.

The reputation-maximizing university also adopts a selective admission standard, as students are attracted to an institution where other students are thought to be superior in talent and promise, and the passing standards in courses are higher because of the competition that high-quality students engender among themselves.

The elements of reputation for high quality are mutually reinforcing: a highly reputed faculty attracts high-quality applicants for study, and outstanding original research—especially in the laboratory sciences—needs the involvement of exceptionally talented graduate students. There are, however, problems with this picture of the reputational benefits to be gained from shrewd allocation of extra resources:

1. The gains in reputation from investments in exceptionally promising personnel and facilities arrive after a considerable time lag.

2. The choices are attended by uncertainty. Will this year's most promising junior-level appointment become a star five or ten

years hence? Is the current, and expensive, star-quality full professor likely to lose energy and drive? Will the "hot" field of today be obsolete and uninteresting tomorrow?

3. The university is unlikely to have sufficient extra resources to make reputation-enhancing investments everywhere, and it must therefore ration its choices.

4. Enhanced reputation helps to attract extramural research grants and foundation support, and it makes it easier to get prospective students to swallow increased tuition, but it may be quite problematic in terms of net budgetary equilibrium. The ability of the institution to attract enough additional resources at the margin to pay for its investments in reputation is by no means assured. The situation is reminiscent of the problem of profitability in Division 1A intercollegiate football: the "winning" football programs fill the stands, receive postseason bowl bids, and have lucrative television contracts, more than justifying the university's investment in them. The "losers," on the other hand, with scarcely lower budgets, do not break even.

A department or program that is authorized to offer the Ph.D. or other doctorate should demonstrate its ability to:

1. Offer a high-quality and highly reputed degree, as an important benefit to the university's reputation

2. Attract excellent doctoral candidates and find funds to cover the exceptionally high costs of graduate enrollment

3. Provide the special facilities and resources required for doctoral research

Any department of marginal academic quality that is not crucially needed as a teaching resource by other departments and programs should be phased out or consolidated, to save the indirect as well as direct costs of its operation. If needed as a teaching resource, it may need to continue to operate as a service department, but not to offer advanced degrees of its own.

The above rules, it should be emphasized, apply to situations *not* involving change in instructional technology or in the opportunities to break open new domains of knowledge and lay the basis for new curricula. These issues belong in the realm of dynamics and typically require significant and risky investment over a period of time. We consider these questions of dynamics in a later section of this chapter.

Efficiency and Productivity in the Provision of Administrative Services

Analysis of higher education costs in the 1970s disclosed that costs of administrative services and student support tended to expand relative to the direct costs of academic departments. Howard Bowen (1980) and Earl Cheit (1971) provided illuminating data and explanations. Bowen pointed to expansion of support services as enriching the institution's "living standard." Cheit calculated that in the late 1960s increased costs of campus security added one full percentage point to general and administrative costs.

Massy (1990) suggests the model of the "academic ratchet." A university responds whenever it can to insistently expressed needs of all sorts and to demands for greater convenience of operation. Departments seek more clerical staff and more course advisers. Administrative offices "always" need more people than their current budgets permit. And so on.

The first questions to ask are: Must the university provide the service in question? To whom? Who pays? And who performs the service?

Every student uses the services of the admissions office, the enrollment system and registrar, and the student account billing system. These, then, must normally be built into student services budgets and paid for from student fee revenue. The security and safety of the campus and its population is another universal service of great importance.

Some services, such as access to buildings for those with physical disabilities, are needed and demanded by only a fraction of the campus population but are mandated by law or are part of the moral expectations of the campus community. Other services for which demand is relatively small are not mandated by law. These are candidates for special fees, for elimination, or for redirection of the student or faculty member to an external vendor.

Computerizing High-Volume Administrative Services

Many efficiency improvements in high-volume administrative services depend on investment in systems design, hardware, and software for computer-based operations. Universities have now designed effective computer-based systems to take care of many accounting, record-keeping, and transactional functions, especially for those services that are universal in demand. Some now have students undertake their course registration by touch-tone phone, which then makes it possible to generate the class list by computer and even, if there is a priority scheme, to enforce the enrollment limits on a course.

In many administrative areas, databases capable of being easily updated and accessed help the staff of service units to work more efficiently.

Some administrative activities, however, are not amenable to cost-reducing investments in computerization. Streamlining, in these cases, is a matter of designing more efficient administrative methods or adopting "best practice" techniques employed by other organizations with more or less comparable functions.

"Outsourcing"

University administrators are also examining new possibilities for "outsourcing"—obtaining a given service from an external vendor rather than producing it internally. When this approach is adopted, it can capture available efficiencies and also remove the monopoly of an internal service unit that previously has faced no effective limit on its overhead charges. Among the candidates for outsourcing are: food services, parking administration, building repairs and minor renovations, and equipment servicing and repair.

The mode of organization that should be adopted depends in part on the scale of the organizational units within the university. Some administrative services, such as the financial accounting system, must be centrally controlled and provided in order to ensure coherence and uniformity. In other cases, an administrative service with many delivery points may be usefully decentralized, control of service delivery being given to the management of each academic or administrative entity needing the service.

Academic Support Services

Academic support services include departmental administration, the university libraries, and computer facilities.

Departmental Administration

Departmental administration is, by design, under continual scarcity pressure. A small cadre of administrative personnel is supposed to maintain departmental records, conduct all types of transactions (accounting, personnel, and student records), and see to the clerical support needs of faculty. Keeping budgets under tight control is necessary but a continual work overload is no guarantee of true efficiency and does not contribute to good morale or workload management.

In scientific and engineering fields, technicians and laboratory maintenance workers and assistants keep teaching laboratories functioning. Research laboratories employing state-of-the-art equipment are still more expensive to operate, and they usually depend on extramural research grant funds.

Forcing departmental efficiency by minimizing slack and keeping service demands in excess of capacity does have some beneficial effects, but it may also discourage good organization of tasks. Department-level accounting, preferably on-line, can help the department chair and the management services officer keep expenditures within budget. A more comprehensive approach to sound departmental management can be achieved by means of responsibility center accounting and controls.

Investments in personal computers and arrays of computers connected in local area networks (LANs), together with the training of academic support personnel—and faculty!—in their effective use, can improve the effectiveness of service delivery. Universities tend to lag behind commercial organizations in their efficient use of business systems and processing networks. The objective of investing in more equipment is to upgrade the work and responsibilities of the administrative staff and to reduce staff numbers.

Libraries

Library collections and services that support undergraduate curricula are smaller and far less expensive than the research library collections. Some universities, such as Princeton, point with pride to their undergraduates' access to open-stack research collections. Public universities with much larger student populations set up a separate undergraduate library of two to three hundred thousand titles and design the separate facility to have large amounts of study space for commuting students' use.

The cost of collection building in research libraries necessarily increases over time, as the number of new books published annually and the number of serial publications (journals and monographs) grows. Technical books have increased in price much faster than the CPI, and professional journals have had even faster rates of price inflation. Libraries perforce practice increasingly severe selection and culling, to make best use of acquisition budgets. Interlibrary loan systems make it possible, with some delay, to fill gaps in meeting research needs. Interuniversity agreements for division of labor between libraries may lead to structural redesign: coordinated allocations of acquisition budget and specialized librarianship that saves money in each field. (Difficulty of access is a problem, however. Faculty at the cooperating institutions are likely to be unhappy about the inconvenience of consulting library collections at other universities.)

Specialized databases have become important as a new type of library resource for the student and the scholar. These require annual subscription or specific access charges—either way, a new cost of library operation. Some "futurists" dream of the pure electronically based (or "virtual") library in which all the information the library contains can be computer-accessed and subject to computer analysis (Mitchell and Saunders, 1991; Nelson, 1990; Rosser and Penrod, 1990). As yet, though "virtual reality" is available in coin-operated arcade games, the virtual library does not quite exist. Once the large initial investment costs are made, a virtual library may well be cost-effective, as it would have small space requirements for book storage, less acquisition processing, a different method of putting library materials at the disposal of the user, and increased user power to tour material and select what is needed for the purpose at hand. So far, however, the electronic databases that are coming into use add their own costs and do not reduce other library costs to an appreciable extent.

On-line catalogues and bar-coded identification of books have already made bibliographical search activity and circulation services more efficient.

Head librarians at universities are continually confronted with the challenge of deciding when a particular subcollection warrants its own branch library and library staff. Budgeted cost is minimized by maintaining the entire collection in one place and under one set of administrative managers. On the other hand, a special collection can offer a richness that is fed by the interest of key scholars in collection building and by the use of exotic materials. Branch libraries and special collections, therefore, compel library administrators to examine trade-offs between minimum cost (via centralized administration), geographical convenience on a large campus, and the incentives to create high collection quality.

Computing Services

Computer usage in the university of the 1990s is far ahead of what was imagined two decades ago, when universities struggled to finance a large mainframe machine to provide both batch processing and time-shared service. (In batch processing, a data file and application program are fed directly into the central machine. Processing is completed and the computed results are printed at the machine. Currently, this method is used only for high-volume administrative jobs such as the processing of financial accounting reports and for very large problems in the sciences and in engineering. Time-sharing developed as a means for connecting a set of users interactively to the mainframe from their own simple terminals. Personal computers can now connect with the mainframe computer to retrieve data or to direct complex computations, although for many purposes their own stand-alone capacity is sufficient.) Personal computers, engineering workstations, and LANs have proliferated; faculty members assume the right to an appropriate personal machine, and many students have their own as well. Advances in design and power of intermediate-sized machines and their operating systems now cast doubt on the need for the central supercomputer, though many major research universities own one— either a Cray or an IBM.

Software, and software site licenses, have become as costly and important as the hardware investment itself. The vast increase in computing capacity at every major university has undoubtedly boosted learning efficiency and has increased accessibility and power for numerous kinds of research, including research in the humanities. Rationalization of the spreading use of machines, systems, and software has become all but impossible, and decisions to acquire are, in large part, decentralized to departments, research teams, and the individual user. Computerization is in this sense out of control—a victory in search of a general! The saving grace is that prices have fallen at a sufficiently rapid rate to prevent computer acquisition, maintenance, and software costs from becoming overwhelmingly burdensome. There is little systematic indication, however, that this vast increase in academic computing has resulted in reductions of other academic costs. A few universities, led by Drexel University and Carnegie-Mellon University, adopted the requirement that each student be equipped with a self-financed personal computer, thereby shifting some institutional costs to the student. This made it possible for instructors and departmental administrators to send both instructional materials and administrative messages to students by electronic mail ("e-mail"). The requirement was also intended to stimulate increased use of computer-based instruction.

Productivity-Enhancing Redesign in Administrative and Academic Support Services

Many administrative services and some academic support services can be improved by adapting to the university environment the best-practice methods developed in the business and governmental sectors. In other cases, solutions to problems can be found in computer software, either purchased off the shelf or customized for the institution by the software manufacturer. Both admissions and enrollment procedures have been transformed by such means. Some universities have also had success with their own systems design and applications software, although this is a difficult area to manage well.

Whether computer based or not, many administrative and academic support services call for periodic assessment leading to an investment in task reorganization and overhaul. Often, external consultants—who have the advantage of detachment from the internal pressures of the organization—are engaged to undertake the necessary systems work, recommend applications software or database management packages, and assist in implementation of the new organization of work by undertaking training and transitional guidance.

A brief for searching redesign of administrative frameworks in universities is the CAUSE paper by Penrod and Dolence (1992). In keeping with their focus on information resources and strategic planning, the approach emphasizes the critical role of database creation and on-line access to information in the streamlined organizational unit. Their paper, on "re-engineering," advocates a combination of analysis leading to task reorganization, changes in the authority structure that promote greater decentralization and performance-oriented management, and extensive reliance on computer-based data. Sizable initial investments, a transitional interval, and intensive staff training are necessary to make this reform agenda workable. In administrative areas of greatest long-term significance to it, a university would do well to consider investment commitments of this type and magnitude.

Dynamic Efficiency: Investing in Educational Innovations

We now consider the most challenging and difficult productivity issue: investing to bring about major improvements in the effectiveness of the educational process itself. It is noteworthy that both university administrators and university funders display essential pessimism about achieving this goal. The administrators defend the existing internal processes of the university institution, which are deeply conservative. The funders assume that nothing can be done to bring about qualitative change. Private universities such as Harvard, Princeton, and Cornell seek multibillion dollar additions to endowments, which will help to preserve the institution, but they do not emphasize research and development investment to reduce instructional costs. As for public universities, governors and legislators who face budget crises typically concentrate their fire on what they regard as inappropriate (but modifiable) allocations of current faculty effort. That is, the budget gap would be greatly reduced "if every professor is required to teach one more course per year." Universities competing on academic quality and research eminence resist this pressure toward increases of teaching load and of the student-faculty ratio.

The university environment is quite hospitable to incremental improvements in education, and these take place regularly. Professors update lecture notes, write new textbooks for their own students and students elsewhere, design new courses, experiment with computers or in-class demonstrations, and participate in occasional curriculum redesign. A well-funded university, in fact, makes provision for professorial development time, and for other investment related to such incremental improvements.

New Curricula and Academic Structures

In contrast, many of the more sweeping proposals for academic reform and innovation die aborning; or, if they are launched as experiments, their life is brief. Experimental colleges and interdisciplinary degree programs within larger university campuses often cannot survive the first major budget squeeze or the first academic review. The basic reason is that faculty members are grouped into a politically durable array of academic departments. These departments are strongly reinforced by disciplinewide connections, loyalties, and perspectives. Academic arrangements that do not conform to the departmental structure lead a precarious life.

Some academic fields do undergo a significant transformation over time. Cross-disciplinary research, for example, results in a body of new knowledge and findings. Only later are the curricula and academic units created to reflect this knowledge in new regular courses and departmental faculty appointments. Biophysics is a case in point; now, the broader revolution in the biological sciences gives rise to regrouping of activities and faculty in that entire field.

Professional schools are, of course, the other major structural exception to the rule of conformity with the academic disciplines. With their external professional and practitioner constituencies, and their ability to attract funding, such schools are able to survive in the university setting.

The lesson seems clear: if a new academic design and structure is in fact needed as a response to a social need or a learning opportunity, it should either be compatible with the departmental organization at the university or be provided with separate organization and funding as an autonomous unit. While such an organization may be a genuine innovation, it is unlikely to improve productivity as compared with other entities that have a similar intellectual style.

Task Reorganization: Active Learning and Distance Learning

A public university campus is traditionally designed to provide a large lecture course at the introductory level (with discussion sections or laboratory sessions led by graduate students); intermediate-sized classes at advanced undergraduate levels; and small seminars and tutorials for the doctoral students and postdoctoral fellows. This design controls unit costs in undergraduate education, supports graduate students through teaching assistantships, and reserves individuated attention to those advanced areas of discourse in which problems are unstructured and unresolved.

This design is often criticized as exactly wrong in the allocation of instructional attention and costs. It is said that the beginning student needs the most help and the most intensive motivational support, whereas the more advanced students can learn effectively on their own. The problem is in part structural: large inflows of students enter each subject area at the introductory stage, then, at more advanced levels, each specialized course attracts a relatively small number of enrollees. Cost control becomes a matter of choking off the proliferation of small-enrollment advanced courses. The replacement of the introductory large-lecture course with some other format is not considered an option under any circumstances.

Treisman noted that Asian undergraduates in mathematics courses did exceptionally well, and he traced this to their membership in small study groups in which the students helped each other to learn. He has experimented with the formation of small study groups among students from other cultural groups, and these have had positive effects on learning success. (See Hofstede, 1991, for comments concerning culturally significant styles of learning.)

Grouping students into small cooperative teams for the learning process is an alternative strategy to the conventional "lecture and section" design. The professor in charge of the subject would then have a new set of tasks—organizing and monitoring the groups. Additional time and effort would be justified by the improved student performance. But what could be changed or eliminated from the typical course format?

How about giving up the big lecture? Introductory physics and introductory economics were two subjects for which careful, large-scale investments in video lectures were made. (Harvey White, a Berkeley professor, did the physics course, and John R. Coleman, then of Haverford College, did the economics.) The front-end investments, substantial in both cases, were financed by foundations. Textbook publishers have now begun to develop video formats for the high-volume courses in some social science fields, and their efforts may herald new possibilities for changes in course organization.

In more general efforts to deliver course instruction effectively to widely scattered audiences, the Open University in Britain and NOVA in the United States have developed extensive syllabi, course notes, and broadcast lectures. "Distance learning," as it is called in the higher education literature, enables delivery of instruction without the cost (to the student as well as the institution) of assembling students in classrooms. The Open University does, however, provide study and discussion sessions at numerous locations, and these carry more of the instructional responsibility, in fact, than is undertaken by the more heavily publicized TV broadcasts.

Another design for "distance learning" is used in the College of Engineering at the University of California, Berkeley. Closed-circuit TV pipes the professor to engineers (most of them practitioners enrolled for brush-up or added specialization) assembled in classrooms at their companies. Telephone lines are kept open so that students can ask questions of the instructor, thus providing, to some extent, the advantages of interactive learning.

In contrast to books and instructional videos, broadcasts for distance learning have not gained widespread acceptance. Even videos, more flexible in usage though they are, have not ordinarily substituted for professorial time in instruction; most professors use them, if at all, as adjuncts to their regular classroom presentations, to illustrate key points or provide capsule reporting of situations. These technologies have not penetrated far as replacements for the traditional classroom colloquy between instructor and student. Adoption or nonadoption is often a decision made within the local academic department, and not at some other, efficiency-promoting level in the university. Departments have limited incentives to adopt radically different course formats. Also, professors may object, quite rightly, that material produced for an indeterminately large and heterogeneous student population does not meet the needs of their specific student groups. Finally, both budgeting and financing issues confront university users of the new technologies. Questions of fee payments for usage (a charge per student?) and of regular updating of the material are difficult to resolve.

Another possibility is to shift more of the instructional process to the computer. Bell Laboratories developed a high-powered interactive package, Writer's Workbench, to teach expository writing. Self-paced courses in calculus, with interactive modules for self-administered quizzes, have been on the market for some years. Software packages for learning foreign languages now include sound for pronunciation instruction, as well as pictorial images and printed words. Courses have even been developed (mainly focused toward the business manager) to facilitate creative problem solving, with the user being prompted to decompose the stated problem and explore imaginative approaches to a solution. Perhaps these fragmentary efforts will be joined by other attempts at substitution of computer power for professor power.

There are numerous unanswered questions about task reorganization and the uses of technology for university course instruction. Students appear to learn more successfully when they are enthusiastic and highly motivated, when they are in productive study groups or receive other positive support in the learning process, and when they have a mix of designed structure and creative opportunity that is matched to their level of knowledge. It is baffling to confront these issues, for the traditional incentive system of a university does not give specific rewards to the faculty member for intensifying student motivation and success.

The formidable problems and costs of designing and producing wholly new instructional materials that rely on the new technologies seriously inhibit their exploitation. Much more extensive development funding from the National Science Foundation and from private foundations may be required, as well as the formation of consortia of universities willing to cooperate in implementation for the purpose of fostering qualitative change. Knowing that periodic reinvestments would be required to freshen and improve the materials, funders and academic decision makers will be cautious in moving ahead. Because initial investment would be large, it is likely that the main focus will be on materials for entry-level courses.

Chapter Fifteen

Retrenchment,
Restructuring,
and "Re-engineering"

As we saw in Chapter Fourteen, greater efficiency and productivity can be pursued both in the university's ongoing or "steady" state and on the university's dynamic path, where variables are subject to change and the university can reorder the technologies on which it relies. Here we focus on the issue of reshaping units of the university. By reexamining their objectives and functions, the university's leadership can identify the features of these units that are essential to the institution and redesign operations so that the use of resources becomes fully cost-effective.

Restructuring: Confronting Proliferation

Downsizing of large organizations often occurs when costs are acknowledged to be out of control or when the organization's efforts are producing the wrong products. Large organizations—including universities—tend to obey laws of bureaucratic accretion, under which functions are added and the hierarchy grows as units proliferate. Additional coordination and support functions then appear necessary. A corporation that loses markets and faces stronger competition may respond by seeking major cost reductions or by reshaping product lines. Many not-for-profit organizations confront similar pressures. In this chapter, we compare strategies employed by universities with those used in for-profit corporations; this is a useful, though perhaps painful, conceptual device for raising unexpected questions.

"Delayering" and Consolidation

Large organizations may come to question whether their administrative overhead, intermediate management layers, and operating units are delivering "value added" in relation to their costs. Operating units—whether the Fisher-Price division of Quaker Oats or the Department of Philosophy at UCLA—can be subjected to reasonably direct evaluation. For a corporate division, profits and return on investment (corrected for risk) can be calculated, and if the division is performing poorly, it can be reorganized or liquidated.

A university can use systematic judgmental evaluations of academic quality and research performance; as to instruction, it can use quantitative measures of "student credit hour production," assess the topical design and comprehensiveness of courses, and undertake qualitative measures of the depth, freshness, and vitality of teaching. Where an academic performance appears to be inadequate, however, the university's remedies are difficult to manage institutionally.

Incomplete though these indicators of value added are, they are clearer in their directional implications for operating units than are the judgments that can be made about management layers and administrative staff and support services. The fact that such elements contribute to output indirectly, and that their impact must be imputed rather than directly measured, renders moot the question of value added. Corporate restructurings of the 1980s and early 1990s, such as the elimination of intermediate management layers at the General Electric Company, may have been prompted as much by the question, "What kind of organization do we want to have?" as by doubts concerning value added.

It is noteworthy that in the 1980s, support expenditures at universities rose far more rapidly, in percentage terms, than direct expenditures of academic departments. Some increases occurred as a result of new external regulatory and reporting obligations. But beyond that effect is the tendency for expanding financial resources at a university to be poured into support activities rather than into direct academic services for teaching and research—an interesting reflection of the implicit priorities of institutional life, and also an indicator of where budgetary power resides at a university (Massy, 1990; Massy and Wilger, 1991).

One motive for downsizing an organization is to capture a margin for innovation. A high-technology corporation may fear being left behind in the competitive race. A contract research organization may seek to concentrate resources on activities that are of greatest potential for future funding and research payoff.

Two gambits that are common among for-profit corporations—leveraged-buyouts and takeovers—have almost never been adopted by universities. However, the rapid consolidation movement of the 1990s in community hospitals and health maintenance organizations (HMOs) demonstrates that nonprofit status alone does not immunize against drastic restructuring. Universities are not, in principle, exempt from consolidation. More will be said on this issue in a later section.

Short-Term Actions for Retrenchment

"Retrenchment" connotes a set of short-term responses to adverse conditions. These, and the reasons for them, are discussed here; later, we will discuss the longer-term approaches to major institutional reorganization and what is coming to be known as "re-engineering."

Retrenchment is not only short-term in its motivation and its intended effects; the actions it entails are typically designed to be adopted and implemented rapidly.

If the trigger for action is immediate financial and budgetary stringency, the initial phase of retrenchment is consumed by the task of gaining control over the current cash position and cash flow. Only when this has been accomplished can other, less urgent issues be dealt with. Major universities have seldom faced immediate threats of closure for lack of ability to meet payroll and pay the bills, but every year, thirty to fifty colleges do close their doors. The University of Bridgeport faced such severe financial problems in 1991 that it became willing to entertain the possibility of alliance with a subsidiary of the Unification Church.

When the immediate cash position and cash flow are adequately defended, two basic alternative strategies then present themselves to the financially troubled institution: radical recentralization and restructuring from the top; or a systematic effort to galvanize the board, the senior administration, and the academic and administrative units—including their rank and file staff members—in a joint, organizationwide effort to reshape the institution toward viability.

The traditional methods of cutting costs are: squeezing, eliminating, postponing, and shifting. Though short-term in their rationale, their effects—positive and negative—are often long-lasting. All of them involve paring down the organization and controlling it more heavily. Complaints can be minimized somewhat if the mix of reductions and postponements is arrived at through internal consultations.

Two contrasting management styles for retrenchment are radical recentralization, and an open administrative approach.

The Strategy of Radical Recentralization

A corporate retrenchment involving radical recentralization is ordinarily spearheaded by the chief executive officer. It falls into five phases:

1. Operating units receive new and demanding targets for cost reduction and revenue expansion, with the indication that each unit manager will be accountable for results—to be reported weekly, monthly, and quarterly. Any expenditures not contributing to the stated short-term goals are to be eliminated. Hiring freezes and personnel reduction targets may be included as separate provisions.

2. Internal audit and task teams may review units that are regarded as particularly shaky.

3. The CEO sets in motion a process to identify the "losers" among the operating units. Decisions are then made to sell or liquidate any units failing the test of immediate cash-flow and profit contribution.

4. The managers and supervisors of the remaining units are motivated powerfully, by a combination of money incentives and fear, to meet their targets.

5. Top management addresses the pruning of management layers, support staff units, and other "indirect" functions. (If the corporation's R&D budget is eliminated or cut severely, this signals that top management is focused on short-term survival goals only.)

A college or university in extremis might undertake radical recentralization as a desperation measure—an alternative to immediate closure and bankruptcy. Its governing board would have to find a chief executive able and willing to pursue in the academic setting the array of actions just described for corporate recentralization. The board and executive would first have to agree that draconian measures are absolutely necessary and would have to communicate this credibly to internal and external constituencies.

Colleges and universities, however, typically exude an air of permanence. Most constituencies would find it hard to believe that drastic measures are necessary, unless there had previously been a sequence of lesser—but painful and well-publicized—steps toward economizing. Substantive recentralization actions would provoke resistance. Faculty would defend tenure as a right and as a legal, philosophical, and organizational issue. Employees and their organizations would defend job rights. Students would display intense anxiety, to the point that a tuition-based institution might lose students and revenues. Alumni and other supporters would likely be divided and disaffected.

Besides these resistances, the executive administration would confront inadequacies of information and of administrative competence in trying to carry through the reductions necessary for fiscal survival. Even if fiscal measures are temporarily successful, there remain fundamental questions about the academic viability of the reduced institution.

Reshaping the Institution: Measures for the Long Term

Reshaping the institution through reorganization and reform is directed to the goal of assuring long-term viability. More compatible with a university's institutional norms, this strategy is often pursued as an open approach to retrenchment and restructuring, but the process is appreciably more time-consuming than radical recentralization. Changes of the magnitude required for longer-term viability provoke institutional resistance, political gambits, and demands for procedural exactitude, all of which may delay or paralyze the effort.

The Difficulties of Implementing Retrenchment Policies

The university is typically committed, in principle, to the conduct of education and research in all fields of fundamental scholarship and most or all of the recognized professions. A mandate of comprehensiveness is the rule, although specific institutional history or fiscal caution may justify omission of some fields or professions. At the same time, the faculty of the university is likely to have a predilection for the most advanced levels of teaching—doctoral programs and postdoctoral scholarly dialogue—while the institution faces claims for comprehensive programs in undergraduate education. These various philosophical commitments inhibit adoption of systematic processes of program review that might lead to either elimination or reinforcement of programs.

Faculty departments are typically collegial, deliberative, and consensual in their academic decision making; as Massy (1990) argues, this approach often spills over into administrative areas. The law of bureaucratic expansion is also in evidence, with accretion of personnel and coordination the common result. Massy points further to a general belief in "upward-only adjustment" with respect to salaries and position levels, staff cadre sizes, and the boundaries of academic and administrative units.

Two further issues plague the academic administrator and reformer: lack of consensus on the necessary elements of academic program design in each field, leading to the presumption that the academic department or other unit should always be somewhat larger than it already is; and lack of agreement concerning academic quality and how to achieve and sustain it, which facilitates defense of whatever is being done and demands for additional capabilities.

When the State of Washington experienced a sharp drop in fiscal resources in the early 1980s, the University of Washington at first experienced the same percentage reductions as other agencies. In 1981, the state government declared a fiscal emergency, and the university followed suit by declaring one of its own. Temporarily, the state permitted shifting of resources from capital reserves so that a previously announced 10 percent cut would be reduced to 5.5 percent. Immediate cuts were concentrated in support services, to give time for review of academic program reductions.

The university proceeded with a longer-term analysis to determine where to shrink the size of the institution while maintaining quality. The Faculty Senate set criteria, the president identified thirty-two programs for possible elimination, and faculty committees reviewed all of them in 1982–83. Of the targeted programs, nineteen were eventually eliminated. Forty-two faculty members, half of them tenured, were affected: six retired, one resigned, and the rest were relocated to other programs. An early retirement scheme then enabled the university to speed the process of contraction (Olswang, 1987).

Program Review and Administrative Consolidations

We have cited the expansionary tendency of bureaucracies to grow over time and encompass more functions. Massy (1990) discusses another source of growth: the "administrative lattice," which acquires increasing numbers of interfaces or linkages between units. This phenomenon means that *even without any rise in output,* the increasingly elaborated administrative system grows in cost and complexity.

Management studies can show whether administrative units should be overhauled or consolidated. Methodologies for such cost-effectiveness studies have been applied both to academic and administrative functions in higher education (Balderston, 1993). Administrative units that warrant consolidation have few institutional defenses against redesign, unless a senior administrator with access to the governing board is able to provide political protection.

The preconditions for worthwhile administrative consolidation are:

1. A systematic determination that the old authorities, processes, and technology are deficient in function and/or excessively costly

2. A plan for improvement, via infrastructure investment, organizational redesign, and the retraining of personnel

3. An implementation decision by top management, with follow-through to ensure that the entire plan is fulfilled.

Personnel regulations or collective bargaining contracts may provide rights of continued employment, and workers displaced by reorganization may in some cases need to be provided new assignments elsewhere. Nearly all administrative consolidations entail short-term transition costs, to be much more than offset by long-term performance improvements and cost savings. (We discuss below the concept of "re-engineering," which has gained recent popularity in connection with administrative reorganization.)

Elimination of Academic Programs

Restructuring includes the prospect of eliminating unsustainable academic programs. The following are examples:

- Numerous dental schools have closed. Five leading schools have reorganized teaching and research programs with the help of planning funds from the Pew Charitable Trust. The reason: fluoridation of the water supply has greatly reduced cavities, so that dental practice has perforce shifted toward periodontics, diseases of the mouth, reconstructive and cosmetic surgery, and other specialties.

- The University of Pennsylvania made a determination to close three academic departments in order to economize ("For Lack of Money . . .," 1993).

- UCLA determined in 1993–94 that its School of Library Sciences would be folded into its School of Education.

- Yale University, seeking to make significant cuts in faculty numbers by phasing out some departments, decided in 1991 to close its Department of Sociology, then settled for downsizing. Conflict and hostility attended the decision-making process, and in May 1992, Yale's president, Benno Schmidt, announced his intention to leave the presidency (Bernstein, 1992).

- San Diego State University decided to eliminate its departments of anthropology, chemistry, and German, because of severe reductions in appropriations from the State of California. More broadly, Chancellor Barry Munitz of the California State University announced that if the state's appropriation fell by 8 percent for 1992–93, 2,200 employees—including 340 tenured and nontenured faculty—would have to be laid off (Gordon, 1992).

Closing out an academic department will save resources, but the major savings will be delayed. A hypothetical sequence of closure actions might look like this:

1. When the closure decision is announced, faculty and administrative staff positions are frozen to facilitate capture of funds released by personnel departures.

2. The department is put on notice to achieve budget reduction targets during the current year and avoid equipment acquisitions and other unnecessary expenses.

3. Nontenured ladder-rank faculty are given the obligatory one year of notice. Lecturers and graduate teaching assistants are terminated to the extent not immediately needed to staff existing courses, and all are gone by the beginning of the second year.

4. Tenured faculty are nudged toward voluntary early retirement. Some may be offered retirement bonuses, in order to save longer-term salary costs.

This hypothetical sequence shows that the full amount of budgeted expenditure for "the current year" cannot be saved immediately. Rather, certain major costs carry over into succeeding years. Also, continuing incremental costs of graduate students and undergraduate majors who are still in the pipeline will be claimed by departments obliged to absorb them. If the eliminated department has been a significant drawing card for enrollment, there will also be losses of undergraduate tuition revenue.

The history of the use of program reviews as a basis for eliminating or consolidating academic programs is mixed at best. Such reviews are unpopular within the academic establishment of the university; they are time-consuming and often expensive (involving outside reviewers who are paid stipends as consultants); and their advice is painful to implement. We discussed academic program review in Chapter Thirteen. (Balderston, 1985, provides a detailed discussion of a program review episode.)

The Politics of Futurity

Resistance to information sharing at the University of California during a cycle of universitywide program review was a reminder that academic administrators and faculty organizations are fierce defenders of their "turf." In that instance, the contest occurred between levels of a public university system. Academic administrators and academic senate committees on some campuses defended their autonomy ("turf") by refusing to allow a universitywide task force to read and use campus evaluations of academic departments.

Within a given campus, boundaries between disciplines, departments, and programs are likely to be contested from time to time. In the retrenchment wars of the early 1990s, for example, certain language departments with small enrollments were vulnerable to consolidation into neighboring, larger departments because the faculty cadre had to be large enough to cover the curricular essentials, and the resultant cost per student was much greater than in a high-volume department. The small departments resisted the loss of autonomy (again, "turf"). Academic administrators and entrepreneurs ordinarily prefer downsizing over outright abolition of an academic department or a research unit. The authorization and initiation of an academic department and its programs requires elaborate procedural review over a period of years in most universities. This authorization is, in effect, a "hunting license" for future reputation. Once abolished, a department may never be reinstated, and the ambitions of the field's advocates may be permanently thwarted.

The "politics of futurity" takes a special form in a multicampus public university system. The chief officer of each campus is typically ambitious to enlarge the range of programs offered there. The academic plan of the campus is therefore likely to set forth a rationale to strengthen existing departments and programs, to obtain approval for the offering of doctoral study in the strongest of them, and to initiate new departments and professional schools in additional areas. Comprehensiveness is the objective, and the campus administration and faculty use the planning process as a means of advocacy for future expansion.

Given this deep expansionist bias, a change of perspective is required if the imperative is to consolidate and retrench instead of to grow. Only if financial pressures are severe, or if certain programs can be identified as lacking in future enrollment, resource attraction, or long-term quality, is downsizing willingly considered. Regular evaluation of program quality as a normal element of institutional oversight can provide a healthy background for consolidations if these do become necessary.

The Costs of Academic Program Elimination

Eliminating an academic program, as we saw earlier, does not immediately result in reduction of the budgeted costs of the program. A university typically attempts to preserve the jobs of regular tenured faculty, regular nontenured faculty, and full-time lecturers. Career administrative staff members may also be protected from immediate termination. Thus, the first burden of job loss falls on part-time lecturers and on recently hired, probationary, and part-time staff employees. Termination of career staff and of regular faculty usually requires substantial notice—six months or one year—and severance pay. Responsible employers also attempt to provide outplacement services and other transition assistance to the terminated employee.

When an academic program is eliminated, its undergraduate student majors and graduate students who are in the program pipeline cannot be abandoned. The university seeks to maintain enough of the program to graduate these students; if this cannot be done, it attempts to reassign these students to "close neighbor" programs. Discouraged students may, however, withdraw from study or may shift to other institutions, resulting in loss of tuition and fee income—a partial offset to the budget savings.

The affected students, staff, and faculty benefit from as much lead time as possible before their program actually closes down, but providing such lead time also postpones the realization of the needed cost savings.

The reduction in faculty numbers and in the variety of courses offered also imposes indirect costs on the university. Other programs may require or strongly recommend that their own majors take certain courses in the affected program; students may find that desired elective courses are fewer and are oversubscribed. (An example: a department of classics is likely to be vulnerable to elimination because it has few undergraduate majors and few graduate students; but other departments—the "living" languages, history, archaeology, and others—count on it as the teaching resource for their undergraduate majors and their graduate students.)

Cutbacks in course offerings result in patchwork adjustments of curricula and in delays in student progress toward completion of degree requirements. The affected faculty and other academic defenders of the eliminated program are certain to criticize the decision to eliminate the program as damaging to the academic quality of the university.

The Ideal Candidate for Elimination

Given the difficulties and the institutional pain that ordinarily attend program cutbacks and eliminations, it is possible to identify the characteristics of the "ideal candidate" for program elimination. Such a program is an isolate in the body academic, not depended on by other curricula or departments. Its subject matter may be under attack as lacking in coherence or in appropriateness to the academic standing of the university and to its mission. The program has a reputation for mediocre scholarship and poor quality of instruction, and a low percentage of its degree candidates completes the degree. Its graduates cannot be placed in jobs for which they were trained.

Programs in Marxist economics in the universities of the former Eastern Bloc countries apparently have many of the features of the ideal candidate for program elimination. Many of these universities have struggled to redefine the study of economics and are coping, slowly, with the elimination of the now-discredited programs and their redundant academic staffs.

Selective Priority as a Basis for Strengthening Academic Programs

Eliminating an academic program does make it possible to redirect certain academic resources to other purposes, as well as to reduce total budgets. Displaced faculty may be reallocated to areas needing additional personnel, and they will strengthen those areas if they are appropriately qualified and are motivated to contribute. Administrative staff, building space, and facilities are also released by program closure, and other programs benefit from reallocation of these resources.

In some instances, it is possible to arrange merger or consolidation of academic departments that are too small to be viable on their own. Unfortunately, such mergers are often difficult to bring off, especially if the original creation of the departments in question was necessitated by doctrinal conflicts or political tensions in a predecessor department. A university that has subjected its academic organizations to careful study of what is required for viability—in terms of faculty size, enrollment, and facilities—can invoke these standards in identifying the candidates for consolidation.

Program eliminations and consolidations must be permanent if the university is to obtain long-term institutional benefits. If an academic program is eliminated in one year only to be resuscitated a year or two later, the cost of the mistaken decision amounts to the combined costs of the shutdown and the start-up.

Administrative Reorganization and Re-engineering

A recent buzzword in the study of organizational change is "re-engineering," which argues for greater decentralization, greatly increased reliance on information technology, and the empowerment of administrative staff members to take substantial initiative and local responsibility. Penrod and Dolence (1992) prescribe a sweeping reform program for the campus, spearheaded by the director of information technology. His or her mandate would be to build the infrastructure for fully reshaped and newly linked administrative entities.

The drive toward a decentralized, networked organization draws on contemporary reasoning and empirical findings in the field of organizational behavior. Often, information technology is seen as the impetus to this type of change.

In principle, the reorganization of administrative entities in a university offers the promise of improved quality of services. Whether it will also produce net economies is another question.

Two kinds of preparatory investments are essential. First, it is necessary to analyze the demands that the administrative apparatus must satisfy. What outcomes are required, and what volume as well as quality of service is needed? If a new system is to rely extensively on information technology, integrated databases, and cross-communication, there can be no presumption that existing administrative units and the jobs of their staffs will continue to have validity. Comprehensive redesign of each organizational unit and the tasks performed by it is what justifies the term "re-engineering." Joined with this redesign is a substantial investment in retraining, as the networked organization requires initiatives, skills, and teamwork abilities greater than those demanded in a more traditional bureaucratic organization.

Second, the information infrastructure required to satisfy the new organization and its ways of doing business requires systems design, selection of hardware and communications, and design and installation of software and interfaces. Existing, commercially available software for applications such as accounting and admissions administration ordinarily need to be modified to fit the unique needs of the particular university. Seldom can the design of a general-purpose applications package mesh perfectly with the organization's authority and communication structure.

A task force within the University of California's central administration studied the question of the desirable mode of administrative organization for a wholly new campus. Its report, *Sustaining Excellence in the 21st Century* (University of California, 1991b), offers a challenging perspective on the advantages of the highly decentralized, networked organization. The University of California, Los Angeles, issued its own prospectus for reform and reorganization, *Transforming Administration at UCLA* (1991). In 1993, University of California President Jack Peltason empaneled a universitywide task force on Improved Management Initiatives (IMI), headed by UCLA Chancellor Charles Young. Four major IMI reports signal in their titles a strong vision of innovative organization: "Developing the UC Workforce for the 21st Century" (December 1993), "A New Balance—From Transactional Control to Accountability for Results" (January 1994), "Report of the Workgroup on Capital Programs" (January 1994), and "Empowerment with Accountability" (March 1994).

The two types of major investment called for by extensive reorganization consume money, personnel, and time. UCLA's plan has the merit of distinguishing between the less costly elements of a program, which can be implemented in the shorter term, and the more expensive elements that will be brought to fruition only after a significant time lag.

When the requisite investments in reorganization, retraining, and strengthened infrastructure have been made, the networked organization promises substantial economies as well as notable improvements in outcomes—that is, in the quality of administrative services that it provides in support of the academic enterprise.

Reorganization for Long-Term Gains

When it is possible to take a completely fresh look at the tasks, functions, and authorities of an organization, as well as at the options for the best supporting technology, permanent improvements in the efficiency of resource use are brought within grasp.

Universities can capture long-term savings and productivity improvements more easily in administrative support areas than in the conduct of academic programs for instruction and research. One reason is that it is possible to acquire fairly quickly the organizational designs and the computing software for such areas as accounting, student record keeping, and administration of personnel. In the conduct of university-level instruction, on the other hand, the universities themselves are responsible for defining what is to be accomplished and what range of capabilities must be put in place.

While there are numerous piecemeal efforts toward improvement of instruction, universities do not commit significant resources to the study and redesign of their instructional efforts. Conventional short-term "saving" on the academic side usually implies increasing class sizes, narrowing the course offerings, and increasing the teaching load—and all of these are customarily associated with a decline in academic quality. An innovative reorganization of academic work, to achieve more and better outcomes for given resources used, requires the active involvement of faculty, administration, and students themselves. The achievement of such reorganization is most likely to come in a context where changes and improvements in the conduct of instruction can be adopted continuously. This in turn depends on the creation of incentives to identify, evaluate, and reward innovation.

The steps that are necessary to achieve the long-term cost savings of the networked organization require strong leadership as well as substantial resources and time for implementation. These steps lead toward job enlargement and team formation as well as toward extensive decentralization.

The immediate pressures of retrenchment tend in precisely the opposite direction: toward heightened control of first-level decisions through mechanisms of expenditure approval; and toward increased workload in currently defined jobs, accompanied by dimmer prospects for reward and advancement.

Most traditional techniques for cut, squeeze, and cost reduction are negative in character. A hiring freeze leaves random vacancies in each administrative unit, to be coped with ad hoc by the remaining personnel. Because the organization is undergoing shrinkage, the most mobile and ambitious administrative employees are likely to be the first to leave if they can get other jobs. The remaining staff members face heavier workloads at the same time as they are subject to the threat of reduced hours and pay, or of layoff. Morale spirals downward, to be met by an even greater intensity of supervisory pressure.

Expenditure controls are intensified, shrinking the range of initiative of lower-level decision makers. Training, equipment expenditures, facilitating services, and investments in information technology are reduced or eliminated, to cut costs.

This traditional set of actions to compel a more reduced use of resources, it should be noted, induces people at all organizational levels to protect themselves by concentrating on the approved essentials and directing all available efforts toward immediate workload demands. From this perspective, the decentralized and networked organization, with its extensive reliance on local initiative and information technology, could seem to appear as an irony, a fantasy, and a paradox. Examples from experience, and modern organizational analysis, tell us that it need not be so.

In the corporate setting, Unisys was able to effect a drastic downsizing (one-third of its workforce) while retaining the energetic loyalty of the employees who remained. General Motors Corporation invested in the Saturn automobile development, and the program achieved radical innovations in the organization of work as well as in the coordination of product design with manufacturing processes. Worker involvement was so intense that when GM's upper management sought to mandate a major expansion of manufacturing output to meet heavy demand, workers at the Saturn plant took to wearing black armbands in defense of their commitment to intense quality control.

Critical to the success of "re-engineering" are openness of decision making, involvement of the rank-and-file employees and enlargement of their job responsibilities, and redesign of both the organizational units and the individual and group incentives that govern compensation and advancement. These measures are not less feasible in the administrative activities of the university than in the for-profit corporation. It is not so clear that academic units will yield to the same prescriptions for reform.

Chapter Sixteen

Ensuring Viability, Change, and Excellence

What kinds of change by universities will be required to ensure their viability? To impart stability? To foster excellence? These strategic questions can be addressed now that we have dealt with the nature of university organization, key resources, programs and quality, and leadership and change management.

Managing for Viability

We are used to thinking of universities as all but immortal organizations—as, indeed, many examples of the species appear to be. But their future viability is not, in fact, ensured. Universities experienced a long period of growth in size, numbers of institutions, complexity, and visibility following the end of World War II. This has made them, in the 1990s, quite sensitive to external pressures. The major universities have deep constituency support from students, alumni, and individual donors, but their hold on the attention of federal research agencies weakened during the latter 1980s and early 1990s. (See Nichols, 1993.)

State governments, facing financial stresses of their own, did not succeed in keeping pace with inflation in their budgetary support. Universities themselves began to retrench and reorganize in many areas, but they have not yet committed themselves to those uncomfortable changes in academic organization that would be required to prevent costs per student from rising over time. In the first edition of *Managing Today's University* (1974b), there were no chapters on "Efficiency and Productivity" or "Retrenchment, Restructuring, and Re-engineering." These are now essential topics.

Financial Crisis

Nonsurvival, at its most unequivocal, is evidenced by disappearance through bankruptcy or involuntary closure. Each year, from 1960 through 1992, there have indeed been institutional casualties—an average of about ten per year, most of them private, nonuniversity institutions. The prime financial indicators of mortal crisis are a steep increase in bank borrowings to meet current payroll, the beginnings of serious defaults on commitments and contracts, and the loss of internal control. A less clear-cut but still classic manifestation of nonsurvival is a drastic, involuntary change of mission and functions. Viability does not, of course, mean that the university continues to operate in exactly the same manner over time. Universities, like other organizations, do adapt to new circumstances, and this adaptation is, indeed, a sign of a healthy organization. What is at stake is the preservation of the university's basic self-definition and commitments, while it evolves in programmatic scope and in other ways compatible with its mission and its place in the spectrum of postsecondary institutions.

Institutional Crisis

Besides financial risks, universities may face threats to survival from internal institutional crisis (sometimes involving also the surrounding local community) and dangers from political intrusion or ideological assault. During the 1960s, many U.S. universities had great difficulty holding together under near-siege conditions, when they were centers of the social turmoil associated in great part with protest against the Vietnam War. Demonstrations sometimes escalated into confrontations and sit-ins, and from there to violent conflict with the police, both on campus and in the streets. Such episodes exposed weaknesses in university policies and procedures and resulted in numerous changes in the relations between the institution and the student. In loco parentis was for the most part abandoned, standards of student conduct were made much more specific, and due process procedures became much more elaborate.

U.S. universities bent, but on the whole they did not give way to the pressures of that era, except for the cancellation of final examinations at some institutions in May 1970, at the time of the invasion of Cambodia. The parliaments of several European countries reacted against similar events in continental universities by mandating sweeping changes in the statutes of university governance and new requirements for internal democratization. These reached much farther into the mechanisms of institutional power than was the case with U.S. university reforms.

Political interventions and ideological controls have a long and ignoble history, reaching back to the demands of church and monarch for obedience, and persisting to our own time as the Bolshevik revolution asserted demands for party conformity in the Soviet Union and the Nazi regime gained dominance over the great German universities. Political repression can have a long aftermath. For example, Charles University in Prague came under firm Stalinist control after the "Prague Spring" of 1968; when at last Czechs and Slovaks overthrew communist rule in 1989, the university confronted painful problems of reorganization and of reinstatement of those previously persecuted. The Czech parliament's "screening law" required examination of the status of any civil servant (including university staff) who had been a collaborator with the secret police. Beyond this, questions existed concerning the academic competence of some who had allegedly been appointed to professorial positions through exceptional party patronage. The People's Republic of China continues, with varying intensity, to require political conformity of Chinese university faculty and students.

Most political meddling in U.S. higher education is directed against public universities by key figures in state government, although those with long memories still wince at the witch-hunt atmosphere of the McCarthy period in the early 1950s.

Sometimes, state intrusion is associated with straightforward political patronage: examples are control of construction contracts for university buildings and politically inspired arrangements to hire favored consultants or law firms. Interference is more serious when directed toward political control over academic activities, appointments, or utterances. Academic leaders are obligated to resist these forays, by seeking broad public understanding of the wrongs done by political intrusion. Because universities are indeed important institutions, with responsibility for educating a nation's future leaders, passions may be aroused by unpopular advocacy. A public university is best situated to resist if it has well-protected autonomy as well as sturdy leadership.

Conditions for Long-Range Viability

The most critical factors for long-range viability are a sound structure of governance (including provisions protecting autonomy and self-direction) and a deep and widely accepted commitment to academic values. Financial viability and effective, prudent leadership and management are almost equally important.

A university probably prospers best with a steady, sustainable trajectory over time, avoiding excessive oscillations in enrollment, programs, and funding. Very rapid growth entails risks, as a large volume of faculty recruiting often involves a higher than average percentage of mistakes. After a period of substantial growth, holes in the age distribution of faculty persist for a long time, and mistakes of haste in program expansion are only slowly rectified. There are, of course, some counterexamples: a few universities, such as Chicago and Stanford, started with heavy donor sponsorship, had farsighted presidential leaders, and developed into major universities quickly. The University of California, San Diego, grew rapidly to major-university stature from its origins in the Scripps Institution of Oceanography.

The period of cooling out after rapid growth is functionally somewhat similar to absolute retrenchment, although the distress may be temporary. Promotions and new assignments are harder to come by. The budgetary margin becomes far less elastic. The excitement of expansion is replaced by stabilization and lowered morale. Decisions are more affected by the feeling of trade-off: if we do commit to this, we must give up something else.

When budgets must be cut absolutely, the negative consequences of ad hoc retrenchment can be severe. As was discussed in Chapter Fifteen, much depends on whether cuts are made in view of longer-range as well as immediate impacts.

Control agencies in many states, as the creatures of the governor and legislature, often respond to fiscal pressures by attempting to squeeze greater efficiency out of the public institutions they control: "Absorb additional enrollment, and do it without proportionate increase in budget." The faculty is a major target, as pressures mount for higher teaching loads and increased throughput.

Finally, a sustainable path requires continual efforts to engage and retain the support of numerous external and internal constituencies of the university. In public higher education, the cry is for increased accountability. This means not only good financial disclosure but also the issuance of reports that show how well (from some particular viewpoint) the institution is performing: rates of persistence to the degree; evidence of a long faculty workweek and adequate teaching load; and other reports in response to emerging public pressures.

But private institutions, equally, need to tell their story well. One index of the increased intensity of constituency relations is the large volume of house organs, publicity documents, and newsletters that any university disseminates. These come not only from the president's office but from all those units and entities that are seeking to anchor their support. The old sense that a university could maintain itself in quiet isolation has long since been replaced by the urgency of cultivating constituency support.

Managing for Excellence

The concept of academic excellence has its absolutes, but as a practical matter, it usually involves comparisons and distinctions. If there is a best, there is by implication a second best, a mediocre, and a worst. In the central functions of teaching and basic scholarship, the appreciation of excellence in each field almost always has to be the province of knowledgeable peers in that field. This makes the students, the senior administration, and the general body of the faculty dependent on testimony and evidence from specialists within the university and—if their opinions are sought—those at other institutions. The administration and the general faculty can make some assessment in accordance with generalized standards of academic performance, but these are not likely to extend to the fine differences between good performance and what is construed by experts to be outstanding.

Excellence, then, is assessed on the basis of academic judgments and reputation, and reputation operates with lags: a quite short lag among the cognoscenti, longer ones for the peers in the discipline as a whole, and still longer ones for academia in general, for administrators, for most students, and for the wider public. Because of these lags, a university is both the beneficiary and the victim of its past. Many of the things it does have only long-range impact on the impressions of excellence circulating within its own ranks and conveyed to other institutions.

Some of the hallmarks of excellence do have an impact in a short time, and others that have only long-term implications are taken by competitors as significant signals of intentions. A university that is able to attract a star professor—someone who has acquired wide reputation early and still has a substantial period of intensive scholarly productivity ahead—adds immediately to its reputation in that specialist's field. In addition to contributing personal productivity, the star is often a nucleating force for attracting grant funds, doctoral candidates, and junior faculty.

Short-term steps that have long-term implications for the excellence of work in a given field include: institutional commitments of building space, equipment funds, library acquisition funds, and allocations of faculty positions and operating budget.

One of the few certainties about academic work is that if the people are very good, they are likely to achieve very good results. Thus, tightening of admission standards, aggressive recruitment of outstanding students, and an effort to make the most promising junior faculty appointments are assurances for the long range and are taken as signals of intentions by the academic community generally. The actual consequences do not become evident until much later, as students complete their thesis research and enter the job market and as junior faculty establish scholarly reputations.

Publishable research is the dominant vehicle of scholarly contribution in most conventional fields. There are exceptions—in the fine arts, in architectural design, and sometimes in law or medicine. In all of these, distinction may result from evidence of creativity in doing rather than saying. Published research generally has to survive peer-group screening by journal editors, and good work gets fairly rapid feedback in most fields. Qualitative originality, as distinct from a high general level of scholarly effort, is hard to bring off and hard to predict.

When a nucleus of faculty proposes a new degree program or research center according to a new intellectual design, they seek sponsorship from the university (as well as from extramural funding sources). This confronts the administration and the faculty organization with a high-risk choice. If there is no defined peer group, there is no ensured feedback, which is worrisome; yet, in some cases, a new design can be productive and influential, and the university that has underwritten a qualitatively new venture that proves successful gains reputation and a head start.

Although there exist a few cross-institutional comparative measures of curriculum and teaching quality—for example, performance of undergraduate students in tests of aptitude for graduate school—

the basis for a reputation for teaching excellence, even within the local communication networks of one university, is often uncertain. Because the status quo is always less than ideal and the frontier of knowledge is changing, evidence of changes is often taken to be a correlate of quality. Such changes include overhaul of curricula, updating and redesign of particular courses, and experiments with new and more effective methods of teaching. The administration can stimulate such efforts by providing funds and time for the necessary work. Together, faculty and administration can bring a higher level of attention to teaching quality and innovation; they can also provide incentives by ensuring that good teaching performance is rewarded at the time of faculty personnel reviews and that poor teaching is subject to penalties.

Sometimes a program or a whole institution can gain celebrity for its styles of teaching and learning, or for exceptional student achievement. To achieve this requires long-range attention from the administration and the faculty. A strong reputation for excellence of instruction, once achieved, is self-reinforcing because it attracts able students. At its best, a university conveys a special atmosphere of concern for learning that contributes to the quality of work done by both students and faculty. The cultural, aesthetic, and communicative dimensions of the institution and the breadth of opportunity to explore them determine the quality of student life and bind together the academic community. Here, the administration and the general faculty organization are vitally important forces. They provide facilities and funds for cultural activity on a broad front and ensure that actions are taken to promote excellence in these fields.

In allocating resources for excellence, the leadership of a university has to rely on developing and using good consultative mechanisms rather than trusting a few individuals to make the crucial decisions. The process begins with academic appointments and promotions. Though pay scales and other aspects of compensation have to be competitive, they are no insurance against mediocrity. What is essential is to have high standards of quality in all significant dimensions. These standards of faculty achievement must be enforced firmly and fairly and propagated as norms throughout the faculty.

Beyond this, the administration, in cooperation with the faculty, needs to review the quality of academic operations and make courageous, discriminating choices. Universities have been subject to funding cycles. During periods of rapidly increasing resources, improvements could often be financed out of the growth margin. As growth has slowed down, this strategy has become impracticable for most universities, yet investment in improvements and in occasional new programs remains essential. The solution is selectivity among academic programs; failure to be selective burdens the university with more programs than it can afford to maintain at a high standard of excellence.

A deserved reputation for excellence improves the claims of a university on its loyal constituencies and on the larger society: funds from these sources become obtainable for projects that further reinforce quality. Like an athlete who must constantly test his or her personal limits, the university cannot afford not to be actively striving for excellence.

But a policy of sustained pressure toward excellence has its price, and may even endanger an institution's survival prospects. Some commitments to excellence are costly in resources. Many have long gestation periods before results are known and appreciated and entail significant risks that results will not be favorable. This is true of the bets placed on key areas of research and on faculty personnel. Because many commitments balloon in size over time, the university may all too easily discover that its aggregate of program demands is unsustainable. Furthermore, constituency support may be jeopardized when, on behalf of excellence and academic principles, the institution becomes embroiled in internal controversy or takes an unpopular stand in defense of a program or individual. This has happened repeatedly in academic history, both in the United States and abroad.

Putting It All Together

What any one university should do to find an equilibrium between the goals of viability and excellence depends on its particular circumstances and on the values of those who are directing it. Nevertheless, it is possible to outline a general approach to the problems and opportunities of the university that brings together the various analytical perspectives examined in preceding chapters.

A set of institutional aims must be identified, then translated into guiding policies and program obligations. All of the university's constituencies must be consulted. The essential values of the university must be honored and supported while the institution works to formulate its aims. Some criteria can be applied during this process: compatibility of aims; effectiveness and mutual reinforcement of programs; and acceptability to the most important constituencies.

Every university of consequence has existed for some time and has accumulated a heritage of commitments. How can the institution move from this historical base into the future it desires?

A Series of Value Dimensions

Institutional aims can be seen as points along a number of value dimensions. Some of the polar alternatives that present themselves are:

- Broad or highly selective enrollment policies
- Utilitarian or idealistic and critical philosophy
- Applied or fundamental research
- Local or national and cosmopolitan concerns
- Short-range or long-range intellectual focus
- "Basic start" education or education at the most advanced levels of scholarship and in the graduate professions

- Popular or high-status values and style
- Value added or absolute achievement focus

Suppose that only two of these value dimensions needed to be considered—say, broad versus selective enrollment and local versus cosmopolitan concerns. An institution that chose only one point along each of these dimensions could be represented as a point in a two-dimensional diagram such as Figure 16.1. The figure illustrates the positions of three institutions: one that is highly selective and emphasizes cosmopolitan interests; another that has a popular base of enrollment and a local set of interests; and a third whose commitments are spread over a zone rather than being concentrated at one point.

**Figure 16.1. Three Types of Institutions,
in Two Value Dimensions.**

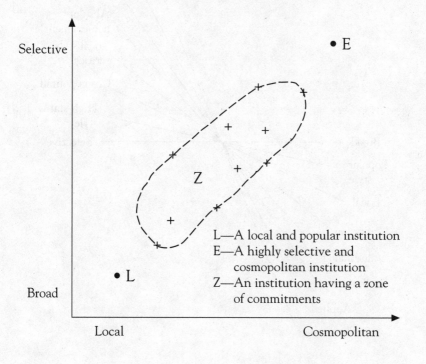

But, as we have seen, there are many value dimensions to be taken into account. It would not be possible to draw a diagram that represented the combination of all value commitments in multidimensional space. We can, however, suggest a crude visual projection from the many dimensions down to one plane, and this is done in Figure 16.2. Later on, we will locate the commitments of an institution separately in each of these dimensions.

**Figure 16.2. Projection of Numerous
Value Dimensions to the Plane.**

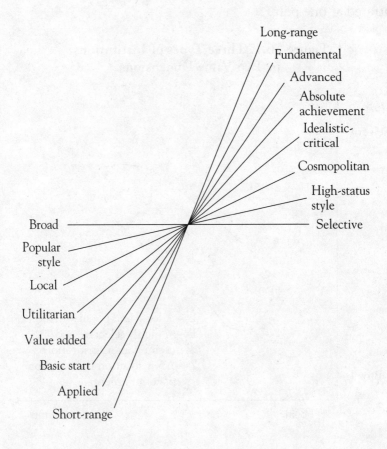

University Constituencies and Value Dimensions

We now proceed to a few observations about these value dimensions and the kinds of constituency interests that are attracted to them.

First, the faculty constituency. In order to connect with the worldwide community of scholars in a field, university faculty members in the basic disciplines emphasize the selective, the critical, the fundamental, the cosmopolitan, the long-range, and education at the advanced levels. In the graduate professions this commitment is tempered by some emphasis on the utilitarian. Some faculty do have a commitment to education of students for a basic start, and some to a philosophical orientation that speaks to student interest in the short-range and the "relevant." But often, the claims they make for resources and curricular changes conflict with the interests of discipline-oriented colleagues. Problem-focused and value-focused curricular proposals challenge the conventional academic organization, whether the topic is social ecology, conservation and natural resources, women's studies, or Third World studies.

Faculty and applied research groups in the health professions, law, engineering, urban planning, agriculture, and business management have clientele, curricular, and problem-solving research interests that are often local, popular, and utilitarian. At the same time, they must deal with scholars in the basic disciplines whose work serves as background for their own. The strongest professional schools have a combination of values that may cause a particular set of tensions: they favor highly selective admission and emphasize utilitarian interests and the cosmopolitan concerns of the profession, yet they draw on, and contribute to, fundamental theories and knowledge as they strive to break new ground in professional practice.

External Constituencies and Value Dimensions

Each external constituency sees some points along the value dimensions that it finds attractive, some to which it is indifferent, and some that arouse repulsion or outright conflict. An external agency that provides funding for basic research in a scientific field is likely to have a positive interest in what the advanced students in that field can contribute to a project, whereas it will seek safeguards against the diversion of grant resources to introductory instruction or to applied or utilitarian research. The liberals in a state legislature usually welcome evidence that a publicly supported institution is responding to the needs of young state residents for first-time access to higher education; but they may be skeptical about admission of out-of-state and foreign students or about graduate programs in exotic foreign languages and abstruse areas of science and the humanities.

Jeffersonians and Jacksonians

How can universities come to terms with the dominant themes of contemporary democratic society, particularly the egalitarian forces that are proving to be so powerful both in western Europe and the United States?

In the American context, there are two versions of egalitarianism. The Jeffersonians are believers in equality of opportunity and in struggle for individual gain and growth on the basis of individual merit. The Jacksonians and the levelers regard justice in the society as requiring equality of condition and results. Unusual intellectual attainment is reasonably compatible with the Jeffersonian ideal, but to the Jacksonians, intellectualism is suspect. As Hofstadter (1963) pointed out in his brilliant book, *Anti-Intellectualism in American Life*, Americans have always favored lots of education but they have been deeply ambivalent about intellectuals and ideas. The rugged man of common sense is better, and more to be trusted, than the effete intellectual snob.

On another aspect of the egalitarian position—the question of the university's influence on the concentration or diffusion of power in the society—the responses of the modern-day Jeffersonian and Jacksonian are not so clearly differentiated. The Jeffersonians have always favored maximum diffusion of power. They applaud the university if it is shown to assist the diffusion process and inhibit concentration. The Jacksonians and the levelers, on the other hand, are interested in what the system delivers to the mass of people and in closing the gap between those at the top and those at the bottom. They are willing to use the power of the state to accomplish these ends—for example, via income redistribution plans. If the university adds to the amount that society delivers to the mass of people and adds to the state's capacity to control the economy and equalize delivery, the Jacksonians may be more in favor of the institution than the Jeffersonians are. (And if the university is a supplier of facilitating ideas for Jacksonian interventions, so much the better!)

Mapping Institutions onto the Value Dimensions

Some institutions have a cluster of commitments at one end of all of these value dimensions. A technical-vocational institution of postsecondary instruction might well classify itself as open-admission, applied, utilitarian, and local, giving its students a basic start and maximum educational value added, providing a relatively short exposure to relevant training, and operating according to popular values and style. A community college that emphasizes general liberal arts education, on the other hand, prepares students to go on toward completion of the baccalaureate degree at a four-year college or university, and it may well give greater accent to fundamental learning, absolute achievement, and the idealistic-critical functions of education.

At the opposite pole from the technical-vocational institution are the most elite institutions, such as Oxford and Cambridge in the United Kingdom, the *grandes écoles* in France (more than the French universities), and in the United States, a relative handful of great private universities beginning with the Ivy League. Perhaps the purest cases in the United States are Rockefeller University, which has very few students, all at the graduate level, and the Institute for Advanced Study at Princeton, which has no students at all.

There is an appearance of easy compatibility between the value commitments and the educational programs designed to realize them at the institutions occupying the two ends of the spectrum: the technical-vocational community college and the elite private university. These two polar cases are illustrated in Figure 16.3.

Figure 16.3. Comparing a Technical-Vocational Institution and a Major Private University.

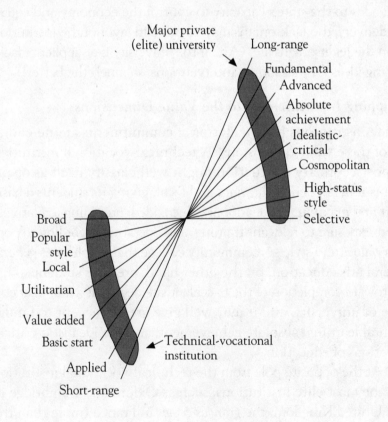

But where do the great state universities fit—Michigan and Michigan State, Wisconsin, Illinois, Ohio State, Minnesota, and of course, California? These universities can be shown to be operating *simultaneously* at several points in each of the pertinent value dimensions, making educational, research, and service commitments to meet diverse constituency claims. But more than this, these public universities are reflections of a democratic vision that has for a long time combined, in some state of tension, the Jeffersonian and the Jacksonian themes.

It is clear that the local citizenry will give strong funding and other backing to the community college. Constituency support for the major private university is also easy to characterize: the best money is contributed by people already dead; the next best by foundations and agencies that finance basic research and scholarship; then come tuition income and current alumni giving; and finally, endowment support provided by the living rich and the great corporations. The great university is discreet in cultivating establishmentarian support, for it has to guard its independence. Its faculty, through critical and humane scholarship, illumines and contributes to the high culture, and the high culture is inescapably and properly in a state of tension vis-à-vis both the establishment and the mass society.

The great private university, seeking the best student and faculty talent wherever they can be found, approximates the Jeffersonian ideal. The argument for the role of such universities in American society can be put this way:

Fundamental science and discovery are essential to feed the applied and the utilitarian, which would soon atrophy without a stream of new basic findings. (Further, it is necessary to have fundamental discovery nearby, for lead time is essential in the game of application.) A shelter for idealistic, critical, and visionary scholarship is necessary to the body social and philosophical; otherwise, complacency, philistinism, and sentimentality will overtake both the establishment and the conservative mass of the population. High selectivity and emphasis on the most intensive and advanced levels of education are essential for the preparation of future leadership. A relative handful of people at the top end of the distribution of talent and energy serves as the driving force of a society, and on the quality of this aristocracy of merit the welfare of the mass of people depends. As a national and cosmopolitan institution, the university contributes to, is in touch with, and attracts the very best of human inquiry and experiment all over the world, and it would be hampered in its task if it were provincial. The egalitarian critic can be assured that the great private university pursues its elite role without regard to race, creed, or gender, demanding only extraordinary talent in all those it accepts as students or appoints as faculty. The essence of such an institution is absolute devotion to academic excellence.

The elite university enhances the competitive power of a nation and the flowering of its civilization. In so doing, it sustains the well-being of the entire society.

The great private university can promise to serve as a gateway to leadership and eminence for the ablest people, whatever their origins, provided that it is seeking them out and helping them to overcome barriers (including the financial and the psychic) to attendance and to academic success.

Public universities have a more diversified, more dangerous, and thus more interesting set of relations between their value commitments and programs than do private universities, and they have to elicit support from the democratic political process and from many publics in a much more direct way. The public university competes with other major universities in the United States and abroad and also stands in a symbiotic relation with them. Scholarly talent circulates, ideas travel and are judged, and these universities make a dominant contribution to scholarship and to evolving standards of excellence.

Complex Value Commitments of the
Major Public University

A great public university is different from, and can be more than, a great private university. For illustration, Figure 16.4 maps out the several points of commitment of this sort of university, with respect to both institutional aims and programs.

Are the commitments compatible with each other? If there are some incompatibilities or conflicts between aims, what strategies

Figure 16.4. A Major Public University.

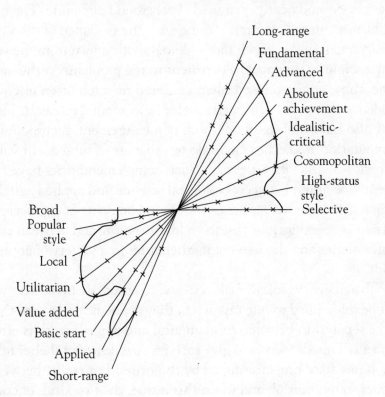

can a university adopt to bring them into harmony? Or must it consider giving up some of them?

Where the university's aims include several points along the same value dimension, these may be complementary and reinforcing or they may be independent of each other, but they are rarely in direct conflict as basic aims. The issue of trade-off generally arises when it is necessary to allocate scarce resources to programs that are, inescapably, in competition for institutional funds, space, and the attention of faculty and staff.

Complementarity is exemplified in the relationship between fundamental research in a discipline and problem-centered research. The latter, dealing with a problem of technology or social policy, does not depend neatly on a single background discipline. The best problem-centered research is done with the guidance of powerful theory and sound research methodology, both drawn from the several disciplines that may be pertinent to the problem. At the same time, those engaged in problem-centered research often uncover evidence that poses new questions for fundamental research. They may also have to develop methods of measurement, techniques of computation, and other methodology that are of subsequent value in basic scientific investigation. Such complementarities have frequently occurred between biological science and applied agricultural research; between physics and several branches of engineering; between economics and business administration; and between pure mathematics and the users of mathematics in a variety of applied fields.

To achieve organizational focus and to ensure that resources will not be misapplied to one task when they are dedicated to another, some separation between fundamental and applied work is often prudent. This also serves to give each group a degree of shelter from the immediate pressures faced by the other. But traffic between them is often fruitful, and when this is true, the two kinds of commitment are complementary.

Elements of complementarity and "jointness" in the operation of educational programs have already been discussed. Let us now consider a possible case of conflict in aims by supposing that a university commits itself to open admission in some areas (for example, psychology or business) and selective admission in others (for example, mathematics or electrical engineering), and that it attempts to emphasize both a large improvement in learning for students (large educational value added) and high absolute achievement. Suppose that the broadly selected students are put into the same courses (for example, in computer science or political science) with the highly selected, and suppose also that the standard accepted by students and faculty is one of high absolute achievement (enforced by a high minimum passing standard and by special recognition for those who excel). The highly qualified students will for the most part do well, and they will set the pace of achievement. Some of the less qualified students will also excel, and more, by struggling hard, will meet the acceptable minimum standard of performance. But in the conventional organization of instruction, a much larger fraction of the less qualified students than of the more qualified ones will have academic difficulties.

Some strong public universities have operated in this way. A broad spectrum of students is eligible to enroll and to try, but the attrition rate for academic reasons is very high among those not well prepared or strongly motivated. Inflicting failure on a large number (and percentage) of students imposes heavy and often damaging burdens on them, and the policy is therefore increasingly branded—in this egalitarian age—as unacceptable. If the odds are well-known to prospective students, those not prepared for the high risks may self-select away from such an institution.

There are, however, several ways to design the organization of instruction to reduce the incidence of failure. One is to separate the streams of students, both by areas of motivation and interest and according to initial level of mastery. The students who need more initial help can then get it, at the appropriate pace, while those of exceptional preparation and ability progress more rapidly toward advanced courses. A second approach is to individualize the learning process, so that each student receives individual guidance and facilitation from competent and patient faculty. This approach is far more expensive in faculty time than the first. It also reduces the stimulus that students get from interaction with those who excel. The third approach is the most difficult to bring off. It entails keeping a broad spectrum of students together, using the superior performers as examples to be emulated, and employing their talents to help less qualified students meet the standard of acceptability.

These three approaches can be labeled *stratification, individualization, and mutuality*. All three can be found to some extent in public universities. But the second requires much more budget per student than public universities have conventionally been permitted, and only now are innovative uses of information technology promising to change the cost pattern. The third approach calls for organizational inventions that have not as yet emerged in significant numbers or been widely applied. New emphasis on "active learning"—project teams, study circles, and field involvements—can potentially show the way toward greater mutuality in the learning process.

The public university has interesting challenges to meet in building an educational organization that will serve its institutional aims. These are far more complicated than the design of institutions of the polar types shown in Figure 16.3. However, the educational setting of the strong public university offers the potentially excellent student far more challenge and access to learning at the frontier than could be provided in a purely local and popular institution, because the university enjoys complementarities between its superstructure of graduate education and research and its undergraduate programs. The public university, by the devices just discussed, can also meet the needs of a broader spectrum of students than can the purely elite institution. However, the full range of educational designs and approaches to mutuality of learning has still to be worked out.

As for the question of constituency support, it is essential to state first that though public universities, like private universities, are infused with commitments to the deepest, and often most controversial, questions of philosophical and social values, they are not politically partisan enterprises. Furthermore, public universities need all the friends they can win and keep on terms that are compatible with their institutional integrity. Ideally, each public university should be capable of engendering the support and loyalty—in different aspects of its operations—of constituencies ranging from the conservative to the left-of-center.

Because a university has to defend its essential institutional principles of operation, however, and because events compel it to defend the unpopular, the university faces periodic criticism from one constituency or another. No university should give up its essential mandate, and none should give up the attempt to harmonize, where it can, divergent social interests and support. These commitments keep the public university in a relationship of constant tension with the coalitions of support it seeks to build and maintain.

A public university's institutional aims, commitments, and approaches to constituency support may seem to lack the natural coherence that is found in an institution designed definitively at one end of the value spectrum or the other. But the public university is based on a view of how a democratic society ought to function—not choosing between social justice and excellence, but regarding both aims as essential and in the long run, compatible. Whether the great public university will continue to be viable depends essentially on whether society in general continues to embrace this double commitment.

The many friends a public university has among the establishmentarians are friends it needs, and this point must be emphasized both to the establishmentarians themselves (who occasionally may doubt the public university's need for them and their need for it) and to the egalitarians, who have many differences of view with the Establishment. As has been argued earlier, the university needs to serve as a meeting point for the major interests and themes of society, which would be ill-served indeed if every significant institution had to be exclusively in one camp or the other.

Specifically, the establishmentarians are needed by the public university because they hold much of the power and influence in the great corporations, the leading professions, the trade unions, organized agriculture, and other important interest groups. In the long view, the public university can be seen to serve these interests significantly, for it contributes to the vitality of social institutions, of technology, and of the economy.

The establishmentarians are also a major support and audience for high culture. At the same time, they control the mass media, which tell us all that it is fitting for us to know about ourselves. In the major professions—law especially, but also the health care and administrative professions—they supply leadership and thoughtful action. Not only does the public university help to train the new recruits in these professions; it also depends on the perspective they later bring to their leadership roles.

Finally, there is the essential need for financial support. The establishmentarians control the great foundations, and these foundations are important indeed to universities, because—when they are doing as they should—they provide much seed funding for experiments and ideas that can qualify for major governmental support only after they have been worked up to the point of significant promise.

Also, the rich among the establishmentarians (they are not all rich, only highly influential) have given heavily to both private and public universities. The former have always relied on large private donors, but public universities have an increasingly urgent case for similar benefactions, to assist in providing a margin of excellence.

Universities must depend substantially on other sources of funds. The establishmentarians are important here too, through their influence in state capitals and in Washington. The egalitarian political leader works for various changes in the established order and especially toward redistributions in favor of the poor, the young, the old, and the wage worker—in other words, most of the people. For obvious reasons, this power base is not as solid as that of the establishmentarians, even though it is much more populous and therefore potentially decisive at the ballot box. The public university should respond to egalitarian concerns by engaging in aggressive recruitment of potentially qualified students from low-income and minority origins and by providing help toward reforms and innovations in the classic areas of mass concern: elementary and secondary education; employment; health care; and improvement of housing, safety, and other conditions of urban life.

It is to be hoped that the egalitarians will appreciate the reasons for which the public university is in touch with and asks the support of the establishmentarians. One may also hope that establishmentarians in their turn will understand that the public university has to explain itself to, cultivate, and respond to egalitarian interests.

Egalitarian concerns to which the public university can properly respond include the removal of financial barriers to educational opportunity, provision of a wide diversity of offerings of instruction, and expansion of the graduate professions in areas of prime social need. Public universities are also strongly accountable now for their performance in attracting minority students and women to their programs and to their faculty and staff. The public university is part of a spectrum of institutions in a state, and it therefore has to contribute to the overall educational capability of the state system in numerous ways. Finally, the public university has to respond positively to demands for applied research of a problem-solving nature, and it is obliged to offer a wide range of public services to government and to the community.

Managing for Change

A university cannot rest. As we have seen, an active faculty and student body bring about continual incremental changes in the content of individual courses and fairly frequent changes of curricular structure. But the accumulation of new knowledge and the demands of a restless society create many new intellectual and academic opportunities of more major scope. Alert faculty members and university leaders need to determine which opportunities must be pursued out of the precious margin of internally available resources; which ones should be initiated if new external resources can be attracted; and which ones are not of high enough priority or not truly appropriate to the university's self-defined mission.

Making Way for New Academic Commitments

New opportunities sometimes arise in the basic scholarly disciplines, usually on the strength of new theory and evidence. Some others come in multidisciplinary form; they may be harbingers of new fundamental scholarship, or their significance may be for application, policy studies, or the active professions. Indeed, new subprofessions may come into being as occupations evolve, and these may justify initiation of new professional degrees and curricula.

Winnowing out obsolete programs to make way for new ones is good advice in principle, but as shown in Chapters Fourteen and Fifteen, the process is both difficult and painful. Yet the constraints on a university's growth rate and eventual size make it essential to reach priority judgments as to what should no longer be supported, so that a margin of resources for change can be created.

Innovations for Increased Efficiency

In the 1990s, the demand for efficiency within the university is insistent. Administrative processes and systems, as discussed above, can be reshaped and improved readily if the leadership is good and the institution is willing and able to invest in changes at the front end. Changes with significant potential impact do require investment: redesign of organizational processes and incentive systems; information technology support; reassignment and training of personnel.

It would be reasonable to aim at a stable level of cost per student year in constant dollars. However, the setting of such a goal shocks the university system, for to achieve it *while permitting academic and staff salaries to keep pace with other sectors of society* would require steady productivity improvements, both in administration and in academic operations. The lessons and opportunities discussed in Chapters Fourteen and Fifteen become important institutional priorities if the university does adopt such a goal. If it does not, it becomes an ever-weaker claimant on available subsidy funds, public and private, and the danger of loss of autonomy increases over time.

Assessment of the University's Path

To manage change, an institution needs to mobilize extensive information and feedback about its performance. Internal information from students, faculty, and staff can be elicited regularly; we have already discussed how important this is in efforts to maintain and improve quality. Comparative information about the strengths and weaknesses of programs becomes available periodically when national assessments are made. Journalistic and other ratings are less reliable, but when they are publicized, it becomes necessary to reckon with both their actual implications for quality and their effect on public perceptions. Special program reviews can focus on particular programs that are at a critical juncture and can help to prescribe a course of action.

Administrative units and services have no less need to monitor performance and obtain feedback. Management improvement depends on it.

Allocation of Programs and Functions Among Universities

As resources become more constrained, universities should also seek economies by entering into consortium and cooperation agreements. Funders will insist on some of these—for example, the sharing of capital and operating costs of major research facilities. In other instances, universities that are close enough neighbors can enact course-interchange agreements, library sharing, and other cooperative efforts that either cut costs or broaden academic opportunities, or both. Cooperative agreements are most likely to succeed when none of the cooperating entities need give up visibility, reputation, or control, and when the benefits are great enough to justify adjustment pain and institutional sacrifice.

Public and private universities in a region compete for enrollment in numerous degree programs and offerings. When there is high demand, a university can maintain a relatively uncompetitive program and still attract enrollment—albeit, of relatively less qualified students. But a weak program (usually associated with a weak faculty group) does not attract external research and support funding, and it does little for the overall reputation of the institution. Even though the competitive pressure among universities does not drive out weak programs quickly, it may discourage the university from continuing a weak program unless it sees a way to invest for a significant qualitative improvement.

The public universities in a state or region are likely to confront explicitly a number of questions of allocation of programs. The state government, as a major funding source, can force consideration of priorities. How many academic programs in specialized field X, or how many professional schools of type Y, should the state finance, and on how many campuses? How many doctoral programs and major research commitments should the state support in each field? The multicampus university system has a choice: it can either have in place its own process for determining reasonable answers to these questions, or it can wait until a fiscal crisis unleashes political initiatives via the budgetary route. The 1990s will probably see some public universities follow the second approach, but there is advantage in proactive academic leadership, review, and management of the kind entailed in the first.

More complicated, but also worth considering, are issues of public-private cooperation and competition in the allocation of academic programs. Very little has been done to attempt to "manage" at this margin of the university sector. The unending pressure to upgrade, seek larger academic reputation, and broaden programs operates as a backdrop against which the question of proliferation needs to be considered. In the past, state governments have often responded positively to arguments for the initiation of new graduate degrees and programs at the public universities. Thus, more and more universities have entered the doctoral program sweepstakes; once in the game, they compete vigorously for research funding and other resources, for only in this way can they strengthen program quality and reputation. These forces of proliferation do not face clear-cut, obvious barriers, although the results may be disappointing enough eventually to disillusion the state funders. The university sector is likely to face this problem for a long time to come.

Looking Ahead: The Effective Research University

A slow-growth economy and tight federal and state budgeting must be assumed for the indefinite future. Yet there is a basic alternative to the university that is cramped by obsolescence, pinched in its budgetary resources, and beset by problems of morale and even purpose. The alternative is to build a new set of institutional capabilities for effective leadership, both in academic operations and in administration. While the healthy university of the future honors its institutional values and its structures, it is dedicated to a rate of change sufficiently rapid to produce rising productivity of administration, faculty, and academic programs, and even of students themselves.

It is easiest to sketch the profile of change in administrative services. Administration will be substantially "delayered," and task activities will be re-engineered and organized for responsible initiative, with appropriate incentives—in pay and recognition—for high performance and innovation.

Academic programs will be selected for excellence, and some (in public universities) will be selected as responses to intense social needs and thus for their special contributions to institutional viability. Low-quality academic and professional degree programs will be phased out after appropriate evaluation and priority review. Doctoral programs will be subject to regular quality assessment, and low-quality programs will either be phased out or boosted by investment to bring about drastic quality improvement.

Instruction at all levels will be cost-controlled. Advanced-placement study in high school, assignment of remedial and introductory college courses to community colleges, and more intensive use of summer sessions will enable the efficient university to concentrate its undergraduate instruction on what it can do best: teach at intermediate and advanced levels. This will improve utilization of facilities and staff. The array of courses for undergraduates and graduate students will be pruned to concentrate on offerings with at least a respectable minimum enrollment.

Major efforts to incorporate interactive computer and multimedia technology into instructional processes will result, at last, in some substitution of capital for labor in instruction. Leading institutions will make significant front-end investments in the design and development of these computer and multimedia packages and will offer them on a royalty basis to other institutions or for use in distance-learning programs.

The effective university will be responsive to student demand in its program offerings and will seek to improve its performance in persistence to the degree and shorten the time to the degree in both undergraduate and graduate programs. Such improvements will benefit the student, the student's family, and (in a public university) the state's finances.

The university will couple its selection of high-quality graduate programs with aggressive institutional support of research in those fields, and it will assign low priority in special facilities, funding, and research library resources to programs that are designed as service programs and are not budgeted for research and doctoral study. It will finance more research from internal institutional sources and by soliciting support from private sources as well as state and federal research agencies. It will strengthen ties with industry for research support in selected areas.

The faculty will include a larger percentage of nonladder teachers, and ladder faculty will be chosen and retained on rigorous quality and performance standards. Compensation may increasingly be split between a "base" for normal duties of teaching and departmental research and a series of optional pay components for institutional duties and innovative course development using new technologies. Intervals of intensive faculty research will increasingly be financed via "buyouts" of time on extramurally funded projects or special institutional funds, not simply financed through normal department budgets.

Academic support needs, beginning with the library resource, will be administered in accordance with academic priorities, so that deep research collections will be maintained only in key areas selected for doctoral and advanced professional education. The library will depend more and more on computer-based and electronic-storage systems. University consortia and sharing arrangements will intensify, so that scholars who need materials not in their own libraries will have reasonably prompt access to library materials.

Academic and administrative space will be budgeted in departmental operating budgets and thus be subject to more effective self-management, and space will be monitored for effective utilization.

Student services, where not universal to the whole student population and financed via compulsory student fees, will be offered on the basis of student demand at voluntary fees intended to cover costs. Increasingly, such services will be student directed.

The senior administration and academic leadership will reserve a significant portion of the operating budget for continued investment in improvements and innovations. Oversight committees in the major fields will be empaneled to identify new directions of innovation in the conduct of existing programs and to explore potential new programs that may be deserving of formative investment.

The effective university will continually seek corporate and individual private support, as well as governmental support, for its priority programs. It will avoid seeking funds for low-quality programs unless these are scheduled for drastic overhaul. It will promote academic alliances and partnerships with other institutions, public and private, in order to enhance opportunities for its students and faculty.

This profile of the effective research university of the future is within the reach of many private and public universities today. To achieve a high level of effectiveness, however, the university will have to seek out talented academic and administrative leadership to manage the many crucial relationships with constituencies and cooperating institutions. These relationships provide the basis for continuing strength in funding and play a key role in the design of cooperative arrangements that widen opportunities while economizing resources. The presidency will enunciate directions of institutional priority and development that will have been worked out within the university and with its key constituencies. A further function of the presidency will be to oversee the selection and reward of those who take the special burdens of relational leadership, both within the institution and with its partners.

Thus, we end as we began. The significant universities of the world vary greatly in age, size, legal form of organization, institutional style, and mode of financing. Yet they have in common the coupling of teaching and research, the offering of a diversity of programs up to the most advanced stages of systematic learning, and the implicit commitments to humane ideals and scholarly interests that cross the boundaries of governments.

If this book has clarified how universities manage themselves, justify society's support, and are guided to fulfill their aims, it has accomplished its purpose.

Let me end, then, on a note of faith. Universities will survive in the service of a good society, for despite their crankiness and their unsettling qualities, they are essential to it. They operate by internal processes that require high personal motivation on the part of scholar and student and confer a great deal of individual latitude. This gives them a character that may be a hopeful portent for other kinds of organizations in postindustrial society.

References

Academic Senate, University of California, Berkeley. *Report of the Special Task Force on Faculty Diversity*. Berkeley: Academic Senate, University of California, 1991.

Acherman, H. "Termination of Degree and Research Programs." *International Journal of Institutional Management in Higher Education*, 1984, 8(1), 67–78.

Anderson, C. "'Strategic Research' Wins the Day." *Science*, 1993, *259*(5091), 21.

Anderson, M. *Imposters in the Temple: American Intellectuals Are Destroying Our Universities and Cheating Our Students*. New York: Simon & Schuster, 1992.

Astin, A. W. *What Matters in College? Four Critical Years Revisited*. San Francisco: Jossey-Bass, 1993.

Baker, W. D. "Higher Education's Facilities and Instrumentation Needs." Statement from the vice president, budget and university relations, Office of the President, University of California, before the Subcommittee on Science, Research and Technology, Committee on Science and Technology, U.S. House of Representatives, Washington, D.C., Oct. 22, 1985.

Balderston, F. E. "Financing California's System of Higher Education." In N. J. Smelser and G. Almond (eds.), *Public Higher Education in California*. Berkeley: University of California Press, 1974a.

Balderston, F. E. *Managing Today's University*. (1st ed.) San Francisco: Jossey-Bass, 1974b.

Balderston, F. E. "Academic Program Review and the Determination of University Priorities." *International Journal of Institutional Management in Higher Education*, 1985, 9(3), 237–248.

Balderston, F. E. "Organization, Funding, Incentives and Initiatives for University Research: A University Management Perspective." In S. A. Hoenack and E. L. Collins (eds.), *The Economics of American Universities*. Albany: State University of New York Press, 1990.

Balderston, F. E. "Cost-Effectiveness Methodologies for University Decisions." In G. L. Schmaedick, *Cost-Effectiveness in the Nonprofit Sector*. Westport, Conn.: Quorum, 1993.

Balderston, J. B., and Balderston, F. E. (eds.). *Higher Education in Indonesia: Evolution and Reform*. Berkeley: Center for Studies in Higher Education, University of California, 1993.

Barnard, C. I. *Functions of the Executive*. Cambridge, Mass.: Harvard University Press, 1938.

Becher, R. A. "The Demand for 'Quality Assurance' in British Higher Education." Unpublished paper presented at a colloquium at the Center for Studies in Higher Education, University of California, Berkeley, Apr. 1992.

Berg, D. J., and Hoenack, S. A. "The Concept of Cost-Related Tuition and Its Implementation at the University of Minnesota." *Journal of Higher Education*, 1987, 58(3), 276–305.

Bernstein, R. "The Yale Schmidt Leaves Behind." *New York Times Magazine*, June 14, 1992, pp. 32, 46, 48, 58, 64, 66.

Birnbaum, R. *How Academic Leadership Works: Understanding Success and Failure in the College Presidency*. San Francisco: Jossey-Bass, 1992.

Bloom, A. *The Closing of the American Mind*. New York: Simon & Schuster, 1987.

Bowen, H. R. *Investment in Learning*. San Francisco: Jossey-Bass, 1977.

Bowen, H. R. *The Costs of Higher Education*. San Francisco: Jossey-Bass, 1980.

Bowen, H. R., and Douglass, G. K. *Efficiency in Liberal Education: A Study of Comparative Instructional Costs for Different Ways of Organizing Teaching-Learning in a Liberal Arts College*. New York: McGraw-Hill, 1971.

Bowen, W. G. "Economic Pressures on the Major Private Universities." In U.S. Government Printing Office, *The Economics and Financing of Higher Education in the United States: A Compendium of Papers Submitted to the Joint Economic Committee, Congress of the United States*. Washington, D.C.: U.S. Government Printing Office, 1969.

Bowen, W. G., and Rudenstine, N. L. *In Pursuit of the Ph.D.* Princeton, N.J.: Princeton University Press, 1992.

Bowen, W. G., and Sosa, J. A. *Prospects for Faculty in the Arts and Sciences*. Princeton, N.J.: Princeton University Press, 1989.

Breneman, D. W. *The Ph.D. Production Function: The Case at Berkeley*. Berkeley: Ford Foundation Program for Research in University Administration, Report P–16, University of California, 1970.

Breneman, D. W. *An Economic Theory of Ph.D. Production*. Berkeley: Ford Foundation Program for Research in University Administration, Report P–8, University of California, 1971a.

Breneman, D. W. *The Ph.D. Degree at Berkeley: Interviews, Placement, and Recommendations*. Berkeley: Ford Foundation Program for Research in University Administration, Report P–17, University of California, 1971b.

Broad, W. J. "Big Science Squeezes Small-Scale Researchers." *New York Times*, Dec. 29, 1992, p. C1.

Bromley, D. A. *The National Research and Education Network Program: A Report to Congress.* Submitted by the director, Office of Science and Technology Policy, in response to a requirement of the High Performance Company Act of 1991 (P.L. 102–194). Washington, D.C.: Executive Office of the President, Office of Science and Technology Policy, 1992.

Buckley, W. F. *God and Man at Yale: The Superstitions of Academic Freedom.* Chicago: Rignery, 1951.

Burrough, B., and Helyar, J. *Barbarians at the Gate: The Fall of RJR Nabisco.* New York: HarperCollins, 1990.

California Higher Education Policy Center. *Time for Decision: California's Legacy and the Future of Higher Education.* San Jose: California Higher Education Policy Center, Mar. 1994.

California Postsecondary Education Commission. *A Capacity for Learning: Revising Space and Utilization Standards for California Public Higher Education.* Report no. 90–3. Sacramento: California Postsecondary Education Commission, 1990.

Callan, P. *The Higher Education Policy Vacuum.* Report no. 93–2. San Jose: California Higher Education Policy Center, 1993a.

Callan, P. "Indexing Student Fees to Instruction Costs at CSU Is a Bad Idea." *Sacramento Bee,* June 1, 1993b, p. 11.

Carlson, D. *The Production and Cost Behavior of Higher Education Institutions.* Berkeley: Ford Foundation Program for Research in University Administration, 1972.

Carnegie Commission on Higher Education. *Dissent and Disruption.* New York: McGraw-Hill, 1971.

Carnegie Foundation for the Advancement of Teaching. *A Classification of Institutions of Higher Education, 1994 Edition.* Princeton, N.J.: Carnegie Foundation for the Advancement of Teaching, 1994.

Cartter, A. M. "Scientific Manpower for 1970–1985" *Science,* 1971, *172,* pp. 132–140.

Cheit, E. F. *The New Depression in Higher Education.* New York: McGraw-Hill, 1971.

Chronicle of Higher Education, Almanac Issue, 1994, *41*(1).

Clark, B. R. *The Higher Education System.* Berkeley: University of California Press, 1983.

Close, F. *Too Hot to Handle: The Case of Cold Fusion.* Princeton, N.J.: Princeton University Press, 1991.

Coase, R. H. *The Firm, the Market, and the Law.* Chicago: University of Chicago Press, 1988.

Cohen, M. D., and March, J. G. *Leadership and Ambiguity: The American College President.* New York: McGraw-Hill, 1974.

Cole, J. R. "Balancing Acts: Dilemmas of Choice Facing Research Universities." *Daedalus*, 1993, *122*(4), 1–36.

College Entrance Examination Board. *The College Handbook, 1992*. New York: The College Board, 1992.

Cornford, F. M. *Microcosmographia Academica: Being a Guide for the Young Academic Politician*. Cambridge, Mass.: Dunster House, 1923.

"Cracks in the Ivory Tower." *Science*, 1992, *257*, 1196–1201.

Cyert, R. M., and March, J. G. *A Behavioral Theory of the Firm*. Englewood Cliffs, N.J.: Prentice-Hall, 1963.

Day, D. N. "The Management of Organized Research Units at the University of California, Berkeley: Size, Politics, and Interdisciplinarity." Working Paper CP–399. Berkeley: Center for Research in Management Science, University of California, 1976.

DePalma, A. "MIT Ruled Guilty in Antitrust Case—Judge Says It Conspired to Fix Amount of Aid to Students." *New York Times*, Sept. 3, 1992, pp. A1, A13.

D'Souza, D. *Illiberal Education: The Politics of Race and Sex on Campus*. New York: Free Press, 1991.

Economic Consulting Services, Inc. *A Study of Trends in Average Prices and Costs of Certain Serials over Time: Prepared for the Association of Research Libraries*. Washington, D.C.: Economic Consulting Services, Inc., 1989.

Ehrenburg, R. G. "The Flow of New Doctorates." *Journal of Economic Literature*, 1992, *30*(2), 830–875.

El-Khawas, E. *Campus Trends 1993*. Washington, D.C.: American Council on Education, 1993.

Evangelauf, J. "A New 'Carnegie Classification.'" *Chronicle of Higher Education*, Apr. 6, 1994, pp. A17–A26.

"For Lack of Money, Penn May Drop 3 Departments." *New York Times*, Oct. 14, 1993, p. A10.

Gade, M. L. *Four Multicampus Systems: Some Policies and Practices That Work*. Washington, D.C.: Association of Governing Boards of Universities and Colleges, 1993.

Garbarino, J. W. "Creeping Unionism in the Faculty Labor Market." In M. S. Gordon (ed.), *Higher Education and the Labor Market*. New York: McGraw-Hill, 1974a.

Garbarino, J. W. *Statement, Hearings on Collective Negotiation in Higher Education*. California Legislature, Joint Committee on Postsecondary Education, Apr. 19, 1974b.

Garbarino, J. W. *Faculty Bargaining*. New York: McGraw-Hill, 1975.

Gilmour, J. E., Jr. "Participative Governance Bodies in Higher Education: Report of a National Study." In R. Birnbaum (ed.), *Faculty in Governance: The*

Role of Senates and Joint Committees in Academic Decision Making. New Directions for Higher Education, no. 75, San Francisco: Jossey-Bass, 1991.

Gordon, L. "CSU Plans to Lay Off 2,200 Unless State Helps." *Los Angeles Times,* June 6, 1992, p. B–1.

Gourman, J. *The Gourman Report: A Rating of Graduate and Professional Programs in American and International Universities.* Los Angeles: National Education Standards, 1989a (5th ed.) and 1993a (6th ed.).

Gourman, J. *The Gourman Report: A Rating of Undergraduate Programs in American and International Universities.* Los Angeles: National Education Standards, 1989b (7th ed.) and 1993b (8th ed.).

Hambrick, D. C. "The Top Management Team: Key to Strategic Success." *California Management Review,* 1987, *30*(1), 88–108.

Hambrick, D. C., and D'Aveni, R. A. "Top Team Deterioration As Part of the Downward Spiral of Large Corporate Bankruptcies." *Management Science,* 1992, *38*(10), 1445–1466.

Hansen, W. L., and Weisbrod, B. A. *Benefits, Costs and Finance of Public Higher Education.* Chicago: Markham, 1969.

"Harvard University." *Change Magazine,* 1990, *22*(5), 18.

"The Higher Education Amendments of 1992: What They Mean for Colleges and Students." *Chronicle of Higher Education,* 1992, *38*(48), A20–A23.

Hirschhorn, L., and Gilmore, T., "The New Boundaries of the 'Boundaryless' Company." *Harvard Business Review,* 1992, *70*(3), 104–115.

Hitch, C. J. *Decision-Making for Defense.* Berkeley: University of California Press, 1965.

Hofstadter, R. *Anti-Intellectualism in American Life.* New York: Knopf, 1963.

Hofstede, G. *Cultures and Organizations: Software of the Mind.* New York: McGraw-Hill, 1991.

Huber, R. *How Professors Play the Cat Guarding the Cream.* Fairfax, Va.: George Mason University Press, 1992.

Hutchings, P., and Marchese, T. "Watching Assessment: Questions, Stories, Prospects." *Change Magazine,* 1990, *22*(5), 12–38.

Ingram, R. T., and Associates. *Governing Independent Colleges and Universities: A Handbook for Trustees, Chief Executives, and Other Campus Leaders.* San Francisco: Jossey-Bass, 1993a.

Ingram, R. T., and Associates. *Governing Public Colleges and Universities: A Handbook for Trustees, Chief Executives, and Other Campus Leaders.* San Francisco: Jossey-Bass, 1993b.

Jenny, H. H., and Wynn, G. R. *The Golden Years: A Study of Income and Expenditure Growth and Distribution of Forty-Eight Private Four-Year Liberal Arts Colleges, 1960–1968.* Wooster, Ohio: College of Wooster, 1971.

Jenny, H. H., and Wynn, G. R. *After the Golden Years*. Wooster, Ohio: College of Wooster, 1972a.

Jenny, H. H., and Wynn, G. R. *The Turning Point*. Wooster, Ohio: College of Wooster, 1972b.

Johnstone, D. B. *New Patterns for College Lending: Income Contingent Loans*. New York: Columbia University Press, 1972.

Jones, L. V., Lindzey, G., and Coggeshall, P. E. (eds.). *An Assessment of Research-Doctorate Programs in the United States*. 5 vols. Washington, D.C.: National Academy Press, 1982.

Keller, G. *Academic Strategy*. Baltimore, Md.: Johns Hopkins Press, 1983.

Kerr, C. "Why Every Institution Wants To Be Berkeley, Harvard or Swarthmore." *Change Magazine*, 1991, 23(3), 8–15.

Kerr, C. *Higher Education Cannot Escape History: Issues for the Twenty-first Century*. Albany: State University of New York Press, 1994a.

Kerr, C. *Troubled Times for American Higher Education: The 1990s and Beyond*. Albany: State University of New York Press, 1994b.

Kerr, C., and Gade, M. L. *The Many Lives of Academic Presidents: Time, Place and Character*. Washington, D.C.: Association of Governing Boards of Universities and Colleges, 1986.

Kerr, C., and Gade, M. L. *The Guardians: Boards of Trustees of American Colleges and Universities — What They Do and How Well They Do It*. Washington, D.C.: Association of Governing Boards of Universities and Colleges, 1989.

Krueger, A. B., and Bowen, W. G. "Income-Contingent College Loans." *Journal of Economic Perspectives*, 1993, 7(3), 193–201.

Magner, D. K. "Job Market Blues." *Chronicle of Higher Education*, 1994, 40(34), pp. A17, A20.

Mamet, D. *Oleanna*. 1992.

March, J. G., and Olsen, J. P. "Institutional Perspectives on Governance." Unpublished paper, Graduate School of Business, Stanford University, 1994.

Marcuse, H. "Repressive Tolerance." In R. P. Wolff, B. Moore, Jr., and H. Marcuse, *A Critique of Pure Tolerance*. Boston: Beacon Press, 1969.

Massy, W. F. "Productivity in Higher Education: Conclusions from a Preliminary Study." Discussion paper. Stanford, Calif.: Stanford Institute for Higher Education Research, Stanford University, 1990.

Massy, W. F., and Wilger, A. "Productivity in Postsecondary Education, A New Approach." Paper presented at the annual research conference of the Association for Public Policy Analysis and Management. Stanford, Calif.: Stanford Institute for Higher Education Research, Stanford University, 1991.

Matkin, G. W. *Technology Transfer and the University.* New York: Maxwell Macmillan International, 1990.

Metzger, W. P. "The 1940 Statement of Principles on Academic Freedom and Tenure." In W. W. Van Alstyne (ed.), *Freedom and Tenure in the Academy.* Durham, N.C.: Duke University Press, 1993.

"Minorities in Science: The Pipeline Problem." 1st Annual Report. *Science*, 1992, *258*, 1175–1237.

Mitchell, M., and Saunders, L. "The Virtual Library: An Agenda for the 1990s." *Computers in Libraries*, 1991, *11*(4), 8–11.

National Center for Education Statistics. *Digest of Education Statistics 1993.* NCES 93–292. Washington, D.C.: U.S. Goverment Printing Office, 1993.

National Research Council. *Postdoctoral Appointments and Disappointments.* Washington, D.C.: National Academy Press, 1981.

National Science Board. *Science Indicators—1986.* Washington, D.C.: U.S. Government Printing Office, 1986.

National Science Board. *Science and Engineering Indicators—1991.* NSB 91–1. Washington, D.C.: U.S. Government Printing Office, 1991.

Nelson, N. "Electronic Libraries: Vision and Implementation." *Computers in Libraries*, 1990, *10*(2), pp. 6, 8, 10, 12–13.

Nelson, R. R., and Winter, S. G. *An Evolutionary Theory of Economic Change.* Cambridge, Mass.: Harvard University Press, 1982.

Nerad, M., and Cerny, J. "From Facts to Action: Expanding the Educational Role of the Graduate Division." *Council of Graduate Schools Communicator*, special ed., May 1991, pp. 1–12.

Nichols, R. W. "Federal Science Policies and Universities: Consequences of Success." *Daedalus*, 1993, *122*(4), 197–224.

Olswang, S. G. "Financing Financial Distress: A Case Study of the University of Washington." *Higher Education*, 1987, *16*(2), 145–154.

Office of Management and Budget, United States Government. "Cost Principles for Educational Institutions," Circular A-21, Revised editions 1979, 1982, 1991, 1993. Washington, D.C.: Federal Register.

O'Reilly, C. A., III, and Flatt, S. "Executive Team Demography, Organizational Innovation, and Firm Performance." Unpublished paper. Haas School of Business, University of California, Berkeley, 1989.

O'Reilly, C. A. III, Snyder, R. C., and Boothe, J. N. "Executive Team Demography and Organizational Change." In G. Huber and W. Glick (eds.), *Organizational Change and Redesign: Ideas and Insights for Improving Managerial Performance.* New York: Oxford University Press, 1993, pp. 147–175.

Penrod, J., and Dolence, M. "Reengineering: A Process for Transforming Higher

Education." Professional Paper Series, no. 9. Boulder, Colo.: CAUSE, 1992.

Pfeffer, J. *Managing with Power: Politics and Influence in Organizations.* Boston, Mass.: Harvard Business School Press, 1992.

Pfeffer, J., and Moore, W. L. "Average Tenure of Academic Department Heads: The Effects of Paradigm, Size, and Departmental Demography." *Administrative Science Quarterly*, 1980, *25*, 387–406.

Pfeffer, J., and Salancik, G. R. "Organizational Decision Making as a Political Process: The Case of a University Budget." *Administrative Science Quarterly*, 1974, *19*, 135–151.

Prewitt, K. "America's Research Universities Under Public Scrutiny." *Daedalus*, 1993, *122*(4), 85–100.

Princeton Today, 1992, Summer.

Radner, R., and Miller, L. S. *Demand and Supply in U.S. Higher Education.* New York: McGraw-Hill, 1975.

Rodarmor, W. "TKO in Sociology." *California Monthly*, 1992, *103*(1), 16–19.

Rosovsky, H. *The University: An Owner's Manual.* New York: W. W. Norton, 1990.

Rosser, J. M., and Penrod, J. I. "Computing and Libraries: A Partnership Past Due." *Cause/Effect*, 1990, *13*(2), 21–24.

Rothblatt, S. (ed.). *The OECD, the Master Plan, and the California Dream: A Berkeley Conversation.* Berkeley: Center for Studies in Higher Education, University of California, 1992.

Rupp, G. E. Inauguration address, unpublished paper, Columbia University, Oct. 4, 1993.

Searle, J. *The Campus War.* New York: World, 1971.

Shapiro, H. "Voyage of Discovery in a Pluralistic Society." Commencement Address. *Princeton Today*. Summer, 1992, p. 12.

Simon, H. A. *Administrative Behavior.* New York: Macmillan, 1947.

Smart, T., Engardio, P., and Smith, G. "GE's Brave New World." *Business Week*, Nov. 8, 1993, pp. 64–70.

Smelser, N. J. "The Politics of Ambivalence: Diversity in the Research Universities." *Daedalus*, 1993, *122*(4), 37–54.

Smolla, R. A. "Academic Freedom, Hate Speech, and the Idea of a University." In W. W. Van Alstyne (ed.), *Freedom and Tenure in the Academy*. Durham, N. C.: Duke University Press, 1993.

Solmon, L. J., and Taubman, P. J. (eds.). *Does College Matter?* San Diego, Calif.: Academic Press, 1973.

Stigler, S. "Competition and the Research Universities." *Daedalus*, 1993, *122*(4), 157–196.

Trow, M. "Managerialism and the Academic Profession: The Case of England." Working paper 93–15. Berkeley: Institute of Governmental Studies, University of California, 1993.

University of California, Office of the President. *Report of the Universitywide Task Force on Faculty Rewards*. Oakland: Office of the President, University of California, 1991a.

University of California, Office of the President. *Sustaining Excellence in the 21st Century: A Vision and Strategies for the University of California's Administration*. Report by the New Campus Administrative Support and Ancillary Services Planning Group. Oakland: Office of the President, University of California, 1991b.

University of California, Office of the President, Improved Management Initiatives. *Developing the UC Workforce for the 21st Century*. Oakland: Office of the President, University of California, 1993a.

University of California, Office of the President, Improved Management Initiatives. *Report of the Workgroup on Capital Programs*. Oakland: Office of the President, University of California, 1994b.

University of California, Office of the President, Improved Management Initiatives. *A New Balance—From Transactional Control to Accountability for Results*. Oakland: Office of the President, University of California, 1994a.

University of California, Office of the President, Improved Management Initiatives. *Empowerment With Accountability*. Oakland: Office of the President, University of California, 1994b.

University of California at Los Angeles. *Transforming Administration at UCLA*. Los Angeles: Office of the Chancellor, University of California, 1991.

Van Alstyne, W. W. (ed.). *Freedom and Tenure in the Academy*. Durham, N.C.: Duke University Press, 1993.

Walker, D. E. *The Effective Administrator: A Practical Approach to Problem Solving, Decision Making, and Campus Leadership*. San Francisco: Jossey-Bass, 1979.

Weathersby, G. B., and Balderston, F. E. *PPBS in Higher Education Planning and Management*. Berkeley: Ford Foundation Program for Research in University Administration, University of California, Report P–16, 1970.

Williamson, O. E. *Markets and Hierarchies: Analysis and Antitrust Implications*. New York: Free Press, 1975.

Williamson, O. E. *The Economic Institutions of Capitalism: Firms, Markets, Relational Contracting*. New York: Free Press, 1985.

"Yale Installs Dean as Its 22nd President." *New York Times*, Oct. 3, 1993, p. 16.

Yamada, M. M. "Joint Big Decision Committees and University Governance." In R. Birnbaum (ed.), *Faculty in Governance: The Role of Senates and Joint Committees in Academic Decision Making*. New Directions for Higher Education, no. 75, San Francisco: Jossey-Bass, 1991.

Zumeta, W. *Extending the Educational Ladder*. Lexington, Mass.: Heath, 1985.

Index